PRESIDENTIAL VOICES

PRESIDENTIAL VOICES

Speaking Styles from George Washington to George W. Bush

ALLAN METCALF

Houghton Mifflin Company
Boston   New York

Visit our website: www.houghtonmifflinbooks.com

ISBN-13: 978-0-618-44374-1
ISBN-10: 0-618-44374-6

Library of Congress Cataloging-in-Publication Data

Metcalf, Allan A.
  Presidential voices : speaking styles from George Washington to George W. Bush /
Allan Metcalf.
     p. cm.
  Includes index.
  ISBN 0-618-44374-6
  1. Political oratory--United States.   2.   Presidents--United States--Language.
3.   Rhetoric--Political aspects--United States.   4.   Communication in politics--United
States.   5.   Presidents--United States--Biography.   I.   Title
  PN4193.P6M48 2004
  352.23'8'0973--dc22

                                                                    2004005742

Manufactured in the United States of America

Book design by Catherine Hawkes, Cat & Mouse

QUM 10 9 8 7 6 5 4 3 2 1

For Maja Natasha Metcalf

A new voice!

And for Mary Wambach

The voice of experience.

Table of Contents

Preface

How should you talk if you're president of the United States—or if you want to be?

That is the question that motivated this book. What do Americans want from their president? Soaring oratory or plain speaking? Dignified or down-to-earth speech? Highfalutin or homely address?

These questions have been on my mind ever since I had the opportunity to attend one of President Eisenhower's press conferences more than forty years ago. He had been criticized for excessive informality, if not ungrammaticality, unbecoming a president in those unrehearsed situations. Did he speak with proper presidential dignity and authority? I offer my answer to that question in chapter 6.

But the catalyst for this book was a more recent event, the accession of George W. Bush to the presidency in 2001. As I listened with continuing fascination to the linguistic legerdemain of the current president of the United States—his *misunderestimate*, his *women of cover*, his *arbo-tree-ist*, his *embetterment of mankind*—the question of presidential language was thrust on me again. Heck, it was thrust on all of us. How could a malaprop man—a guy whose speech mangled the toniest of high-class educations—manage as president to speak for all Americans and be taken seriously?

To find a satisfying answer, I had to write my own book. Countless books have been written on the policies of the presidents, the rhetoric they have employed, their character, the minutest of their daily habits, but their language has been dealt with only glancingly. Other books have focused on what the presidents said or on what oratorical devices they used. This book is not about what they said,

ix

but about the language they employed in saying it, and why they said it that way.

There's another reason for studying the language of the presidents: because we can. There are gaps in what we know about the English language during the first century of our republic, but we do know a lot about the presidents. If we are looking for a category of speakers to exemplify American English from the very beginning of the United States to the present day, we can do no better than pay attention to the presidents.

For the history of American English, the presidents are an unparalleled resource, because so much has been recorded by and about them, including their speech. For the latter half of our presidents, going back as far as Grover Cleveland in the late nineteenth century, we have actual voice recordings. For the first half, George Washington through Chester Arthur, voice recordings do not exist (though Lincoln's "phonautograph," now lost, was taken in 1863 on a machine that was a precursor of the spectrograph that acoustic linguists use nowadays), but we do have copious written texts, as well as contemporary comments and scholarly studies. So one reason for paying linguistic attention to the presidents is the same as George Mallory's reason for climbing the Himalayas, "because they are there" on the record, in a way that few other Americans of any era are.

The presidents have all been, so far, white and male, and the Constitution requires that they be native-born and over the age of 35. Otherwise, though, they represent a wide variety of the American experience. Among the 42 presidents are those who began life very rich and those who began very poor, those with a postgraduate education and those who were hardly schooled at all, soldiers and civilians, professional politicians and complete amateurs. Their temperaments range from Reagan's calm to Nixon's frenetic neurosis; from Washington's imperial bearing to Jefferson's genteel democracy to Jackson's rough populism; from Theodore Roosevelt's drive and Lyndon Johnson's relentless ambition to Rutherford B. Hayes's reluctance and Warren G. Harding's sentiment expressed in his declaration before the Republican Party held its 1920 convention, "The only thing I really worry about is that I might be nominated."

By studying the voices of the presidents, furthermore, we can learn about American ideals. We have elected to have our presidents speak for us, even if we haven't actually elected all the presidents. What styles of speaking have we thus privileged and presumably admired?

Admittedly, to learn about the lives—and the speaking ability—of the presidents is to become persuaded of the truth of the maxim that anyone can grow up to be president. The election of every president, except the first, was in some measure accidental. In every presidential election there have been others as bright, as experienced, as ambitious as those who became president, and indeed there have been occasions when others got more votes.

Sometimes all it takes to become president is being next in line. Although the United States does not have royalty, it does have a position analogous to that of heir apparent—the vice presidency. That officeholder has little to do except take over for a dead, resigned, or incapacitated president. It's a roll of the dice, but it happens often enough. Eight presidents died in office (W. H. Harrison, Taylor, Lincoln, Garfield, McKinley, Harding, F. D. Roosevelt, and Kennedy), and one more resigned (Nixon), so the chances have been better than one in five that a person would assume the presidency simply by occupying the office of vice president.

So it would be far from the truth to claim that Americans have chosen all their presidents. In the early days of the republic, especially, the electoral college was well shielded from the voting public, and the voting public itself was only a minority of the whole population. In later times, more Americans have been able to vote for president, but not every president has received a majority of the popular vote.

Nevertheless, once in office, a president commands our attention, if not always our respect. We attend to our presidents' pronunciation as well as their pronouncements.

The only exception to the accidental presidency has been George Washington. No one else was seriously considered for the first presidency of the United States, and no one else ever has been chosen by a unanimous vote of the electoral college—twice. If there had been a popular vote for president in 1788 or 1792, Washington would have won by a landslide.

Washington set the pattern and established precedents for all subsequent presidents—thank goodness, because for one thing he established the precedent of retiring to private life after two terms rather than maintaining a grasp on power as long as possible. With Washington in mind, even the most ambitious of later presidents have had to moderate their aspirations. Presidents like Lincoln and the Roosevelts may have stretched the limits of their constitutional authority, but they were still bound by those limits. In language, too, and in speaking styles, Washington set a pattern that no successor could or can ignore, as the first chapter will explain.

The rest of the first part of this book is an overview of presidential styles from the days of the founders to the present. The first century of the presidency was the great age of oratory. By no means were all the early presidents great orators, but some were masters of that formal style of speechmaking, and they are celebrated in chapter 2. In the twentieth century, new technology and changing styles made oratory obsolete and close-up communication crucial. The Great Communicators among those presidents are given their due in chapter 3.

Then other matters come up. What about speechwriters—are the presidents' words really their own? That's the subject of chapter 4. And some presidents have found it to their advantage to portray themselves as down-to-earth, but only one really succeeded. That's chapter 5.

With presidents always under close scrutiny, it's no wonder that many have been accused of faulty language. Chapter 6 looks at the leading candidates for blunderer-in-chief.

Deliberately or accidentally, presidents have introduced new words into the English (or American) language. The leading neologists (inventors of new words, to use a word Jefferson relished) are the subjects of chapter 7.

The regional accents of the presidents and changing fashions in presidential pronunciation are explored in chapter 8. Chapter 9 moves from reality to fantasy, concerning itself with the actors who portray presidents as Hollywood would have them.

And chapter 10 gives practical advice on how you should talk when you become president.

I was expecting to find a typical presidential style. Instead I found variety. And yet, drawing on the example of past presidents, it's possible to estimate what manner of speaking might suit a president best. It's not that one size fits all; what makes an outstanding speaker, or an effective one, has changed over the past two centuries. In their own speechways, the presidents illustrate the changing ideals. And from the varied ways of speaking of recent presidents, we can deduce lessons for the presidents of the rest of the twenty-first century.

But that's not the end of it. There are two ways this book could have been organized: thematically by topic, or chronologically by president. I have taken advantage of both, even though it means a little overlap. Following these general chapters, then, come short chapters on the distinctive qualities of the language of each of the 42 presidents. Not every president gets equal opportunity. Some just weren't as outspoken as others.

A Note on Sources

Abundant indeed are the sources of information on the presidents. To consult them all would take many more lifetimes than are available to me, but I am grateful for the tips of the icebergs.

So many sources, first of all, are at one's fingertips on the World Wide Web. For example, I had originally thought to produce a companion CD to go with this book, containing the voices of the 21 presidents whose speech has been recorded. But there is no need. You can hear the voices of the presidents at numerous websites, beginning with those of the Vincent Voice Library at Michigan State University and of Menlo Park in Edison, New Jersey, where Thomas Edison invented the phonograph. For presidents of the twentieth century, there are many sites. I won't give the Web addresses here because they are subject to change, but it is easy to locate them with a moment of Googling.

Also accessible on the Web are all the presidential inaugural addresses and State of the Union messages, and many more presidential documents and recordings. Presidential libraries dot not only the American landscape, but the webscape as well, making it possible to sample the riches of each one by traveling the information superhighway rather than the interstates. Even the *Oxford English Dictionary*, indispensable reference for vocabulary, is available in its latest version only on the Web.

But in this electronic era there are still print publications of first importance for a study like this. In particular I have relied on:

U.S. Presidents as Orators: A Bio-Critical Sourcebook. Edited by Halford Ryan. Westport, Connecticut: Greenwood Press, 1995.

The Presidency and Rhetorical Leadership. Edited by Leroy G. Dorsey. College Station: Texas A&M University Press, 2002.

Presidential Speechwriting: From the New Deal to the Reagan Revolution and Beyond. Edited by Kurt Ritter and Martin J. Medhurst. College Station: Texas A&M University Press, 2003.

Recollections of Thirteen Presidents by John S. Wise. New York: Doubleday, 1906.

Safire's New Political Dictionary (Random House, 1993). It has the stories behind words and phrases like Roosevelt's "New Deal" and Kennedy's "New Frontier," even to the details of which speechwriter (sometimes William Safire himself) was responsible for the creation.

For inspiration and general information on the presidents, I'm grateful for *The American President* by the Kunhardts (Riverhead Books, 1999), a companion to the PBS series of the same name. Very few sources directly address the specifics of a president's language. One that does is *Abraham Lincoln, Public Speaker* by Waldo W. Braden (Louisiana State University Press, 1988). It sifts the voluminous reminiscences of Lincoln to find the few nuggets describing his voice and accent. Augmenting the essential *Oxford English Dictionary* online are the print publications *Dictionary of American Regional English* (4 volumes so far, Harvard University Press, 1985–) and the *Random House Historical Dictionary of American Slang,* edited by Jonathan Lighter (2 volumes so far, 1994–).

Acknowledgments

Colleagues have been generous in helping me locate sources and ask the right questions. I am especially indebted to James Davis of the history department at Illinois College for a wealth of information on presidents of the prerecording era, and to E. Claire Jerry, professor of humanities at MacMurray College, for books and advice on presidents, especially of more recent times.

Others who have helped include Arnita Jones, executive director of the American Historical Association; Malcah Yaeger-Dror of the University of Arizona; Craig Smith of California State University,

Long Beach; and Fred Shapiro of Yale University and Barry Popik of Manhattan, tireless searchers for the origins of words.

At the University of Missouri, Columbia, my thanks go to Peter McCarthy of the Western Historical Manuscript Collection for clippings from the Tamony Collection of American slang, and to Matthew Gordon and the late Donald Lance for inviting me to talk on this subject.

At MacMurray College, I appreciate suggestions by Nadine Szczepanski and Kay Henriksen; manuscript assistance by Erin Klee; and support through a long semester of writing by Alice Dodson, David Fitz, Malea Harney, and Parris Watts, colleagues in the Academic Affairs office.

At Houghton Mifflin, this book was made possible, above all, by my editor, Joseph Pickett, who combines the patience of Job with the persistence of Attila the Hun. I also had important help from Steve Kleinedler, senior editor in the dictionary department; Margaret Anne Miles, art and production supervisor; Brianne Lutfy, editorial production assistant; and Gracie Doyle, publicist, who really knows what she is talking about. Sharp-eyed and punctilious Diane Fredrick copyedited the manuscript.

And I appreciate more than I can say the well-chosen words and encouragement of my wife, Donna. Thanks to all who made this seemingly impossible book possible.

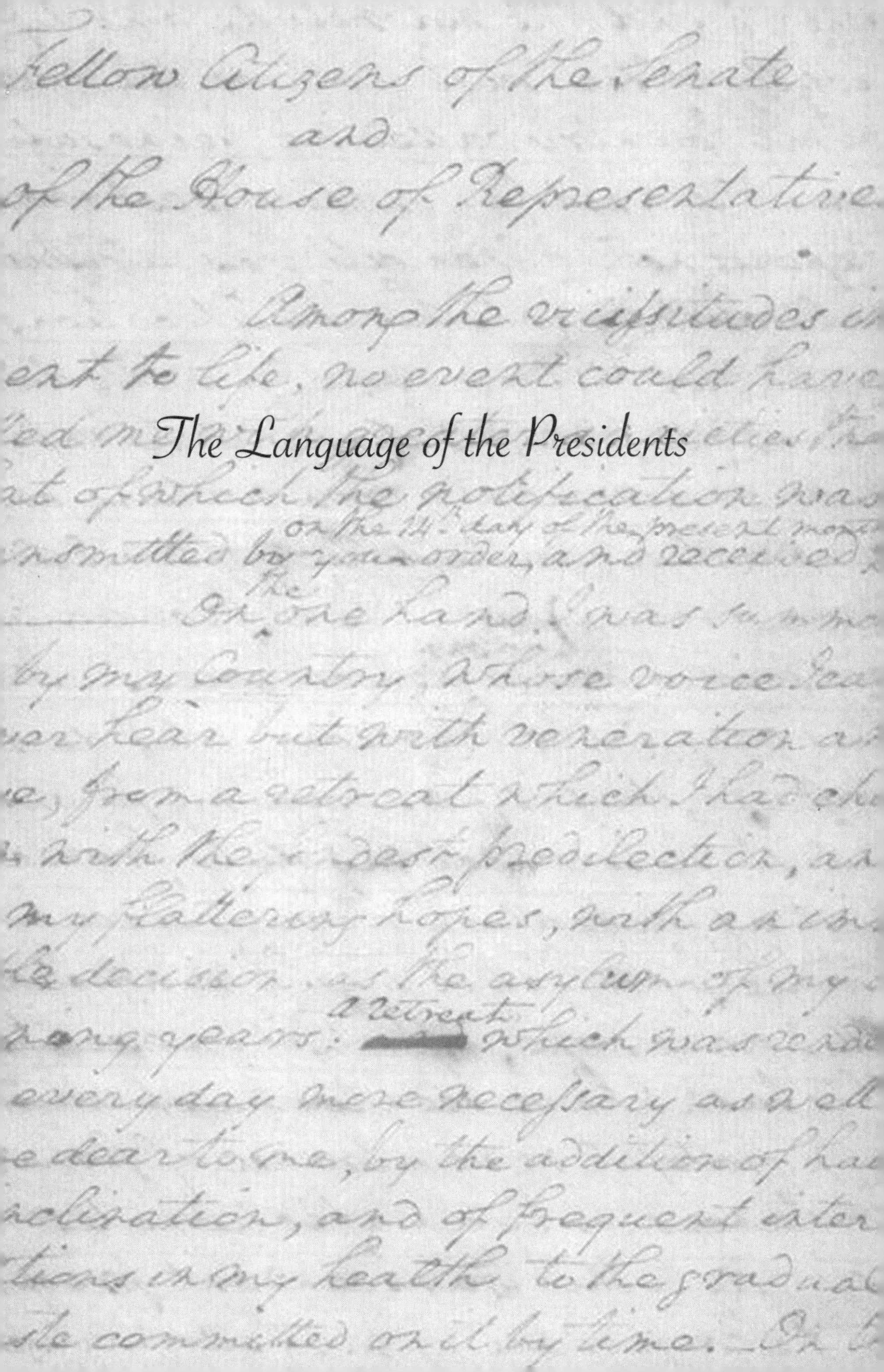

The Language of the Presidents

1 The Original

From our present-day perspective of more than two centuries of presidents, it's hard to imagine the moment just after the ratification of the Constitution in 1788 when the first president remained to be chosen. The new form of government had been determined, but it was still an abstraction, not yet embodied. Without the benefit of experience, those who were starting the American experiment might understandably have had a rather hazy idea of what kind of president they wanted. But they didn't. They had a clearer vision of the presidency than we do today after our roller-coaster ride through presidential greats and mediocrities. The citizens of the newly constituted republic knew exactly what they wanted in a president: George Washington.

It wasn't just that he had led the American army through trials and triumphs to victory in the Revolutionary War. It wasn't just that he had presided over the successful Constitutional Convention. It was also his sense of duty, his integrity, his dignity, and his bearing, cultivated from his youth. Washington possessed the exalted character the new nation needed in its leader.

For it was still the age of kings, another perspective that is hard for us nowadays to imagine. To assume its "equal station" among nations, as the Declaration of Independence phrased it, the new United States of America needed a presiding figure who could stand on equal footing with the great hereditary rulers of Europe. Everyone agreed that that would be Washington. He was America's answer to Europe's royalty, presiding over a nation not by virtue of his ancestry, but by virtue of his virtue.

Not a King

He had every virtue one would hope for in a king, and one thing more: he was democratic. If he hadn't been, we might well have had an American monarchy, and this book (not to mention our country) would be taking a very different shape.

Indeed, Washington very likely could have been king, if he had had a mind to. True, the Constitution specified a term of four years for the presidency. Today that document seems set in stone, so durable is it and so hard to change. But the founders didn't know that. The ink had scarcely had time to dry on the Constitution when the most popular man in America became president. Exactly what character the presidency would assume remained to be seen, and everyone knew it would be largely influenced by Washington's example.

In an age of kings, even the independent American people might have acquiesced to lifetime rule by such a paragon of virtue. But Washington didn't choose to be king. Instead, he became the model citizen of the new republic: first among equals. And that determined the pattern for all who would succeed him in the presidency. If Washington would not be king, nobody could.

In personifying the presidency for the first time, Washington was conscious that he was setting a pattern for all future presidents to follow, and he chose his presidential actions with posterity in mind. For example, he established the pattern of retiring after two terms, a precedent so powerful that it was not overstepped until a century and a half later when Franklin Roosevelt won four consecutive terms. This alarmed enough politicians of both parties that Washington's two-term limit was codified in the Constitution as the Twenty-second Amendment.

Washington also codified the way presidents should talk. He very consciously established what he considered the proper occasions on which a president should speak and the proper way for a president to speak on those occasions.

The Inaugural Inaugural Address

When and how should a president speak? In deciding this question, Washington looked for examples of comparable dignity. He found the

George Washington taking the oath of office on the balcony of the Senate Chamber at Federal Hall on Wall Street, New York City, April 30, 1789.

model for his first speech as president, his inaugural address of 1789, in the British monarch's annual address at the opening session of Parliament. The Constitution makes no mention of an inaugural speech, but Washington's decision meant that every president after him would make one. As he was sworn in before giving his address, he added the words "so help me God" to the oath prescribed in the Constitution, establishing another precedent that his successors would follow.

For that first inaugural, Washington spoke not to the public from the balcony of Federal Hall in New York, where he had taken the first oath of office, but to the members of Congress indoors, following the British model. His style was formal, but his message was one of humility, befitting the man who was First Citizen rather than His Majesty. The very first words of his inaugural address, "Fellow citizens," emphasized democracy and set a pattern followed by nearly every inaugural speech in later years, down to and including George W. Bush's in 2001: "President Clinton, distinguished guests and *my fellow citizens. . . .*"

Washington then followed with a personal statement expressing his willingness to set aside his private desires for the sake of serving his country as a citizen:

> *Among the vicissitudes incident to life no event could have filled me with greater anxieties than that of which the notification was*

> transmitted by your order, and received on the 14th day of the present month. On the one hand, I was summoned by my country, whose voice I can never hear but with veneration and love, from a retreat which I had chosen with the fondest predilection, and, in my flattering hopes, with an immutable decision, as the asylum of my declining years—a retreat which was rendered every day more necessary as well as more dear to me by the addition of habit to inclination, and of frequent interruptions in my health to the gradual waste committed on it by time.

Though this is highly personal, it is also highly formal. He expresses all this sentiment in just two long and elegant sentences, the first of 36 words, the second of 87. Many of the words are stately terms derived from Latin: *vicissitudes, predilection, immutable,* and *asylum* (a now archaic use of that word to mean a safe place of refuge; ultimately from the Greek). The grammar of the two sentences is complex, ornate, and exact, far from everyday language patterns. To be technical for a moment, the first sentence alone ends with a 19-word coordinate postmodifying restrictive relative clause in the passive voice, resulting in two reversals of normal word order. It's perfectly grammatical, but not what someone would be likely to say in ordinary conversation.

Washington continues in similar formal language, discussing his "conflict of emotions" in a sentence of 69 words followed by one of 34:

> On the other hand, the magnitude and difficulty of the trust to which the voice of my country called me, being sufficient to awaken in the wisest and most experienced of her citizens a distrustful scrutiny into his qualifications, could not but overwhelm with despondence one who (inheriting inferior endowments from nature and unpracticed in the duties of civil administration) ought to be peculiarly conscious of his own deficiencies. In this conflict of emotions all I dare aver is that it has been my faithful study to collect my duty from a just appreciation of every circumstance by which it might be affected.

No raw emotions here, but emotions of the utmost dignity suited to this grave occasion of state. After one more 88-word sentence along these lines, Washington invokes the Deity in the most formal of language:

> *It would be peculiarly improper to omit in this first official act my fervent supplications to that Almighty Being who rules over the universe, who presides in the councils of nations, and whose providential aids can supply every human defect, that His benediction may consecrate to the liberties and happiness of the people of the United States a Government instituted by themselves for these essential purposes, and may enable every instrument employed in its administration to execute with success the functions allotted to his charge.*

In the rest of his speech, continuing with the same lengthy sentences, elaborate phrasing, and lofty language, Washington offers "in place of a recommendation of particular measures, the tribute that is due to the talents, the rectitude, and the patriotism which adorn the characters selected to devise and adopt them." It's an elaborate compliment to the members of Congress. Then, in the politest of language, and a 93-word sentence, he lectures against partisanship. In even more formal language, he announces that, as befits a gentleman, he will refuse any salary (but of course he'll happily expect his expenses to be paid), using words like *emoluments* and *pecuniary* to touch on this most delicate of subjects for a gentleman. He concludes his address with a very formal invocation of what one could only, with similar formality, call the Divine:

> *Having thus imparted to you my sentiments as they have been awakened by the occasion which brings us together, I shall take my present leave; but not without resorting once more to the benign Parent of the Human Race in humble supplication that, since He has been pleased to favor the American people with opportunities for deliberating in perfect tranquillity, and dispositions for deciding with unparalleled unanimity on a form of government for the security of their union and the advancement of their happiness, so His divine blessing may be equally conspicuous in the enlarged views, the temperate consultations, and the wise measures on which the success of this Government must depend.*

Take that, kings and queens! Could any monarch speak any better?

As far as his audience was concerned, evidently not. Many of his distinguished listeners were moved to tears, perhaps more by the mere fact of Washington's speaking than by his speech itself or the manner in which he delivered it. Indeed, it was reported that he spoke in a low monotone, hard to hear, and that he too felt the occasion to be so momentous that his hands trembled and his voice quavered. In this also he established a precedent—that a president need not be a great public speaker.

WASHINGTON'S FALSE TEETH

Because George Washington's false teeth made such an impression on his speech, and thus on the example he set for his successors, they call for our attention here.

The popular notion is that Washington had wooden teeth, as depicted in comedian Stan Freberg's revisionist *History of the United States*, where Tom Jefferson is soliciting signatures for the Declaration of Independence:

> Ben Franklin: *Washington? I don't see his name on it.*
> Jefferson: *No, but he promised to sign it.*
> Franklin: *Oh, yeah, that's George for you! Talks up a storm with them wooden teeth—can't shut 'em off! But when it comes time to put the old name on the parchment-o-roonie, try and find him.*

This is wrong in two respects—that the teeth were wooden, and that Washington "talks up a storm." Not that Freberg or his audience would care. But to set the record straight: false teeth never have been made of wood. The saliva in the mouth would soon turn them to mush. Instead, they were made of hard toothlike material, tusks or bones or teeth of animals and humans. Sometimes they were made of gold or silver. As befitted his dignified position and circumstances, Washington got the most advanced dentures of his day from the best dentist in the United States, John Greenwood of New York. ▶

Greenwood made four of the six sets of false teeth Washington wore during his lifetime. In 1789, he made Washington a lower plate with eight human teeth set in hippopotamus bone, with a hole for Washington's one remaining lower bicuspid to hold it in place. Later, when even that one tooth was gone, Greenwood made for Washington the most elegant false teeth in America, with a thin gold plate holding ivory teeth at the top of his mouth, and teeth carved from elephant ivory at the bottom of the mouth. The upper and lower sets of teeth were connected to each other by steel springs, one on each side, that pushed them apart. So Washington had to exert pressure on the plates just to keep his mouth shut.

The false teeth affected Washington's appearance as well as his speech. When Gilbert Stuart made one of his famous paintings of Washington in 1796, he noted, "When I painted him, he had just had a set of false teeth inserted, which accounts for the constrained expression so noticeable about the mouth and lower part of the face."

Washington had had tooth troubles from an early age. He thought that might have been because he liked to crack walnuts with his teeth. The principal treatment for toothache in Washington's day was extraction, and so his teeth went, one by one, removed by the usual local practitioners of dentistry, blacksmiths, and barbers.

His dental troubles might have been embarrassing as well as painful, but they could not be kept private. One letter of his to a dentist in Philadelphia was captured by the British during the Revolutionary War and studied for the military secrets it might disclose. It is now in the Clements Library at the University of Michigan. In his own hand Washington wrote to a Dr. Baker:

New Windsor May 29, 1781

Sir, A day or two ago I requested Col. Harrison to apply to you for a pair of Pincers to fasten the wire of my teeth. I hope you furnished him with them. I now wish you would send me one of your scrapers as my teeth stand in need of cleaning, and I have little prospect of being in Philadelphia soon. It will come very safe by the Post and in return, the money shall be sent so soon as I know the cost of it.

I am Sir Y Very H Serv [Your Very Humble Servant] *G. Washington*

True Brevity and False Teeth

Yet another precedent Washington set in this and other speeches was brevity. His sentences are long, but his speeches aren't. Although his first inaugural address has sentences of extraordinary length, the speech itself is only 1427 words. How long would that take to recite? Well, for example, the rate of speaking for the inaugural addresses delivered between 1989 (George H.W. Bush) and 2001 (George W. Bush, with Clinton in between) ranged between 99 and 114 words a minute. Assuming the lower rate for Washington because of his false teeth, his first inaugural would still have taken no more than 15 minutes to read. In all of his public addresses, Washington rarely exceeded that length. Thomas Jefferson later recalled that he had never heard Washington speak for more than 10 minutes at a time.

Perhaps Washington's brevity stemmed from his celebrated dignified reserve. But just as likely, it was a consequence of his false teeth. They were painful enough to wear; to speak with them was even more of a strain. No wonder his voice on public occasions was the low monotone mentioned above. A contemporary wrote in 1791 that Washington's "voice was hollow and indistinct, owing as I believe, to artificial teeth before his upper jaw, which occasions a flatness." Even 10 minutes of public speaking was an ordeal.

Nonetheless, he did not shrink from what he saw as his obligations. Where the Constitution specified only that the president "shall from time to time give to the Congress Information of the State of the Union, and recommend to their Consideration such Measures as he shall judge necessary and expedient," Washington decided that it was appropriate to do so in person and thus established the tradition of State of the Union speeches. (When Jefferson became president two terms later, he decided State of the Union speeches too closely resembled the custom of a monarchy and sent his in writing, a tradition that persisted for a century.) But these speeches, too, were never long. Washington's first State of the Union address to Congress, in 1790, was shorter than his inaugural, barely a thousand words. His second, also in 1790, was 1425 words; his third, in 1791, about 2300. Thereafter, his State of the Union speeches were generally about 2000 words, except in 1794 and 1796, when they got close to 3000, still much shorter than a present-day

State of the Union address. Not all of his successors would follow him in brevity. So much the worse for them; the great presidential speeches we remember are short.

While setting one precedent in adopting a high, formal, and ornate style in his first inaugural address, Washington set another with his second: speaking plainly and directly. His second inaugural was the shortest and simplest inaugural on record:

Fellow Citizens:

I am again called upon by the voice of my country to execute the functions of its Chief Magistrate. When the occasion proper for it shall arrive, I shall endeavor to express the high sense I entertain of this distinguished honor, and of the confidence which has been reposed in me by the people of united America.

Previous to the execution of any official act of the President the Constitution requires an oath of office. This oath I am now about to take, and in your presence: That if it shall be found during my administration of the Government I have in any instance violated willingly or knowingly the injunctions thereof, I may (besides incurring constitutional punishment) be subject to the upbraidings of all who are now witnesses of the present solemn ceremony.

His first inaugural dwelt on the solemnity, the sublimity, and the mixed emotions of being summoned from retirement to become the first president. Now he's just continuing for another term. That's not such a big deal, he says in effect.

In the second half of the second inaugural he makes a deceptively simple comment that lays down the law about the presidency. By stating the obvious, that he is about to take the oath of office, he implicitly reminds his audience that the Constitution has authority over the president rather than vice versa. If he oversteps the constitutional limits of his office, he will have gone back on his word and will expect to be upbraided by his listeners as well as to incur "constitutional punishment." Few public officials today would dare conjure the potential for their own impeachment in an inaugural address, but Washington was secure enough to use that opportunity to lecture himself and others on the importance of keeping their oath. His seemingly humble and personal statement is a powerful caution for presidents to come that, far from having unlimited powers, they too must "uphold the Constitution of the United States."

As for the brevity of this speech: Maybe it was those teeth again, or maybe Washington was merely exhibiting the other side of the presidency, that of the model citizen rather than ruler of the new republic, first, but among equals. Ever since, just as eloquence has been valued in a president, so has plain speaking.

Meeting Washington's Standards

Perhaps because of Washington's example, the presidency tends to bring out the best in those who hold the office. Maybe it's because of the intense public scrutiny directed at the president; any behavior by a president that is less than noble and principled immediately comes under attack by opponents and comes in for criticism by journalists, historians, and the public. Washington warned about that sort of thing in his second inaugural address. Or maybe it's because the presidents themselves sometimes seem to be awed to be in a line of succession that goes back to Washington himself.

That's not to say all presidents have avoided scandal or behaved nobly, but when they fail to meet the standards of dignity and integrity established by Washington (George, that is, not the city named after him), they are harshly dealt with. Just in recent times we have had two presidents impeached by the House of Representatives for low crimes and misdemeanors: Richard Nixon for authorizing a second-rate burglary, Bill Clinton for his double talk about a personal peccadillo. But even those presidents did their best to serve their country in other respects.

The effect is all the more striking because in the centuries since Washington, chance rather than talent or character has played a large role in determining who has become president. Nine men have emerged unexpectedly from the obscurity of the vice presidency to take over for a president who died or resigned. No matter; the Washington effect has affected them too. One such was Chester A. Arthur, who had headed the corrupt New York Customhouse. When he became president on Garfield's death, he surprised everyone by shunning his former associates and pushing for civil service reform. And Republicans as well as Democrats now applaud the Kansas City machine politician, Harry Truman, who stepped into Franklin Roosevelt's big shoes and became a statesman in his own right.

Many would claim that this doesn't seem to happen to members of the Senate and the House of Representatives. Mark Twain famously said, "Reader, suppose you were an idiot. And suppose you were a member of Congress. But I repeat myself" and "It could probably be shown by facts and figures that there is no distinctly native American criminal class except Congress."

But the president has every encouragement to live up to Washington's standards. Among other things, this means speaking with dignity as the citizen-leader of our great experiment in democracy. And with brevity, too, though that example has sometimes been ignored.

2 The Great Orators

The early years of the Republic through the end of the nineteenth century were the golden age of oratory. What's oratory? Well, it's speaking well, but more than that, it's speaking grandly, majestically. Listening to oratory, even for hours at a time, was a favorite entertainment in the days before movies, television, video games, rock concerts, amusement parks, and the Internet. Our twenty-first-century sensibility is attuned to sound bites. We couldn't swallow a whole long oration even if one were offered. But back in the day. . . .

There have been great American orators, those who kept their listeners spellbound, and then there have been American presidents. Those who have been both can be counted on the fingers of one hand, with the thumb left over. (The thumb belongs to Warren G. Harding, but we'll come to him later.)

George Washington established the precedent that oratorical ability is not a requisite for the presidency. Many other presidents have followed that precedent. Some have had the good sense not even to try to be orators. Others of questionable ability have tried—and descended into bathos. A sad example is the good old general William Henry Harrison, hyped in the 1840 election as hero of a long-ago battle at the Tippecanoe River in Indiana. The 68-year-old gentleman was bathed by a cold rain on the Capitol steps in March 1841 as he delivered the longest inaugural address ever made. The crowd gradually slipped away as he continued for nearly two hours with an oration that began:

Called from a retirement which I had supposed was to continue for the residue of my life to fill the chief executive office of this great

and free nation, I appear before you, fellow-citizens, to take the
oaths which the Constitution prescribes as a necessary qualification
for the performance of its duties; and in obedience to a custom co-
eval with our Government and what I believe to be your expectations
I proceed to present to you a summary of the principles which will
govern me in the discharge of the duties which I shall be called upon
to perform. . . .

Harrison died of pneumonia a month later.

The presidency is a "bully pulpit," in Teddy Roosevelt's words, that can tempt any president to try his hand at oratory, whether he is talented or not. Of course, it doesn't mean that everyone who becomes president is magically gifted with speaking ability. They try their best, but their best often leaves much to be desired.

Great Nonpresidents

Well then, who have been the models of American oratory?

Well, there was Patrick Henry of Virginia, topmost orator at the time of the American Revolution. As far back as 1765, a decade before the Declaration of Independence, he electrified the Virginia House of Burgesses with: "Caesar had his Brutus; Charles the First, his Cromwell; and George the Third–('Treason!' cried the Speaker of the House) may profit by their example. If this be treason, make the most of it!" And a decade later, to the Continental Congress, meeting in Richmond, Virginia: "Is life so dear, or peace so sweet, as to be purchased at the price of chains and slavery? Forbid it, Almighty God! I know not what course others may take, but as for me, give me liberty or give me death!" Just what was needed to stir enthusiasm for the cause, but perhaps a little unseemly for a president. In any case, he was never seriously considered for the presidency.

In the first part of the nineteenth century, with the United States securely established, the U.S. Senate was a place for great oratory. It boasted a "Great Triumvirate" of men who would have been happy to be president: Henry Clay of Kentucky, Daniel Webster of Massachusetts, and John C. Calhoun of South Carolina.

Henry Clay addressing the U.S. Senate on February 6, 1850, pleading for tolerance among arguing factions and for the preservation of the Union.

Clay was famous not only for his speechmaking, but for his ability to resolve political differences through compromise. He was "the Great Pacificator" as well as a champion of speaking well. In his own words: "There is no power like that of true oratory. Caesar controlled men by exciting their fears; Cicero, by captivating their affections and swaying their passions. The influence of the one perished with its author; that of the other continues to this day." And: "I would rather be right than President." Right he was. He was a perennial candidate for president, and was perennially defeated—by John Quincy Adams, Andrew Jackson, and James K. Polk.

Webster was perhaps the top lawyer in the country, arguing cases before the Supreme Court, before he became a senator. He was a strong advocate of a strong federal government. In debate with a South Carolina senator in 1830, he spoke for "Liberty and union, now and forever, one and inseparable!" His oratory was so powerful that Stephen Vincent Benét made him the hero of a short story, "The Devil and Daniel Webster," that declares,

When he stood up to speak, stars and stripes came right out in the sky, and once he spoke against a river and made it sink into the ground. They said, when he walked the woods with his fishing rod, Killall, the trout would jump out of the streams right into his pockets, for they knew it was no use putting up a fight against him; and, when he argued a case, he could turn on the harps of the blessed and the shaking of the earth underground.

In the story, it turns out that Webster had the oratorical skill to defeat the Devil himself on behalf of his client, Jabez Stone. In real life, Webster, too, was a presidential candidate, but he lost that case, in 1836, to Martin Van Buren.

John C. Calhoun was as staunch a supporter of Southern interests as Webster was of the North. He argued for states' rights against the federal government: "The government of the absolute majority is but the government of the strongest interests; and when not effectively checked, is the most tyrannical and oppressive that can be devised." On his deathbed, when the Senate chaplain paid him a visit, he turned away and declared defiantly, "I won't be told what to think!" Calhoun never had a chance as president to check the absolute majority, but of the three in the Great Triumvirate, he came closest to the presidency, serving as vice president under both John Quincy Adams and Andrew Jackson.

Also in the nineteenth century, the great age of oratory, there was the fiery abolitionist Frederick Douglass, the escaped slave: "Where justice is denied, where poverty is enforced, where ignorance prevails, and where any one class is made to feel that society is in an organized conspiracy to oppress, rob, and degrade them, neither persons nor property will be safe." And: "If there is no struggle, there is no progress. Those who profess to favor freedom, and yet deprecate agitation, are men who want crops without plowing up the ground, they want rain without thunder and lightning. They want the ocean without the awful roar of its many waters." Of course in those days, a black man would not have been seriously considered for the presidency.

Nor would a woman. But among the outstanding orators of the time there was Elizabeth Cady Stanton, speaking out for women's rights: "It requires philosophy and heroism to rise above the opinion of the wise men of all nations and races." And: "Nature never repeats herself, and the possibilities of one human soul will never be found in another." And: "So long as women are slaves, men will be knaves."

William Jennings Bryan delivering a campaign speech.

Near the end of the nineteenth century, along came William Jennings Bryan of Nebraska, electrifying the Democratic National Convention of 1896 with "The humblest citizen in all the land, when clad in the armor of a righteous cause, is stronger than all the hosts of error" and "You shall not press down upon the brow of labor this crown of thorns, you shall not crucify mankind upon a cross of gold"—speaking in opposition to the gold standard for money. That speech won him the party's presidential nomination, though he lost the election to McKinley. He won the Democratic nomination again in 1900 with remarks like: "But if it were possible to obliterate every word written or spoken in defense of the principles set forth in the Declaration of Independence, a war of conquest would still leave its legacy of perpetual hatred, for it was God Himself who placed in every human heart the love of liberty." The voters may have admired his orations, but McKinley again took the popular and electoral votes.

The twentieth century brought an end to oratory in the grand old style, for reasons that include the developing technology for broadcasting speech. Oratory became comedy, even when it was serious. The outstanding orator of the U.S. Senate in the mid-twentieth century, Everett McKinley Dirksen of Illinois, was memorable mainly for his quips: "I am a man of fixed and unbending principles, the first of which is to be flexible at all times" and "A billion here, a billion there, and pretty soon you're talking about real money."

The Greatest Presidential Orator

It almost appears that great oratorical ability actually hinders a person from becoming president. But not entirely. Four men have managed to be both presidents and great orators. And the greatest of these was— no, not Lincoln, he's No. 2—George Washington's successor, John Adams.

Adams was so good that we can't know how good he was. He didn't write out his speeches in advance, but spoke extemporaneously. And he mesmerized his audiences so effectively that afterwards they couldn't recall exactly what he said. His grandson Charles Francis Adams, in an 1856 biography of his grandfather, eloquently lamented the lack of a written record of Adams's July 1, 1776, speech to the Continental Congress on behalf of the Declaration of Independence:

> The fires of Demosthenes, of Cicero, and of Burke were lighted at the midnight lamp, for the illumination of the world whilst time shall endure. But Chatham, Patrick Henry, Mirabeau, and John Adams will be handed down as great orators mainly by the concurring testimony of those who witnessed the effects they produced. The "deep conceptions and nervous style," which made Mr. Adams stand forth in the memory of Jefferson, who had the strongest reasons for retaining an indelible impression of the scene, as "the colossus of independence" on the floor of congress, "which," as he further declares, "gave him a power of thought and expression which moved the members from their seats," which sent Richard Stockton home, testifying that he was "the atlas of independence," and the Virginians, never unwilling to give their own citizens the palm, but always susceptible of generous impulses, "to fill every mouth in the ancient dominion with the praises due to the comprehensiveness of his views, the force of his arguments, and the boldness of his patriotism," will be remembered only by this testimony.

So one of the most important speeches in American history, the one that made support unanimous for the declaration "That these United Colonies are, and of Right ought to be, Free and Independent States," is lost except for the breathtaking effect it had.

The Greatest Presidential Oration

Fortunately, however, we do have some written records of John Adams's oratorical skill as president, in particular his crucial inaugural address of 1797. Admittedly, it's easy to miss the great oratorical skill in this speech. At first glance it looks anything but impressive, for either substance or style. In its substance Adams merely stated that he approved of the American Constitution and would do his best to uphold it. In its style it is highly formal and contains the longest sentence of any inaugural address, running on for some 727 words. That would hardly seem to make it such a great speech, even allowing for Adams's skill at delivery. But this initial response is limited by our twenty-first-century need for speed. Take a deep breath, put on your three-cornered hat, and consider it from a Revolutionary perspective of more than two centuries ago.

RIVETING AT 700 WORDS

Here is the conclusion of John Adams's inaugural address, including his 727-word peroration:

> *On this subject it might become me better to be silent or to speak with diffidence; but as something may be expected, the occasion, I hope, will be admitted as an apology if I venture to say that if a preference, upon principle, of a free republican government, formed upon long and serious reflection, after a diligent and impartial inquiry after truth; if an attachment to the Constitution of the United States, and a conscientious determination to support it until it shall be altered by the judgments and wishes of the people, expressed in the mode prescribed in it; if a respectful attention to the constitutions of the individual States and a constant caution and delicacy toward the State governments; if an equal and impartial regard to the rights, interest, honor, and happiness of all the States in the Union, without preference or regard to a northern or southern, an eastern or western position, their various political opinions on unessential points or their personal attachments; if a love of virtuous men of all parties and denominations; if a love of science and letters and a wish to patronize every rational effort to encourage schools, colleges, universities, ►*

academies, and every institution for propagating knowledge, virtue, and religion among all classes of the people, not only for their benign influence on the happiness of life in all its stages and classes, and of society in all its forms, but as the only means of preserving our Constitution from its natural enemies, the spirit of sophistry, the spirit of party, the spirit of intrigue, the profligacy of corruption, and the pestilence of foreign influence, which is the angel of destruction to elective governments; if a love of equal laws, of justice, and humanity in the interior administration; if an inclination to improve agriculture, commerce, and manufactures for necessity, convenience, and defense; if a spirit of equity and humanity toward the aboriginal nations of America, and a disposition to meliorate their condition by inclining them to be more friendly to us, and our citizens to be more friendly to them; if an inflexible determination to maintain peace and inviolable faith with all nations, and that system of neutrality and impartiality among the belligerent powers of Europe which has been adopted by this Government and so solemnly sanctioned by both Houses of Congress and applauded by the legislatures of the States and the public opinion, until it shall be otherwise ordained by Congress; if a personal esteem for the French nation, formed in a residence of seven years chiefly among them, and a sincere desire to preserve the friendship which has been so much for the honor and interest of both nations; if, while the conscious honor and integrity of the people of America and the internal sentiment of their own power and energies must be preserved, an earnest endeavor to investigate every just cause and remove every colorable pretense of complaint; if an intention to pursue by amicable negotiation a reparation for the injuries that have been committed on the commerce of our fellow-citizens by whatever nation, and if success can not be obtained, to lay the facts before the Legislature, that they may consider what further measures the honor and interest of the Government and its constituents demand; if a resolution to do justice as far as may depend upon me, at all times and to all nations, and maintain peace, friendship, and benevolence with all the world; if an unshaken confidence in the honor, spirit, and resources of the American people, on which I have so often hazarded my all and never been deceived; if elevated ideas of the high destinies of this country ▶

and of my own duties toward it, founded on a knowledge of the moral principles and intellectual improvements of the people deeply engraven on my mind in early life, and not obscured but exalted by experience and age; and, with humble reverence, I feel it to be my duty to add, if a veneration for the religion of a people who profess and call themselves Christians, and a fixed resolution to consider a decent respect for Christianity among the best recommendations for the public service, can enable me in any degree to comply with your wishes, it shall be my strenuous endeavor that this sagacious injunction of the two Houses shall not be without effect.

With this great example before me, with the sense and spirit, the faith and honor, the duty and interest, of the same American people pledged to support the Constitution of the United States, I entertain no doubt of its continuance in all its energy, and my mind is prepared without hesitation to lay myself under the most solemn obligations to support it to the utmost of my power.

And may that Being who is supreme over all, the Patron of Order, the Fountain of Justice, and the Protector in all ages of the world of virtuous liberty, continue His blessing upon this nation and its Government and give it all possible success and duration consistent with the ends of His providence.

Closer examination reveals that, in terms of its oratorical purpose and effectiveness, this is perhaps the greatest inaugural address of all time. Greater even than Lincoln's second, his famous "malice toward none, charity for all"? Admittedly not quite—if measured by its long-term impact on American history and its resonance throughout the nation. The world would little note nor long remember what Adams said in his inaugural, and rightly so; it was a speech for the moment, not for all time. But for accomplishing his purpose, for persuading his audience, Adams is without peer among presidents in this address.

The inauguration of Adams marked the first time in the history of the United States that the office of president passed from one person to another. It is now routine and unremarkable that a president peacefully steps down when the term of office is over, even when a detested political opponent is taking over. But that was far from certain when Washington was stepping down. It had never happened before.

Adams spoke, as Washington had done for his inaugurations, not to a crowd outdoors, but to members of the House and Senate and distinguished guests in Congress Hall, Philadelphia. The challenge of his speech was to declare his warm approval of the Constitution and his determination to uphold it—something that might appear unnecessary, but not in Adams's case. He needed to allay the worries of those who thought he wanted the presidency to be more like a monarchy, with a lifetime appointment rather than a limited term. How could he convince his listeners he was sincere?

A lesser speaker might have opened his heart to the audience right away. But that would not have persuaded anyone who doubted his sincerity. Instead, Adams begins by making no demands that the audience believe anything about him. Using detached, impersonal language, he talks about the common history his listeners knew so well:

> When it was first perceived, in early times, that no middle course for America remained between unlimited submission to a foreign legislature and a total independence of its claims, men of reflection were less apprehensive of danger from the formidable power of fleets and armies they must determine to resist than from those contests and dissensions which would certainly arise concerning the forms of government to be instituted over the whole and over the parts of this extensive country. . . .

Even the passive verb *was perceived* contributes to the distancing. Adams had been right in the thick of the movement for independence, but he avoids any personal connection by saying *it was perceived* instead of *we* (or even stronger, *I*) *perceived*. For four paragraphs he continues in this objective vein, inviting approval by stating facts and conclusions his audience would agree with. Then he begins to bring himself in, literally from a distance. He had been in Paris, far from the debates about the Constitution, when he heard about it:

> Employed in the service of my country abroad during the whole course of these transactions, I first saw the Constitution of the United States in a foreign country. Irritated by no literary altercation, animated by no public debate, heated by no party animosity, I read it with great satisfaction, as the result of good heads prompted by good hearts, as an experiment better adapted to the genius, character, situation, and

relations of this nation and country than any which had ever been pro-posed or suggested. . . .

So Adams implicitly declares himself above party and faction, and with full satisfaction in what his countrymen had wrought. He praises the Constitution in the warmest terms and declares his personal attachment to it. And as he speaks of returning from France, the *I* of approval becomes *we* the people, *our* esteem and love, himself included:

> *Returning to the bosom of my country after a painful separation from it for ten years, I had the honor to be elected to a station under the new order of things, and I have repeatedly laid myself under the most serious obligations to support the Constitution. The operation of it has equaled the most sanguine expectations of its friends, and from an habitual attention to it, satisfaction in its administration, and delight in its effects upon the peace, order, prosperity, and happiness of the nation I have acquired an habitual attachment to it and veneration for it.*
>
> *What other form of government, indeed, can so well deserve our esteem and love?*

It must be remembered that Adams's audience was above all the members of Congress. In praising them and the government that the Constitution has established, Adams implicitly credits himself with benevolence:

> *To a benevolent human mind there can be no spectacle presented by any nation more pleasing, more noble, majestic, or august, than an assembly like that which has so often been seen in this and the other Chamber of Congress, of a Government in which the Executive authority, as well as that of all the branches of the Legislature, are exercised by citizens selected at regular periods by their neighbors to make and execute laws for the general good.*

Now that he has fully wrapped himself in the Constitution, step by step, he takes a moment to warn against any party that "should infect the purity of our free, fair, virtuous, and independent elections" and praises his predecessor, General Washington, thereby wrapping himself in Washington's mantle as well. (Washington was right there, giving his blessing to the scene. That helped!) And then comes the peroration, that singular, astonishing 727-word sentence. Hesitatingly at first:

> On this subject it might become me better to be silent or to speak with diffidence; but as something may be expected, the occasion, I hope, will be admitted as an apology if I venture to say that . . .

and then with increasing passion, he declares his fitness for office because of his beliefs in the virtues embodied in the Constitution. There are a number of ways he could have done this. He could have simply stated his beliefs, one after the other, in sentences of conventional length. Or he could have strung together conventional sentences to make one sentence that was 727 words long. But Adams's strategy was different and much more effective in keeping his audience attentive. His 727 words consist mostly of eighteen separate and substantial *if* phrases. Here are the first two:

> if a preference, upon principle, of a free republican government, formed upon long and serious reflection, after a diligent and impartial inquiry after truth;

> if an attachment to the Constitution of the United States, and a conscientious determination to support it until it shall be altered by the judgments and wishes of the people, expressed in the mode prescribed in it;

It's the kind of sentence that creates suspense, because one has to wait till the end for the complete thought: if this, then what? A periodic sentence (as the linguists call it), it contrasts with a compound sentence, which simply adds one statement to another. So the listeners wait after each *if* statement for a finishing declaration. But as President Adams follows *if* statement with *if* statement, the suspense changes. Now the audience no longer waits for the final word, but wonders just how long he will be able to continue with his magnificent, countless *if*s. At last, like a runner who was expected to go a mile and has run a marathon, he ends with a final climactic *if*—an appeal to religious feeling:

> and, with humble reverence, I feel it to be my duty to add, if a veneration for the religion of a people who profess and call themselves

Christians, and a fixed resolution to consider a decent respect for Christianity among the best recommendations for the public service, can enable me in any degree to comply with your wishes,

and then a surprisingly quiet resolution:

It shall be my strenuous endeavor that this sagacious injunction of the two Houses shall not be without effect.

"This sagacious injunction of the two Houses"? He means that his election stands as an injunction to follow Washington's example as president. With this modest ending he implies his own humble acceptance of the great honor accorded him, as Washington had done in his own first inaugural. With that little conclusion, Adams has gone where no president has gone before or since, overwhelming his audience with his sincere belief in the Constitution.

Rarely will one encounter speech, or writing, that undergoes such a drastic change in style from beginning to end. Adams used a dry, impersonal beginning to lead into an impassioned personal declaration at the end, all the more effective because of its contrast with what came before.

And the effect? Well, grown men wept. Washington stood "serene and unclouded," in the words of Adams's letter to Abigail the next day, but aside from the first ex-president there was scarcely a dry eye in the room. Adams added: "All agree that, taken altogether, it was the sublimest thing ever exhibited in America." What, he's so immodest he says his speech is the sublimest? Not quite; he's referring to the whole spectacle. But that's what makes this the greatest presidential oration ever: It was so suited to the occasion, and so effective, that the result was indeed the sublimest thing ever exhibited in America.

Great oratory doesn't necessarily mean a great presidency. Adams, gifted and important as he was in getting the nation started, wasn't such a great president. This great champion of freedom signed into law the Sedition Act of 1798 that made it a crime to criticize the government. He got into such trouble with his own Federalist party that in 1799 he stormed off and retired to his farm in Quincy, Massachusetts, for seven months. But of all the presidents, he was the greatest orator.

The Second Greatest Orator

Is there any doubt that Abraham Lincoln was a great orator? The only question might be whether he should be considered an orator at all, when he was so brief and plainspoken. But his brief, carefully wrought speeches are masterful examples of the art of public speaking. If Adams has first place as an orator, it is because his speeches had such overwhelming immediate effect; Lincoln's took some time to gain their stature. We remember that it was a while before his Gettysburg Address achieved notice over Edward Everett's long oration at the dedication of the Gettysburg cemetery.

Furthermore, not all of Lincoln's presidential speeches were masterpieces. If his only speech as president had been his first inaugural address, he wouldn't even be in the running for great orator. In March 1861 the rail-splitter from Illinois stood on the Capitol steps and tried to bring the Union back together. This was a challenge that would have daunted any orator, because the deed had already been done: seven Southern states had seceded, and four more were considering secession. Perhaps that overwhelming difficulty is why his speech sounds so flat; perhaps it was beyond the power of any orator to undo the secession, and nothing would have been adequate to the occasion. In any case, Lincoln's speech on March 4, 1861, didn't come close.

It's a shock to see how little of the great president is evident in that speech. It includes flat statements such as:

I do not consider it necessary at present for me to discuss those matters of administration about which there is no special anxiety or excitement.

And it contains support for slavery that hardly becomes the man who became the Great Emancipator:

I have no purpose, directly or indirectly, to interfere with the institution of slavery in the States where it exists. I believe I have no lawful right to do so, and I have no inclination to do so.

True, the rather tedious 3600-word speech ends with the stirring "mystic chords of memory." But as chapter 4 will explain, that's an afterthought, proposed by his secretary-of-state-to-be, William Seward. Lincoln originally intended to end with a stark challenge to the secessionists: "In your hands, my dissatisfied fellow countrymen, and not in mine, is the momentous issue of civil war. The government will not assail you, unless you first assail it . . . ," a scolding hardly calculated to conciliate.

He spoke like a lawyer arguing a case—a losing case. Lincoln tried to dissuade the Southern secessionists with two kinds of arguments. The first was that he had no objection to slavery—in its place. The other was that it wasn't legal for a state to secede. There was not much in the speech to appeal to his antislavery Republicans listening intently in the audience, and even less to convince any proslavery Southerners left in his audience that they ought to trust him.

And was his speech effective? No way! Shortly afterwards, Virginia, Arkansas, North Carolina, and Tennessee joined South Carolina, Mississippi, Florida, Alabama, Georgia, Louisiana, and Texas in the Confederacy.

Lincoln's Second Chance

Four long years of war later, Lincoln stood on those same Capitol steps and delivered an entirely different speech, one that does indeed live in the mystic chords of memory. This time the audience was moved first to silence, then in many cases to tears. Lincoln was a changed man and a changed speaker when he delivered his second inaugural, the most profound and poetic of all inaugural addresses. It was much shorter than the first. Indeed, at 701 words, it was shorter than that single long sentence of Adams's speech.

This time as he rose to speak on the Capitol steps, the clouds that had darkened the skies all day parted to let the sun shine on the president and the assembly, as if in blessing. The audience received him with waves of applause, then settled to attentive silence as he began to speak. Like Adams's, his voice was strong, and he could easily be heard even on the fringes of the large crowd.

A long-winded stump speaker in his prepresidential years, Lincoln as president had learned the value of brevity and began his second inaugural by saying so: "At this second appearing to take the oath of the presidential office, there is less occasion for an extended address than there was at the first."

Abraham Lincoln (at the lectern) delivering his second inaugural address from the east portico of the U.S. Capitol building in Washington, D.C. on March 4, 1865. Within weeks he was assassinated by John Wilkes Booth.

Like Adams in his great inaugural, Lincoln began in a matter-of-fact way, drawing his listeners to assent to unexceptional statements about the present situation and the past: "The progress of our arms . . . is . . . reasonably satisfactory and encouraging" (an understatement) and "On the occasion corresponding to this four years ago, all thoughts were anxiously directed to an impending civil war." Nothing exceptional so far, nothing to move anyone to tears; but also something almost self-evident to connect him with the audience.

Then, having brought his listeners to agree with this plain view of the situation, he led them into a deeper meditation on the causes and the meaning of the war. Slaves, he said, "constituted a peculiar and powerful interest. All knew that this interest was, somehow, the cause of the war." *Somehow* is a key word here; it tells his listeners that he is not lecturing them from absolute certainty, but trying to reach an understanding, and inviting them to follow his train of thought. And he admits an equal lack of foresight with his enemies:

> *Neither party expected for the war, the magnitude, or the duration, which it has already attained. Neither anticipated that the cause of the conflict might cease with, or even before, the conflict itself should cease.*

The temptation to claim higher moral ground for his side was irresistible, but after making the claim once, he stepped back from it, again to a position of equal humility before the purposes of God:

> *Both read the same Bible, and pray to the same God; and each invokes His aid against the other. It may seem strange that any men*

should dare to ask a just God's assistance in wringing their bread from the sweat of other men's faces; but let us judge not that we be not judged. The prayers of both could not be answered; that of neither has been answered fully. The Almighty has his own purposes.

And he offered an explanation for the intensity and horrors of the war:

If we shall suppose that American Slavery is one of those offences which, in the providence of God, must needs come, but which, having continued through His appointed time, He now wills to remove, and that He gives to both North and South, this terrible war, as the woe due to those by whom the offence came, shall we discern therein any departure from those divine attributes which the believers in a Living God always ascribe to Him?

No president before or since has offered the opinion that instead of being blessed by God, our country may justly become the object of divine wrath. Yet this view gave meaning to even the bloodiest moments of the bloodiest war in our history:

Fondly do we hope—fervently do we pray—that this mighty scourge of war may speedily pass away. Yet, if God wills that it continue, until all the wealth piled by the bondman's two hundred and fifty years of unrequited toil shall be sunk, and until every drop of blood drawn with the lash shall be paid by another drawn with the sword, as was said three thousand years ago, so still it must be said, "The judgments of the Lord are true and righteous altogether."

A matter-of-fact speech had become a revival meeting, with listeners in tears as he called for repentance and atonement in the now-famous words:

With malice toward none; with charity for all; with firmness in the right, as God gives us to see the right, let us strive on to finish the work we are in; to bind up the nation's wounds; to care for him who shall have borne the battle, and for his widow, and his orphan—to do all which may achieve and cherish a just and lasting peace, among ourselves, and with all nations.

There still was a dry eye or two among the audience, but most were carried along. His speech not only resonated among the victorious supporters of the Union, but enabled a peaceful reconciliation with the South when the war was over, even after his death by assassin. That's sweeping a lot of history under the rug, of course; Reconstruction was no picnic for any Southerners, black or white. But thanks to Lincoln's conciliatory words, together with Grant's magnanimity to the Southern armies after Lee's surrender and Lee's urging his troops to go home and lead peaceful lives, there was no guerrilla fighting after Appomattox. Like Adams's inaugural, Lincoln's second had its desired effect.

Great in Their Time

Much more could be said about Lincoln as a speaker, and that conversation will be continued in the later chapter on Lincoln's presidency. But there are two other presidents who were renowned for their oratory, at least in their own time: John Quincy Adams and James A. Garfield. One earned the epithet "Old Man Eloquent"; the other was the "preacher president." To be sure, they aren't in the same league as Adams and Lincoln, and to a modern sensibility their style of oratory seems more antiquated than Adams's and Lincoln's. But what would you expect? They both were college professors—the one of classical oratory, the other of classics.

In both cases, also, they earned their reputations for eloquence outside of the presidency, Adams after he had served a term as president, and Garfield long before. Since Garfield was assassinated after just four months in office, he had little opportunity to speak in his presidency beyond his inaugural address.

John Q.

John Quincy Adams was perhaps the best-prepared person ever to become president of the United States. From the age of 10 he accompanied his father, John Adams, on diplomatic missions throughout Europe. After a Harvard education focusing on the classics and a few years practicing law, at age 27 he was appointed by President Washington as

U.S. ambassador to Holland. After that he served as a U.S. senator, James Madison's ambassador to Russia and ambassador to Britain, and James Monroe's secretary of state, in which role he wrote for that president what became known as the Monroe Doctrine.

But from 1805 to 1809 he was also the first Boylston Professor of Rhetoric and Oratory at Harvard, a situation he is said to have preferred to any other. He was never a full-time professor. In fact, he negotiated a nice contract that didn't require him to live in Cambridge or spend the whole year there (he was busy as a U.S. senator), but he did, as the Boylston endowment stipulated, "deliver to the resident graduates and upperclass undergraduates a series of lectures on rhetoric and oratory, based upon 'the models of the ancients.'" Long after he left Harvard, his 1810 *Lectures on Rhetoric and Oratory* were required reading for undergraduates.

Adams was quite classical in his rhetorical stance. He declared in the introduction to his *Lectures*, "A subject which has exhausted the genius of Aristotle, Cicero, and Quintilian, can neither require nor admit much additional illustration. To select, combine, and apply their precepts, is the only duty left for their followers of all succeeding times, and to obtain a perfect familiarity with their instructions is to arrive at the mastery of the art."

And what is that art? In Quintilian's terms, rhetoric is "the good man speaking well." He must be of high moral character; he must be well versed in his subject; and he must speak in a manner suited to the circumstances.

Quincy's inaugural address of 1825 is a calm, straightforward, well-spoken tribute to the Constitution he has sworn to uphold. Like the message it conveys, it is measured and balanced. Its 2910 words include passages like this:

> *The forest has fallen by the ax of our woodsmen; the soil has been made to teem by the tillage of our farmers; our commerce has whitened every ocean. The dominion of man over physical nature has been extended by the invention of our artists. Liberty and law have marched hand in hand. All the purposes of human association have been accomplished as effectively as under any other government on the globe, and at a cost little exceeding in a whole generation the expenditure of other nations in a single year.*

His father's inaugural included that grand suspenseful sentence of over 700 words. The son's has a comfortably culminating, unsuspenseful but satisfying sentence of fewer than 200 words:

Our political creed is, without a dissenting voice that can be heard, that the will of the people is the source and the happiness of the people the end of all legitimate government upon earth; that the best security for the beneficence and the best guaranty against the abuse of power consists in the freedom, the purity, and the frequency of popular elections; that the General Government of the Union and the separate governments of the States are all sovereignties of limited powers, fellow-servants of the same masters, uncontrolled within their respective spheres, uncontrollable by encroachments upon each other; that the firmest security of peace is the preparation during peace of the defenses of war; that a rigorous economy and accountability of public expenditures should guard against the aggravation and alleviate when possible the burden of taxation; that the military should be kept in strict subordination to the civil power; that the freedom of the press and of religious opinion should be inviolate; that the policy of our country is peace and the ark of our salvation union are articles of faith upon which we are all now agreed.

The diplomat-statesman-scholar-senator-turned-president was well received on that inaugural day, but no one shed a tear. There was no need to persuade, no crisis to confront, no urgent measures to pursue. It was, as he said later in the inaugural, "a period of profound peace."

What earned Adams his reputation as "Old Man Eloquent" was his brilliance as a member of the House of Representatives for the last 16 years of his life. When Southerners tried to prevent the House from debating petitions against slavery, he outmaneuvered them by starting debates on whether the petitions should be received in the first place. It's a bonus that he was a good guy, speaking out against slavery, for the rights of Indians, and for the right of women to petition (citing the authority of the Bible):

Are women to have no opinions or actions on subjects relating to the general welfare? Where did the gentleman get this principle? Did he find it in the sacred history—in the language of Miriam the prophetess, in one of the noblest and most sublime songs of triumph that ever met the human eye or ear? Did the gentleman never hear of Deborah, to whom the children of Israel came up for judgment? Has he forgotten the deed of Jael, who slew the dreaded enemy of her country? Has he forgotten Esther, who by her petition saved her people and her country?

And in 1841 he argued before the U.S. Supreme Court the Amistad case, in favor of freeing the slaves who had seized control of their ship and sailed it to America. Adams's speech extended over two days and lasted nine hours. It included fierce denunciations:

I am ashamed! I am ashamed that such an opinion should ever have been delivered by any public officer of this country, executive or judicial. I am ashamed to stand up before the nations of the earth, with such an opinion recorded as official, and what is worse, as having been adopted by the government:—an opinion sanctioning a particular course of proceeding, unprecedented among civilized countries, which was thus officially sanctioned, and yet the government did not dare to do it.

And he concluded with a warning of mortality, invoking the examples of the Supreme Court justices before whom he had argued a case in 1809 who were now gone:

Where are they all gone! Gone! All gone!— Gone from the services which, in their day and generation, they faithfully rendered to their country. From the excellent characters which they sustained in life, so far as I have had the means of knowing, I humbly hope, and fondly trust, that they have gone to receive the rewards of blessedness on high. In taking, then, my final leave of this Bar, and of this Honorable Court, I can only ejaculate a fervent petition to Heaven, that every member of it may go to his final account with as little of earthly frailty to answer for as those illustrious dead, and that you may, every one, after the close of a long and virtuous career in this world, be received at the portals of the next with the approving sentence— "Well done, good and faithful servant; enter thou into the joy of thy Lord."

He won. A divided Supreme Court acquitted the Amistad captives, and a year later, with the help of private donations, they were returned to their homeland in Africa, Sierra Leone.

The Preacher President

The fourth of the great presidential orators was James A. Garfield, known as the preacher president. He began preaching in the Church of Christ while a student at Hiram College in Hiram, Ohio, in 1854 and continued preaching regularly until he was elected to Congress in 1863. Evidence of the effectiveness of Garfield's eloquence is his speech at the 1880 Republican convention. Garfield was the campaign manager for one John Sherman, a fellow Ohioan. In nominating Sherman he made a passionate speech that caught the attention of the convention much more than Sherman did. Eventually, after 34 ballots, Garfield himself became the nominee. In those days, nominees stayed home and did not campaign for the presidency, but his speeches and statements from his home in Mentor, Ohio, were so effective that they set a precedent for all future candidates.

His inaugural address was a full 2973 words long. As usual, it praises the Constitution, and as usual for a Republican after the Civil War, it praises the Union, and it also speaks well of the Emancipation:

> *The elevation of the Negro race from slavery to the full rights of citizenship is the most important political change we have known since the adoption of the Constitution of 1787. No thoughtful man can fail to appreciate its beneficent effect upon our institutions and people. It has freed us from the perpetual danger of war and dissolution. It has added immensely to the moral and industrial forces of our people. It has liberated the master as well as the slave from a relation which wronged and enfeebled both. It has surrendered to their own guardianship the manhood of more than 5,000,000 people, and has opened to each one of them a career of freedom and usefulness. It has given new inspiration to the power of self-help in both races by making labor more honorable to the one and more necessary to the other. The influence of this force will grow greater and bear richer fruit with the coming years.*

As well, he argues for education as a solution to problems of race:

> It is the high privilege and sacred duty of those now living to edu-
> cate their successors and fit them, by intelligence and virtue, for the
> inheritance which awaits them. In this beneficent work sections and
> races should be forgotten and partisanship should be unknown. Let
> our people find a new meaning in the divine oracle which declares
> that "a little child shall lead them," for our own little children will
> soon control the destinies of the Republic.

As in the time of John Quincy Adams's inauguration, 1881 fell in a period of relative national tranquillity. In the course of his inaugural address Garfield commented, "The prosperity which now prevails is without parallel in our history." Accordingly, like Adams's, Garfield's speech celebrates accomplishments rather than addressing crises, though he does include concerns like voting rights for blacks (which he favors) and polygamy among Mormons (which he opposes). If Garfield or John Quincy Adams had presided in times of crisis and uncertainty, as John Adams and Lincoln did, the presidential oratory of the former two might have equaled that of the latter.

The Great Bloviator

One last president has to be admitted to the ranks of the great orators: Warren G. Harding of the twentieth century. But just as the thumb is opposed to the fingers, so Harding is opposed to the great oratory of previous centuries. By his own designation, he was not so much an orator as a bloviator.

What's that? Well, in Harding's Ohio the word *bloviate* had been around since the 1850s, an extravagant expansion of the well-known slang expression *blow,* that is, to brag or boast. By Harding's time the word was increasingly obsolete, but Harding used it to mean speaking in an ornate fashion. And he loved to bloviate.

By Harding's time, also, presidential candidates campaigned for office rather than remaining closeted at home. His most famous example of bloviation is a 550-word campaign speech of 1920 titled "Readjustment," about adjusting to peace after World War I. You can hear a recording of him reading it in his hearty voice. It includes this famous height of bloviation, with seven pairs of alliterating opposites:

> *America's present need is not heroics, but healing; not nostrums, but normalcy; not revolution, but restoration; not agitation, but adjustment; not surgery, but serenity; not the dramatic, but the dispassionate; not experiment, but equipoise; not submergence in internationality, but sustainment in triumphant nationality.*

Contrast this with John Adams's 727-word sentence. For all its greater length and weight, that one kept the audience attentive and made a convincing point. Harding's sentence knocks words around like a game of Ping-Pong. A listener can enjoy the game but will hardly grasp the meaning. Some of the pairs make sense, but "not agitation, but adjustment" and "not surgery, but serenity"? Sense has been sacrificed for alliteration.

The great presidential orators had messages to convey. The great bloviator conveyed hot air. The more you try to determine his meaning, the less you can be sure of it. Near the end of the speech, for example, he says, "Let us stop to consider that tranquillity at home is more precious than peace abroad." He doesn't want peace abroad?

"READJUSTMENT"

W arren G. Harding's 1920 Campaign Speech

> *My countrymen, there isn't anything the matter with the world's civilization except that humanity is viewing it through a vision impaired in a cataclysmal war. Poise has been disturbed, and nerves have been racked, and fever has rendered men irrational. Sometimes there have been draughts upon the dangerous cup of barbarity. Men have wandered far from safe paths, but the human procession still marches in the right direction. Here in the United States we feel the reflex rather than the hurting wound itself, but we still think straight, and we mean to act straight; we mean to hold firmly to all that was ours when war involved us and seek the higher attainments which are the only compensations that so supreme a tragedy may give mankind.* ▸

America's present need is not heroics, but healing; not nostrums, but normalcy; not revolution, but restoration; not agitation, but adjustment; not surgery, but serenity; not the dramatic, but the dispassionate; not experiment, but equipoise; not submergence in internationality, but sustainment in triumphant nationality. It's one thing to battle successfully against the world's domination by a military autocracy because the infinite God never intended such a program; but it's quite another thing to revise human nature and suspend the fundamental laws of life and all of life's requirements.

The world calls for peace. American demands peace, formal as well as actual, and means to have it so we may set our own house in order. We challenge the proposal that an armed autocrat should dominate the world, and we choose for ourselves the claim that the representative democracy which made us what we are. This republic has its ample task if we put an end to false economics which lure humanity to utter chaos. Ours will be the commanding example of world leadership today. If we can prove a representative popular government under which the citizenship speaks what it may do for the government and country rather than what the country may do for individuals, we shall do more to make democracy safe for the world than all armed conflict ever recorded.

The world needs to be reminded that all human ills are not curable by legislation, and that quantity of statutory enactments and excess of government offer no substitute for quality of citizenship. The problems of maintained civilization are not to be solved by a transfer of responsibility from citizenship to government and no eminent page in history was ever drafted to the standards of mediocrity. Nor, no government worthy of the name which is directed by influence on the one hand or moved by intimidation on the other. My best judgment of America's need is to steady down, to get squarely on our feet, to make sure of the right path. Let's get out of the fevered delirium of war with the hallucination that all the money in the world is to be made in the madness of war and the wildness of its aftermath. Let us stop to consider that tranquility at home is more precious than peace abroad and that both our good fortune and our eminence are dependent on the normal forward ▸

For a more direct comparison with the great presidential orators, consider a portion of Harding's inaugural address of 1921. Though toned down a little from the level of "Readjustment," it still wallowed in wordiness:

Standing in this presence, mindful of the solemnity of this occasion, feeling the emotions which no one may know until he senses the great weight of responsibility for himself, I must utter my belief in the divine inspiration of the founding fathers. Surely there must have been God's intent in the making of this new-world Republic. Ours is an organic law which had but one ambiguity, and we saw that effaced in a baptism of sacrifice and blood, with union maintained, the Nation supreme, and its concord inspiring. We have seen the world rivet its hopeful gaze on the great truths on which the founders wrought. We have seen civil, human, and religious liberty verified and glorified. In the beginning the Old World scoffed at our experiment; today our foundations of political and social belief stand unshaken, a precious inheritance to ourselves, an inspiring example of freedom and civilization to all mankind. Let us express renewed and strengthened devotion, in grateful reverence for the immortal beginning, and utter our confidence in the supreme fulfillment.

One could either sit back and enjoy the platitudes or find one's teeth set on edge. H. L. Mencken, the curmudgeonly sage of Baltimore, was in the latter camp. He let loose his heaviest artillery on this inaugural address:

Setting aside a college professor or two and half a dozen dipsomaniacal newspaper reporters, he takes the first place in my Valhalla of literati. That is, he writes the worst English that I have ever encountered. It reminds me of a string of wet sponges; it reminds me of tattered washing on the line; it reminds me of stale bean

*soup, of college yells, of dogs barking idiotically through endless
nights. It is so bad that a sort of grandeur creeps into it. It drags itself out of the dark abysm . . . of pish, and crawls insanely up to
the topmost pinnacle of posh. It is rumble and bumble. It is flap and
doodle. It is balder and dash.*

Yet Harding knew what his audience wanted. In an editorial, the
New York Times staunchly defended Harding's style on behalf of the
people, against critics like Mencken:

*It may be boldly maintained that Mr. Harding's official style is ex-
cellent. It carries where finer writing would not go. . . . In the first
place, it is a style that looks Presidential. It contains the long sentences and big words that are expected. The result is a document
which the American in Main Street will glance at and sample here
and there before laying it down with the satisfied verdict, "A great
State paper." . . . It is highly important that a message to Congress
should not only be read by the people but gushed over. . . .*

*It is complained that the President is too verbose and too vague.
But this again is to apply the standards of the cloistered worker in a
literary laboratory to a product meant for all outdoors. . . .*

Harding's bloviation was in fun, not for serious business. When he
wanted to, he could be direct. For example, a month after the inauguration, on April 12, 1921, Harding spoke plainly to Congress:

*First in mind must be the solution of our problems at home, even
though some phases of them are inseparably linked with our foreign
relations. The surest procedure in every government is to put its own
house in order. I know of no more pressing problem at home than to
restrict our national expenditures within the limits of our national income and at the same time measurably lift the burdens of war taxation from the shoulders of the American people.*

But with Harding's death before he could run for a second term, the
epiphenomenon of what Mencken called "Gamalielism" (after Harding's
middle name) was gone for good. The era of oratory was over when the
bubble of bloviation burst.

3 The Great Communicators

Just because oratory went out of fashion in the twentieth century doesn't mean that presidents stopped being effective speakers. The development of new media gave them new and different means of reaching the public, and ushered in the age of the great communicators.

Technology not only made possible but made necessary the change from orator to communicator. The age of oratory was marked by the use of the unaided human voice. Of necessity, to address an audience of any size, a speaker needed to cultivate a strong voice. Abraham Lincoln, to take one example, was famous for having a voice loud (and a little shrill) enough to be heard clearly even at the fringe of a crowd of twenty thousand. The modern communicator, in contrast, is able to speak quietly and conversationally to an audience of any size.

The change began, very slowly, with the invention and development of the phonograph in the late nineteenth century. As is so often the case with new technology, at first there was no inkling that it would have any major effect on people's lives—or on presidential expression. The phonograph was developed originally as a stenographic device for messages transmitted over the newly invented telephone. Telegraph operators could speak the messages over the phone, and the operators at the other end could transcribe them at their leisure from the phonograph record and then deliver the messages in writing.

But there were soon other uses for the phonograph. It was quite a novelty to hear a familiar human voice speaking from a machine, and the phonograph offered an opportunity to preserve voices for the historical record. Naturally, presidents were among the first to have their voices recorded for posterity. Because of that we can hear today, in archives of recorded sound readily available on the World Wide Web, the actual voices of more than twenty presidents, going back as far as Grover Cleveland.

On the Record

From those recordings it is clear that Cleveland and his successors Benjamin Harrison and William McKinley at the end of the nineteenth century were not media-savvy with regard to the phonograph. (They would not have known what to make of the term *media-savvy,* either.) They did not tone down their speaking style for the phonograph, but spoke as if to a large audience. Of course, the early recording machines required the same loud voice as public oratory, so it was necessary to maintain that volume.

But phonographs did force one change that presaged the communication style of the twentieth century. One couldn't speak for long when one made a phonograph record. Harrison's speech, recorded on an Edison wax cylinder in 1889 and archived at the Vincent Voice Library of Michigan State University, lasts a mere 36 seconds. Cleveland's, recorded in 1892, is one minute 21 seconds. McKinley's campaign speech of 1896 is one minute 11 seconds. The presidents used their normal loud public-speaking voices, but they couldn't speak at any length. The evolution toward the modern sound bite had begun.

By the early twentieth century, the potential of the phonograph for bringing popular music and speeches into the home was being realized, and the recording industry was under way. And in the presidential campaign of 1908, the candidates' media advisers (that too would have been an unknown term back then) saw the opportunity to bring the appeals of their candidates into homes and stores coast to coast on phonograph records.

The Mannequins' Debate

For that campaign, phonograph dealers dressed up mannequins of William Howard Taft, Roosevelt's chosen Republican successor, and

William Jennings Bryan, the Great Commoner, the Silver-Tongued Orator of the Platte, and we might add, the Master of the Catch Phrase, carrying the Democratic nomination for the third time. Each mannequin was armed with a phonograph, and each phonograph played a three-minute speech by its candidate. It was a distant forerunner of the televised debates in the latter half of the century.

And it is of particular interest because of the different speaking styles of the two candidates. Phonograph technology had improved so that neither candidate needed to shout. But Bryan talks as if before a vast audience, pausing after every short phrase as if waiting for the echoes to fade away before continuing, while Taft speaks conversationally. You can hear them for yourself on the website of Menlo Park in Edison, New Jersey.

Here's Bryan, the old-fashioned orator, in his famous speech, "An Ideal Republic." The vertical lines indicate pauses.

> *Mr. Chairman | and gentlemen of the committee: | I can never fully discharge the debt of gratitude | which I owe to my countrymen | for the honors which they have so generously bestowed upon me. | But sirs, | whether it be my lot to occupy the high office | for which the convention has named me | or to spend the remainder of my days in private life, | it shall be my constant ambition | and my consoling purpose | to aid in realizing the high ideals | of those whose wisdom and courage and sacrifices | brought this republic into existence. | I can conceive of a national destiny | surpassing the glories of the present | and the past. | A destiny which meets the responsibilities of the day | and measures up to the possibilities | of the future.*
>
> *Behold a republic | resting securely on the foundation stone | quarried by revolutionary patriots | from the mountain of eternal truth. | A republic applying in practice | and proclaiming to the world | the self-evident proposition | that all men are created equal; | that they're endowed with inalienable rights; | that governments are instituted among men | to secure these rights; | and that governments derive their just powers | from the consent of the governed.*
>
> *Behold a republic | in which civil and religious liberty | stimulate all to earnest endeavor | and in which the law restrains every hand | uplifted for a neighbor's injury, | a republic in which every citizen is a sovereign | but in which no one cares | to wear a crown.*

Behold a republic | standing erect | while empires all around are bowed beneath the weight of their own armaments, | a republic whose flag is loved | while other flags | are only feared.

Behold a republic | increasing in population, | in wealth and strength and in influence, | solving the problems of civilization | and hastening the coming | of a universal brotherhood; | a republic which shakes thrones | and dissolves aristocracies | by its silent example | and gives light and inspiration | to those who sit in darkness.

Behold a republic | gradually | but surely becoming the supreme moral factor | in the world's progress | and the accepted arbiter | of the world's disputes, | a republic | whose history, | like the path of the just, | is as a shining light | that shineth more and more | unto the perfect day.

Try saying the last sentence of that speech aloud, pausing where Bryan paused, and you will realize how different it is from ordinary conversation, unless the conversationalist is out of breath. That's the style required by oratory in an auditorium that echoes. Here he isn't in an auditorium, but he speaks as if he were.

And he speaks with a deliberately old-fashioned flavor, especially as it echoeth unto the Bible in the final sentence.

Here for comparison is a competing speech from Taft. Notice the longer stretches uninterrupted by pauses, conversational rather than oratorical, as well as the more down-to-earth language and phrasing. Taft's talk is on "Foreign Missions."

I have known a good many people who were opposed to foreign missions. | I've known a good many regular attendants at church | and sincere members | that religiously, if you choose to use that term, | refused to contribute | to foreign missions. | I confess that there was a time | when I was enjoying a smug provincialism | that I hope has left me now | when I rather sympathized | with that view. | Until I went to the Orient, | until it was thrust upon me the responsibilities with reference to the extension of civilization | in those far distant lands, | I did not realize the immense importance of foreign missions.

The truth is, we've got to wake up in this country. | We are not all there is in the world. | There are lots besides us. | And there are lots of people besides us that are entitled to our effort and our money and our sacrifice | to help them on in the world. | Now no man can study the movement of modern civilization from an impartial standpoint | and not realize that Christianity | and the spread of Christianity | are the only basis for hope of modern civilization in the growth of popular self-government. | The spirit of Christianity is pure democracy. | It is the equality of man before God, | equality of man before the law, | which is as I understand it | the most godlike manifestation | that man has been able to make.

I am not here tonight to speak of foreign missions from a purely religious standpoint. | That has been | and will be done. | I am here to speak of it from the standpoint | of political governmental advancement, | the advancement of modern civilization. | And I think I've had some opportunity to know | how dependent we are on the spread of Christianity | for any hope we may have | of uplifting the people | whom Providence has thrust upon us for our guidance.

I suppose I ought not to go into a discussion here | of our business in the Philippines, | but I never can take up that subject without finding the moral. | It is my conviction that our nation is just as much charged | with the obligation to help the unfortunate peoples of other countries | that are thrust upon us by fate | onto their feet to become a self-governing people | as it is the business of the wealthy and fortunate in a community | to help the infirm and the unfortunate of that community.

It is said that there's nothing in the Constitution of the United States that authorizes | national altruism of this sort. | And of course there is not. | But there's nothing in the Constitution of the United States that forbids it. | What there is in the Constitution of the United States | is a freeing spirit that we are a nation with all the responsibilities that any nation ever had. | And therefore when it becomes the Christian duty of a nation to assist another nation, | the Constitution authorizes it, | because it is part of national well-being.

Taft's voice continues 14, 15, 18, 20 words without a pause, as one might do in uninterrupted conversation. He uses contractions—*I've* and *we've* and *there's*—and starts quite a few sentences with *and*. He qualifies the grand declarations with "as I understand it" and "I think." All in all, it's what you might hear from someone actually speaking in your parlor where you'd be playing the phonograph.

But though his talk is fluent, Taft isn't a particularly memorable speaker; he is not one of our Great Communicators. He's on record here because he was among the first on the record. But he was closely associated with the first Great Communicator of the twentieth century, his predecessor and later his rival for the presidency in 1912, Theodore Roosevelt.

The Bully Pulpit

Roosevelt was a true twentieth-century president. Instead of keeping aloof, he put himself in center stage, invited the spotlight, and put on a show. He happily brought the press and the public close in. He gave reporters their own room at the White House, and he himself published more articles and books than any other president. And he gave speeches and interviews galore.

And what a show he put on when he spoke! He wasn't a great orator; he didn't have a great voice; but he electrified audiences with his energy and combativeness. His teeth snapped when he spoke in his vigorous shrill patrician voice. Long before the term *sound bite* was invented, he was a champion of the art.

In the age of orators, the whole of a speech mattered. It had a cumulative effect greater than the sum of its parts. But in the age of communicators, it's the gems that sparkle within a speech, or a conversation, that catch our attention. Teddy Roosevelt's speeches are for the most part long forgotten. But the astonishing phrases he invented are still the talk of the nation:

> *To a reporter, on returning to the United States after victory at San Juan Hill in Cuba in the Spanish-American War: "I'm in a disgracefully healthy condition! I've had a bully time and a bully fight! I feel as strong as a bull moose!"* (August 14, 1898)

> *"I have always been fond of the West African proverb: 'Speak softly and carry a big stick; you will go far.'"* (Letter, newspaper article, speech, 1900)

> *After luncheon* [President Roosevelt] *invited me to go with him to his office and examine some new German rifles. On arriving there we*

found some very obsequious Germans who, after profound bows, showed their weapons. The President was much pleased with the mechanism of the guns and, seizing one, worked it, threw it up to his shoulder, pointed it out of the window, clicked it, tested it, and finally, with the enthusiasm of a boy, passed it over to me for examination, exclaiming: "By George! Look at it! Ain't that bully?" I wondered whether the Germans had ever heard the Kaiser talking about bully things. (John S. Wise, *Recollections of Thirteen Presidents*, 1906)

Half a dozen of us were with the President in his library. He was sitting at his desk reading to us his forthcoming Message. He had just finished a paragraph of distinctly ethical character, when he suddenly stopped, swung round in his swivel chair, and said: "I suppose my critics will call that preaching, but I have got such a bully pulpit!" (Lyman Abbott, *The Outlook*, February 27, 1909)

"Somebody asked me why I did not get an agreement with Colombia. They might just as well ask me why I do not nail cranberry jelly to the wall. It would not be my fault or the fault of the nail; it would be the fault of the jelly." (*New York Times*, April 9, 1912)

Sometimes his innovative language was so obscure that it required explanation. Well, explanation he was happy to give. It's very hard to succeed in introducing a new word or meaning into the language, but shortly after he had explained what he meant by "The Man with the Muck Rake" in a 1906 speech of that title, *muckraker* became the established name for an investigative journalist. With evident relish, Roosevelt began that soon-to-be-famous speech by explaining his literary reference in detail:

In Bunyan's Pilgrim's Progress *you may recall [he said artfully, immediately providing an explanation for those who didn't recall] the description of the Man with the Muck Rake, the man who could look no way but downward, with the muck rake in his hand; who was offered a celestial crown for his muck rake, but who would neither look up nor regard the crown he was offered, but continued to rake to himself the filth of the floor.*

In Pilgrim's Progress *the Man with the Muck Rake is set forth as the example of him whose vision is fixed on carnal instead of spiritual things. Yet he also typifies the man who in this life consistently refuses to see aught that is lofty, and fixes his eyes with solemn intentness only on that which is vile and debasing.*

Now, it is very necessary that we should not flinch from seeing what is vile and debasing. There is filth on the floor, and it must be scraped up with the muck rake; and there are times and places where this service is the most needed of all the services that can be performed. But the man who never does anything else, who never thinks or speaks or writes, save of his feats with the muck rake, speedily becomes, not a help but one of the most potent forces for evil. . . .

The speech goes on in this vein, criticizing reporters and reformers who dig up dirt. But as is the case with so many new words, once *muckraker* was born, it developed its own character and ever since has been worn as a proud badge by those who would bring wrongdoing to the light of day.

"The Fight Is On"

It should be emphasized once again that TR was not a great orator. But audiences would flock to hear him because—well, they knew he would fight the good fight. And he talked the talk of a fighter, too. Who else would have thought of introducing "hat in the ring" to politics? It was a boxing expression from the Wild West, where the act of tossing the hat in the ring meant that a person was ready to challenge all comers. As he said to reporters at the start of his 1912 "Bull Moose" campaign: "My hat's in the ring. The fight is on, and I'm stripped to the buff." Who wouldn't want to hear a fighter and a talker like that?

When Teddy wanted to fight and talk, nothing could stop him, not even a bullet. In fact, he took a bullet once just as he was about to give a speech. Under such circumstances, every other president has been stopped dead in his tracks, but not Teddy. It was during the wild campaign of 1912, which was eventually won by Democrat Woodrow Wilson because Roosevelt and Taft split the Republican vote. Just before a speech in Milwaukee, TR was shot at close range by a crazed assassin. His folded 50-page speech and his glasses case slowed the bullet to a stop an inch from his heart. Bleeding from the chest, Teddy stepped up to the podium, pulled out the speech to display the bullet hole, and before giving his prepared speech, ad-libbed as follows:

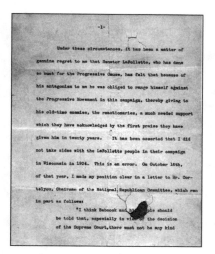

On October 14, 1912, while on his way to give a campaign speech at the Milwaukee Auditorium, Teddy Roosevelt was shot by John Schrank. This first page of the fifty-page address that was in his coat pocket shows the hole the bullet made.

Friends, I shall ask you to be as quiet as possible. I don't know whether you fully understand that I have just been shot. But it takes more than that to kill a Bull Moose. But fortunately I had my manuscript. So you see [holding it up], I was going to make a long speech, and there is a bullet—there is where the bullet went through. And it probably saved me from it going into my heart. The bullet is in me now, so that I cannot make a very long speech, but I will try my best.

And now, friends, I want to take advantage of this incident to say a word of solemn warning to my fellow countrymen. First of all, I want to say this about myself: I have altogether too important things to think of to feel any concern over my own death. And now I cannot speak to you insincerely within five minutes of being shot. I am telling you the literal truth when I say that my concern is for many other things. It is not in the least for my own life. I want you to understand that I am ahead of the game, anyway. No man has had a happier life than I have led, a happier life in every way. I have been able to do certain things that I greatly wished to do, and I am interested in doing other things.

I can tell you with absolute truthfulness that I am very much uninterested in whether I am shot or not. It was just as when I was colonel of my regiment. I always felt that a private was to be excused for feeling at times some pangs of anxiety about his personal safety, but I cannot understand a man fit to be a colonel who can pay any heed to his personal safety when he is occupied as he ought to be with the absorbing desire to do his duty.

Then he set down his manuscript and began talking. His speech lasted more than half an hour, more than 3800 words as recorded by a stenographer. The stenographer's transcript gives us a sense of what it must have been like to be in the audience. The very act of completing the speech became heroic, and Roosevelt frequently reminded his audience of the struggle. It wasn't his declarations of policy that his listeners would remember, but his ad-libbed interjections:

> *I don't know anything about who the man was who shot me tonight. He was seized at once by one of the stenographers in my party, Mr. Martin, and I suppose is now in the hands of the police. He shot to kill. He shot—the shot, the bullet went in here—I will show you.*

It's like Mark Antony's famous speech in Shakespeare's *Julius Caesar,* where he shows off Caesar's wounds to inflame the crowd: "Look, in this place ran Cassius' dagger through: See what a rent the envious Casca made. . . ."

> *Now, friends, I am not speaking for myself at all, I give you my word, I do not care a rap about being shot; not a rap. . . .*
>
> *I am not sick at all. I am all right. I cannot tell you of what infinitesimal importance I regard this incident as compared with the great issues at stake in this campaign, and I ask it not for my sake, not the least in the world, but for the sake of common country, that they make up their minds to speak only the truth, and not use that kind of slander and mendacity which if taken seriously must incite weak and violent natures to crimes of violence. Don't you make any mistake. Don't you pity me. I am all right. I am all right and you cannot escape listening to the speech either.*

His companions on stage kept urging him to cut his speech short and get medical treatment. But the Bull Moose continued to roar:

> *My friends are a little more nervous than I am. Don't you waste any sympathy on me. I have had an A-1 time in life and I am having it now. . . .*
>
> *I am all right. I am a little sore. Anybody has a right to be sore with a bullet in him. You would find that if I was in battle now I*

would be leading my men just the same. Just the same way I am going to make this speech. . . .

I know these doctors, when they get hold of me, will never let me go back, and there are just a few more things that I want to say to you.

And then, instead of stepping down, he set aside further talk of his wounds and talked politics, concluding without self-reference:

I ask you to look at our declaration and hear and read our platform about social and industrial justice and then, friends, vote for the Progressive ticket without regard to me, without regard to my personality, for only by voting for that platform can you be true to the cause of progress throughout this Union.

Throughout most of the speech, however, Teddy had seized the opportunity to deflect attention from his platform to himself. In a sense, like the other Great Communicators, he was the platform. People would be entrusting him with the implementation of Progressive policies. Beyond advocating certain views, the Great Communicators advocate themselves as people you can trust to do the right thing on whatever issue.

Grace Under Fire

No other president has had such a dramatic occasion for a speech. It should be noted, though, that one other Great Communicator, the one who wore the title Great Communicator himself, acquitted himself with graceful words under fire towards the end of the century. Unfortunately, Ronald Reagan was wounded too badly on March 30, 1981, to permit himself more than a few quips. Just before emergency surgery, he said to one of the doctors, "I hope you're a Republican." To which the doctor gallantly replied, "Today, Mr. President, we're all Republicans."

After waking from surgery, Ronald Reagan said to a nurse holding his hand, "Does Nancy know about us?" and then to Nancy, "Honey, I forgot to duck," and then to another nurse, borrowing the epitaph W.C. Fields suggested for himself, "All in all, I'd rather be in Philadelphia."

Fortunately, such occasions are not everyday occurrences. For the most part, the presidential communicators of the twentieth century have been able to present their messages in more tranquil circumstances. At home by the fireside, for example.

Such was the case with the second of the Great Communicators of the twentieth century, Theodore Roosevelt's fifth cousin Franklin D. Roosevelt. Franklin took Teddy as a model, even going to the extreme of adopting the epithet "bully" when he was young. But FDR didn't strip to the buff or call himself a bull moose, even metaphorically. His was a kinder, gentler style of communication. And as Taft and Theodore Roosevelt had used phonograph records to bring their voices into American homes (for both, the 1912 campaign had even more political recordings than the previously mentioned 1908), Franklin Roosevelt used the new medium of radio to the same purpose.

Radio wasn't brand new in the 1930s when Roosevelt used it to get himself elected and his programs approved. Wireless communication had been invented by the Italian physicist Guglielmo Marconi in 1895; commercial broadcasts in the United States started in 1920; and by the end of the twenties, major speeches were frequently aired around the country on radio. But Franklin Roosevelt invented a new way to reach the radio audience: not a speech before a live audience, where the radio listeners would seem to be eavesdropping, but a talk without any other audience than the radio listeners themselves. The president seemed as close and as familiar as if he had stopped in each listener's living room for a chat.

Roosevelt had been president for scarcely a week on March 12, 1933, when he made his first experiment in talking directly to the American people over the radio. It was something new, but then he had just done something else new and astonishing: He had closed the nation's banks. As he explained why he had taken that action, Roosevelt addressed his listeners directly, using *I* and *you*, in long conversational phrases:

> *My friends, | I want to talk for a few minutes with the people of the United States about banking. | To talk with the comparatively*

*few who understand the mechanics of banking | but more particu-
larly with the overwhelming majority of you | who use banks for the
making of deposits and the drawing of checks. | I want to tell you
what has been done in the last few days | and why it was done | and
what the next steps are going to be. . . .*

*. . . And I know that when you understand what we in Washington
have been about | I shall continue to have your cooperation, | as fully
as I have had your sympathy and your help during the past week.*

This new way of speaking quickly acquired a name. CBS reporter
Robert Trout later recalled how the name was introduced:

*The man who actually thought of the phrase "fireside chat" was
Harry Butcher, who at that time was the director and the general
manager of CBS' Washington station. It was his idea that this would
be just the kind of folksy touch that might do for the introduction
for the president. And the whole little introduction was about—The
president is going to talk to you just as if he had come into your home
and sat down beside the fireplace in your living room and gave a sort
of fireside chat.*

The fireside chats were an immediate success with the public. Over
the next few weeks half a million listeners sent letters to the White
House in response, so many that several new staff members had to be
hired to handle the mail. For the rest of his first year as president,
Roosevelt made the talks weekly. Later they became less frequent, but
he continued fireside chats throughout the 12 years of his presidency.
Sometimes, for the benefit of the newsreels, he would deliver his talk
by an actual fireside, reading from his manuscript beside a fire in the
hearth while Eleanor sat nearby, knitting contentedly.

His talks reassured and encouraged the American people, but they
also had a political purpose. In his fireside chats Roosevelt was able to
speak over the heads of the legislators to the voters, so that they could
provide grass-roots support for his measures in Congress.

The fireside chats alone qualify Roosevelt as a great presidential
communicator, but he was adept at traditional modes of public
speaking too. His inaugural addresses (and he had four of them,
twice as many as any other president) introduced memorable phrases

Franklin D. Roosevelt delivering his twenty-first "fireside chat" from the White House on April 28, 1942. In his address, Roosevelt outlined for the general public the seven-point National Economic Policy he had presented to Congress the day before.

and phrasing, such as this from his first inaugural in 1933: "The only thing we have to fear is fear itself: nameless, unreasoning, unjustified terror which paralyzes needed efforts to convert retreat into advance."

A State of War

But FDR's best-known and most effective speech was shorter than any fireside chat, shorter than any of his inaugural addresses. Barely 500 words and barely seven minutes in the reading, including extended applause, it was his call to war on December 8, 1941. He delivered it in the House chamber at the Capitol to members of Congress, but his talk was also broadcast live to the nation, and millions listened. In fact, this speech is said to have had the largest radio audience in history to that time, an estimated 62 million listeners, when the population of the United States was just over 130 million.

For some speeches Roosevelt had had considerable assistance from his speechwriters, but we know that he wrote the Pearl Harbor address himself, dictating several drafts to his secretary and revising it in his own handwriting.

> *Mr. Vice President, | Mr. Speaker, | members of the Senate | and the House of Representatives:*
> *Yesterday, | December 7, | 1941 |*

The president paused frequently, for emphasis. His pauses nailed down that date in American memory.

> *—a date which will live in infamy— | the United States of America | was suddenly and deliberately attacked | by naval and air forces | of the Empire | of Japan.*

That first sentence was a declaration of fact. So were most of the sentences that followed.

> *The United States was at peace | with that nation | and, | at the solicitation | of Japan, | was still in conversation | with its government | and its emperor | looking toward the maintenance of peace in the Pacific.*
>
> *Indeed, | one hour after | Japanese air squadrons had commenced bombing | in the American island of Oahu, | the Japanese ambassador to the United States | and his colleague | delivered | to our Secretary of State | a formal reply | to a recent American message. | And while this reply stated | that it seemed useless to continue the existing diplomatic negotiations, | it contained no threat | or hint | of war | or of armed attack.*

Fact after incontrovertible fact, facts that even the Japanese would have to acknowledge. To get the Congress and the nation to agree to go to war, he was making his case not by declaring his conclusion in advance, but by letting the facts speak for themselves.

In a manner reminiscent of the list of grievances against King George in the Declaration of Independence nearly two centuries earlier, he ended his declaration of facts with a list of Japanese attacks:

Yesterday, | the Japanese government also launched an attack | against Malaya.

Last night, Japanese forces attacked Hong Kong.

Last night, Japanese forces attacked Guam.

Last night, Japanese forces attacked | the Philippine Islands.

Last night, the Japanese | attacked Wake Island.

This morning, the Japanese attacked | Midway Island.

These facts led to the inevitable conclusion:

Japan has, therefore, undertaken a surprise offensive | extending throughout the Pacific area.

So, as he had masterfully presented them,

The facts of yesterday and today | speak for themselves.

There was but one opinion to be reached regarding these facts, he declared. But he let his listeners reach that opinion before he expressed it himself:

The people of the United States have already | formed their opinions | and well understand the implications | to the very life | and safety | of our nation.

And he declared that he simply was following the mandate of his constituency:

I believe that I interpret | the will of the Congress | and of the people | when I assert | that we will not only defend ourselves to the uttermost, | but will make it very certain | that this form of treachery shall never again endanger us.

In the first, factual, part of the speech, only the word *infamy* in the opening statement expressed a judgment on the facts. (He repeated *deliberately* several times, and mentioned *false statements* and *premeditated invasion,* but those were factual extrapolations from the evidence.) But in the conclusion, as he argued for war and expressed confidence in victory, he asserted the righteousness of the American cause and inserted two words of harsh judgment of the Japanese: *treachery* in the statement just quoted, and *dastardly* in his final sentence:

> *I ask | that the Congress declare | that since the unprovoked | and dastardly attack | by Japan | on Sunday, December 7, | 1941, | a state of war | has existed | between the United States | and the Japanese | empire.*

How effective was this speech? It was interrupted by applause three times, with especially long applause just before his statement about interpreting the will of the Congress and the people, which came just after

> *No matter how long it may take us | to overcome this premeditated invasion, | the American people in their righteous might | will win through | to absolute victory.*

Concrete evidence that he persuaded the Congress and the people to commit themselves to war came in the votes that immediately followed. Roosevelt began his speech at 12:30 on that Monday afternoon. At 12:52 the Senate completed a roll-call vote on the war resolution and adopted it by a vote of 82 to 0. At 1:13 the House finished its vote, approving the resolution 288 to 1. Wearing a black armband, the president signed it into law less than four hours later. America had gone to war.

Let the Word Go Forth

The next of the great presidential communicators was John F. Kennedy. After Roosevelt, the nation had heard Truman and Eisenhower, both of them not without skill in communication. But Kennedy kicked it up a notch, not only displaying old-fashioned eloquence, but also being the first president to make full effective use of the new medium of television.

His 1300-word inaugural address in 1961 is remarkably replete with ringing phrases that continue to echo in the imagination:

We observe today not a victory of party but a celebration of freedom. . . .

The same revolutionary beliefs for which our forebears fought are still at issue around the globe—the belief that the rights of man come not from the generosity of the state but from the hand of God. . . .

Let the word go forth from this time and place, to friend and foe alike, that the torch has been passed to a new generation of Americans. . . .

Let every nation know, whether it wishes us well or ill, that we shall pay any price, bear any burden, meet any hardship, support any friend, oppose any foe to assure the survival and the success of liberty. . . .

If a free society cannot help the many who are poor, it cannot save the few who are rich. . . .

. . . the United Nations, our last best hope in an age where the instruments of war have far outpaced the instruments of peace. . . .

So let us begin anew—remembering on both sides that civility is not a sign of weakness, and sincerity is always subject to proof. Let us never negotiate out of fear. But let us never fear to negotiate. . . .

All this will not be finished in the first one hundred days. Nor will it be finished in the first one thousand days, nor in the life of this Administration, nor even perhaps in our lifetime on this planet. But let us begin. . . .

. . . a struggle against the common enemies of man: tyranny, poverty, disease and war itself. Can we forge against these enemies a grand and global alliance, North and South, East and West, that can assure a more fruitful life for all mankind? . . .

In the long history of the world, only a few generations have been granted the role of defending freedom in its hour of maximum danger. I do not shrink from this responsibility—I welcome it. . . .

And so, my fellow Americans: ask not what your country can do for you—ask what you can do for your country. My fellow citizens of the world: ask not what America will do for you, but what together we can do for the freedom of man. . . .

These brief excerpts amount to almost one-third of the entire speech. Even so, this sampling misses many choice phrases. That's because the entire speech consists of choice phrases. It's all main course—there are no side dishes. It's not chocolate chips embedded in a cookie, but one hundred percent chocolate. It's a continuous display of rhetorical fireworks, one after the other.

That makes it brilliant, word for word more brilliant than any speech of any predecessor. But brilliant though it is, it doesn't have the depth, the carefully laid out arguments, the nicely elaborated structure of the great presidential orations of old that start quietly and build to a climax. And it's not intended to.

Kennedy was the first television president—not the first to be televised, but the first to make the most of the new phenomenon of television—and he gave television what it needed, one bright resonant remark after another. The era of the sound bite was beginning. (*Sound bite* itself is a term that emerged in general use about ten years later.) Old-fashioned orators constructed arguments; modern presidents construct quotes, and Kennedy (collaborating closely with his friend and adviser Theodore Sorensen) had the best and the brightest of them.

The Great Presidential Debates

It wasn't just through a feat like his inaugural address that Kennedy took full advantage of television. During the previous year, candidate Kennedy had made the most of the medium in the first televised presidential debates in history—in fact, the first presidential debates in history, televised or otherwise. Until 1960 the nominees of the two major parties had never before met in public debate. That fall they did four times.

The first of the debates was on September 26 in Chicago. Kennedy's opponent was, of course, the untelegenic Richard M. Nixon, later to improve his video skills and become president in his own right. But against the senator from Massachusetts who knew better how to present himself on the small screen, Nixon didn't succeed this time. For this first debate, an estimated 66 million viewers watched the candidates make statements and answer questions from broadcast reporters. The topic was domestic issues, but style mattered more than substance in persuading voters.

And the style to which both candidates had to adjust was this: Their primary audience was not the few in their immediate presence, but the

During the final joint television and radio presidential debate on October 21, 1960, Richard Nixon (left) and John F. Kennedy focused especially on U.S. relations with Cuba.

66 million television viewers, plus millions more listening to the radio. As with Roosevelt's fireside chats, the candidates were in people's living rooms, this time with their images as well as their voices. And the living-room audiences saw the candidates close up, more closely than if they had been in the auditorium with them. So an intimate rather than a formal debating style was appropriate.

In this and the subsequent debates, neither candidate was fully attuned to the television audience. Both still treated it as a formal debate before an auditorium audience. Both labored to outdo the other with facts and figures, and to accuse the other of inaccurate facts and figures. Furthermore, neither one of them had Rooseveltian charm and poise; both often struggled for the proper words. Here's one statement that was a mighty struggle for Nixon:

> *Where our natural resources development—which I also support, incidentally, however— whenever you uh— uh— in— in— uh— appropriates money for one of these projects, you have to pay now and appropriate the money and the eh— while they eventually do pay out, it doesn't mean that you— the government doesn't have to put out the money this year.*

Kennedy too managed to lose control of his sentences:

> *Well, I would say in the latter that the— and that's what I found uh— somewhat unsatisfactory about the figures uh— Mr. Nixon, that*

you used in your previous speech, when you talked about the Truman Administration. You— Mr. Truman came to office in nineteen uh— forty-four and at the end of the war, and uh— difficulties that were facing the United States during that period of transition—1946 when price controls were lifted—so it's rather difficult to use an overall fig- ure taking those seven and a half years and comparing them to the last eight years.

Nevertheless, these two mangled statements reveal a difference in degree of formality between the two candidates. Nixon never addressed his opponent as *you*, always referring to Kennedy in the third person. (When Nixon used *you*, he was referring to the abstract "anybody.") Most of the time Kennedy reciprocated that formality, but in those two sentences he used *you* twice and *your* once to refer to Nixon, and later also slipped in another *you*:

The fact of the matter is, it was a [federal aid to education] bill that was less than you recommended, Mr. Nixon, this morning in your proposal.

Nixon did try *you* with the television audience at one point, at least if *you* were the "average family":

Let's put it in terms of the average family. What has happened to you? We find that your wages have gone up five times as much in the Eisenhower Administration as they did in the Truman Administra- tion. What about the prices you pay? We find that the prices you pay went up five times as much in the Truman Administration as they did in the Eisenhower Administration.

But in other ways, Nixon had the worst of it for stiffness, with state- ments like:

The program that I have advocated is one which departs from the present program that we have in this respect.
I respectfully submit that Senator Kennedy too often would rely too

much on the federal government, on what it would do to solve our problems, to stimulate growth.

And at one point, when moderator Howard K. Smith asked him if he would like to comment on a statement by Kennedy, he replied formally, "I have no comment."

In subsequent debates, both candidates were more poised, but they still did not relax the formality of the debate. Kennedy, however, unlike Nixon, once again used *you* and addressed his opponent directly at one point in the second debate on October 7 in Washington, D.C. (emphasis added):

> *Well, Mr. Nixon uh— I'll just give* you *the testimony of Mr. George Aiken—Senator George Aiken, the ranking minority member—Republican member—and former chairman of the Senate Agricultural Committee testifying in 1959—said there were twenty-six million Americans who did not have the income to afford a decent diet. . . . Now I've seen a good many hundreds of thousands of people who are uh— not adequately fed. You can't tell me that a surplus food distribution of five cents po— per person—and that n- nearly six million Americans receiving that—is adequate. You can't tell me that anyone who uses beans instead of meat in the United States—and there are twenty-five million of them according to Mr. Benson—is well fed or adequately fed.*

In the third debate, on October 13 with the candidates on split screens, Kennedy in New York and Nixon in Los Angeles, Nixon made a statement on the side of dignity, but also stuffiness, scolding ex-president Harry Truman for conduct unbecoming a president:

> *Of course, both er— Senator Kennedy and I have felt Mr. Truman's ire; and uh— consequently, I think he can speak with some feeling on this subject. I just do want to say one thing, however. We all have tempers; I have one; I'm sure Senator Kennedy has one. But when a man's president of the United States, or a former president, he has an obligation not to lose his temper in public. One thing I've noted as I've traveled around the country are the tremendous number of children who come out to see the presidential candidates. I see mothers*

*holding their babies up, so that they can see a man who might be
president of the United States. I know Senator Kennedy sees them,
too. It makes you realize that whoever is president is going to be a
man that all the children of America will either look up to, or will
look down to.*

*And I can only say that I'm very proud that President
Eisenhower restored dignity and decency and, frankly, good language to the conduct of the presidency of the United States.* [Harry
Truman was known to use the epithet "son of a bitch" and other
equally shocking language with regard to his opponents.] *And I
only hope that, should I win this election, that I could approach
President Eisenhower in maintaining the dignity of the office; in
seeing to it that whenever any mother or father talks to his child,
he can look at the man in the White House and, whatever he may
think of his policies, he will say: "Well, there is a man who main-
tains the kind of standards personally that I would want my child
to follow."*

Finally, in the last debate, on October 21 from New York, Kennedy
once more was the only one to relax the formality enough to directly
address his opponent (emphasis added):

*What I downgrade, Mr. Nixon, is the leadership the country is
getting, not the country. Now I didn't make most of the statements
that you said I made. The s— I believe the Soviet Union is first in
outer space. We have— may have made more shots but the size of
their rocket thrust and all the rest— you yourself said to Khrushchev,
"You may be ahead of us in rocket thrust but we're ahead of you in
color television" in your famous discussion in the kitchen.*

And later, even more extensively,

*Well, Mr. Nixon, to go back to 1955. The resolution commits the
president in the United States, which I supported, to defend
uh— Formosa, the Pescadores, and if it was his military judgment,
these islands. . . . In view of the difficulties we've had with the
islands, in view of the difficulties and disputes we've had with
Chiang Kai-shek, that's the only position we can take. That's not the*

position you took, however. The first position you took, when this matter first came up, was that we should draw the line and commit ourselves, as a matter of principle, to defend these islands. Not as part of the defense of Formosa and the Pescadores. You showed no recognition of the Administration program to try to persuade Chiang Kai-shek for the last five years to withdraw from the islands. And I challenge you tonight to deny that the Administration has sent at least several missions to persuade Chiang Kai-shek's withdrawal from these islands.

This was just the beginning of the shift to informality and intimacy in television appearances that would be perfected, if that's the word, by later presidents. By the end of the twentieth century and the start of the twenty-first, Bill Clinton and George W. Bush were revealing themselves candidly, intimately, and unselfconsciously before television cameras like contestants in "reality" shows.

The Great Communicator

But first came the president who earned the epithet "Great Communicator" while in office. Ronald Reagan, with his broadcast and acting experience, was never tongue-tied. It is sometimes said that he needed a script, and indeed as president he did depend on his speechwriters to give him good lines. But his early experience as a baseball broadcaster helped develop his fluency. And his intimate knowledge of the movies not only gave him an inexhaustible store of great lines like "All in all, I'd rather be in Philadelphia" on the unexpected occasion of being shot, but also made him seem a man of the people. So he was able to use Clint Eastwood-ese (from the 1971 movie *Dirty Harry*) in a 1985 speech to the American Business Conference:

I have my veto pen drawn and ready for any tax increase that Congress might even think of sending up. And I have only one thing to say to the tax increasers: Go ahead, make my day.

And finally, he had preoccupied himself with politics for decades before he was first elected to public office as governor of California in

1966. As he wrote about that 1966 campaign, one of his opponent's favorite ploys "was to say, 'Reagan is only an actor who memorizes speeches written by other people, just like he memorized the lines that were fed to him by his screenwriters in the movies. Sure, he makes a good speech, but who's *writing* his speeches?' Well, *I* was writing my speeches."

During his many years as a private citizen, Reagan slowly developed his own political philosophy, moving from being a pro-government admirer of Franklin Roosevelt to an antigovernment advocate of free enterprise. Here's Roosevelt in his second inaugural address of 1937:

> *This year marks the one hundred and fiftieth anniversary of the Constitutional Convention which made us a nation. At that Convention our forefathers . . . created a strong government with powers of united action sufficient then and now to solve problems utterly beyond individual or local solution. A century and a half ago they established the Federal Government in order to promote the general welfare and secure the blessings of liberty to the American people.*
>
> *Today we invoke those same powers of government to achieve the same objectives.*

And pointing in exactly the opposite direction, here's Reagan, an admirer of Roosevelt since childhood, in his first inaugural of 1981:

> *In this present crisis, government is not the solution to our problem.*
>
> *From time to time, we have been tempted to believe that society has become too complex to be managed by self-rule, that government by an elite group is superior to government for, by, and of the people. But if no one among us is capable of governing himself, then who among us has the capacity to govern someone else?*

For many years before that inaugural, Reagan had been developing, polishing, and simplifying his antigovernment, pro-private enterprise position. It is unfair to say that he thoughtlessly reached simple conclusions about the role of government, because he had wrestled with the issues for many years. But it is fair to say that the conclusions he reached after lengthy consideration were simple. As he said in his famous "A Time for Choosing" speech of October 27, 1964, on behalf of the Goldwater-Miller campaign for the presidency (which Democrat Lyndon Johnson won):

They say the world has become too complex for simple answers. They are wrong. There are no easy answers, but there are simple answers.

That 1964 speech, made while he still had never held public office, is a good example of his effectiveness as a communicator. For one thing, he knew his lines, and he had perfected them in front of countless audiences. From 1954 to 1962 he had been host of the *General Electric Theater* on television, and GE began sponsoring him on promotional tours of GE plants around the country, giving what became known as "the speech." Over the years he perfected that speech, choosing and polishing those lines that went over best. "A Time for Choosing" in 1964 was therefore the product of endless rehearsal and improvement.

Like the other Great Communicators, Reagan was brilliant at making the political personal. Here is how he began "A Time for Choosing":

Thank you very much. Thank you and good evening. The sponsor has been identified, but unlike most television programs, the performer hasn't been provided with a script. As a matter of fact, I have been permitted to choose my own ideas regarding the choice that we face in the next few weeks.

I have spent most of my life as a Democrat. I recently have seen fit to follow another course. . . .

We could trust him, he implied, because he was his own man and had figured out for himself what is right. True to his principle that "there are simple answers," his speech continued with those answers:

You and I are told increasingly that we have to choose between a left or right, but I would like to suggest that there is no such thing as a left or right. There is only an up or down. . . .

Some of his simple points were buttressed and illustrated by anecdotes:

> Not too long ago two friends of mine were talking to a Cuban refugee, a businessman who had escaped from Castro, and in the midst of his story one of my friends turned to the other and said, "We don't know how lucky we are." And the Cuban stopped and said, "How lucky you are! I had someplace to escape to." In that sentence he told us the entire story.

Many were buttressed by facts, figures, and arithmetic. Politicians love to quote facts and figures, but Reagan's were decidedly simple:

> Now we are told that 9.3 million families in this country are poverty-stricken on the basis of earning less than $3,000 a year. Welfare spending is ten times greater than in the dark depths of the Depression.
>
> We are spending $45 billion on welfare. Now do a little arithmetic, and you will find that if we divided the $45 billion up equally among those 9 million poor families, we would be able to give each family $4,600 a year, and this added to their present income should eliminate poverty! Direct aid to the poor, however, is running only about $600 per family. It would seem that someplace there must be some overhead.

And later, adding humor to the mix of simple facts and figures:

> We are now going to solve the dropout problem, juvenile delinquency, by reinstituting something like the old CCC camps, and we are going to put our young people in camps, but again we do some arithmetic, and we find that we are going to spend each year just on room and board for each young person that we help $4,700 a year! We can send them to Harvard for $2,700! Don't get me wrong. I'm not suggesting that Harvard is the answer to juvenile delinquency.

Numbers rarely capture an audience's attention, but Reagan knew how to make them entertaining:

We spent $146 billion [on foreign aid]. *With that money, we bought a $2 million yacht for Haile Selassie* [emperor of Ethiopia]. *We bought dress suits for Greek undertakers, extra wives for Kenyan government officials. We bought a thousand TV sets for a place where they have no electricity.*

It should be noted that he gave his "A Time for Choosing" speech before an audience in an auditorium, but he played it for television. He had polished his television manner for nearly a decade, so that must have been second nature to him: facing a studio audience, but with the real audience across the ether. His concern for the television audience is evident in his rapid, fluent delivery. He did not pause | after each phrase | for emphasis | or for applause. The auditorium audience started to applaud several times, but Reagan ignored it and kept right on.

Two years later, he became governor of California—in retrospect not such a strange turn of events for an actor, now that California has elected Arnold Schwarzenegger—and in due course assumed the presidency for most of the 1980s. As president, he had happy speechwriters who appreciated his concern for words well phrased and simple points well made. Like other presidents of the modern age, he is remembered not so much for the overall argumentative structure of his speeches as for his memorable lines and phrases.

The Evil Empire

To take one notable example, consider the "evil empire" speech. Half of his advisers, at least, were horrified at the thought that he would use such a phrase when the United States was hoping to negotiate a nuclear weapons treaty with the Soviet Union. His hardline speechwriters, however, managed to sneak it into a paragraph of an address to the National Association of Evangelicals in Orlando, Florida, on March 8, 1983:

So, in your discussions of the nuclear freeze proposals, I urge you to beware the temptation of pride—the temptation of blithely declaring yourselves above it all and label both sides equally at fault, to

ignore the facts of history and the aggressive impulses of an evil em-
pire, to simply call the arms race a giant misunderstanding and
thereby remove yourself from the struggle between right and wrong
and good and evil.

That was just a small part of a speech that was otherwise concerned with matters like school prayer, parental notification of contraceptives for teenage girls, civil rights, and a possible freeze on the number of nuclear warheads. It was buried so deep in the prepared text of the speech that it escaped the notice of the State Department and the presidential advisers who would have insisted that he delete it. (Incidentally, he also said in that speech, quite prophetically for 1983: "I believe that communism is another sad, bizarre chapter in human history whose last pages even now are being written.") But it was enough to bring the label "evil empire" to everyone's attention. And it played well. The "evil empire" phrase was broadcast over and over again, while the rest of the speech got little notice.

Up Against the Wall

Both Reagan and John F. Kennedy, among other presidents, took the opportunity to confront communism and the Soviet Union at the advanced, isolated Western outpost of Berlin, Germany. Both spoke brilliantly—and characteristically.

On June 26, 1963, John F. Kennedy uttered his famous declaration of American support and empathy for wall-encircled West Berlin:

> *Two thousand years ago the proudest boast was* civis Romanus sum [I am a Roman citizen]. *Today, in the world of freedom, the proudest boast is* Ich bin ein Berliner [I am a citizen of Berlin].

(No, he wasn't mistakenly saying "I am a 'Berliner' jelly doughnut," as some critics later claimed. The statement was understood in its full seriousness by Germans and Americans alike at the time.)

Kennedy's speech glowed with other incandescent lines as well, hammered home with "Let them come to Berlin":

There are many people in the world who really don't understand, or say they don't, what is the great issue between the free world and the Communist world. Let them come to Berlin.

There are some who say that Communism is the wave of the future. Let them come to Berlin.

And there are some who say in Europe and elsewhere we can work with the Communists. Let them come to Berlin.

And there are even a few who say that it is true that Communism is an evil system, but it permits us to make economic progress. Lass' sie nach Berlin kommen. Let them come to Berlin.

Reagan and his speechwriters certainly were aware of what Kennedy had said two decades earlier. They took the occasion to up the ante with an even bolder statement. It came in the middle of Reagan's speech at the Brandenburg Gate in Berlin on June 12, 1987, next to the wall that divided the city. The speech itself was not particularly immortal, but who can forget one paragraph:

General Secretary Gorbachev, if you seek peace, if you seek prosperity for the Soviet Union and Eastern Europe, if you seek liberalization: Come here to this gate! Mr. Gorbachev, open this gate! Mr. Gorbachev, tear down this wall!

This too was something of a stealth statement, inserted among other remarks of a more expected statesmanlike kind. This too was objected to by the State Department and other moderates, to no avail. And as expected, in all of the long speech, this is what stood out. It was a sound bite with real teeth in it. (Once again, Reagan was prophetic. A little more than two years later, the wall was torn down for once and for all.)

It should be mentioned also that some of Reagan's success as a communicator was a result of his sense of humor. Practically every speech of his had a joke or funny story in it. And he was good at ad-libbing humor too. Perhaps his most famous joke was one that made shocking light of the Cold War. As he was testing the microphone before a press conference, he declared:

My fellow Americans, I am pleased to tell you I just signed legislation which outlaws Russia forever. The bombing begins in five minutes.

On June 12, 1987, at the Brandenburg Gate, Ronald Reagan challenged then Soviet leader Mikhail Gorbachev to tear down the wall that divided East and West Germany.

He was kidding, of course. And he would never have said this on the record to anyone. Still, it had the effect he might have hoped for. When Americans learned about it, many were appalled, but many were impressed with his bold insouciance toward the evil empire, just as a generation later many were impressed with George W. Bush's bold insouciance toward Saddam Hussein.

And finally, it should be noted that Reagan was a great debater. Many years of practice in debating policy came in handy, but all he needed to demolish Jimmy Carter in debate in the 1980 election was one from his famous stock of one-liners: "There you go again."

A Near-Great Communicator

Bill Clinton almost makes the pantheon of Great Communicators. He certainly could speak glibly and knowledgeably on almost any issue, and in his "town meetings" he evinced great empathy toward all manner of questioners. What keeps him out of this hall of fame, however, is the use to which he put his great communicating skill in the latter part of his presidency. The *M-word* was his undoing. The famous utterances of Clinton's presidency are not the hopes expressed in his inaugural

("There is nothing wrong with America that cannot be fixed by what is right with America," 1993) or his speeches on behalf of his policies, but phrases like "I did not have sex with that woman" and "It depends on what the meaning of *is* is. If the—if he—if *is* means is and never has been, that is not—that is one thing. If it means there is none, that was a completely true statement."

The Next New Technology

Each new technology has been established for a while before presidents have learned to use it to maximum effect. The latest technology is the Internet, and candidates are making good use of it. But the technology may have to develop further—or users of the technology may have to understand its potential better—before we have a Great Communicator through the Internet. Will bloggers and cell-phone swarmers catapult the likes of Howard Dean into the presidency? They made the former governor of Vermont the front-runner for the Democratic presidential nomination in 2004—until the primaries began and conventional twentieth-century communication made Senator John Kerry of Massachusetts the nominee. But the Internet now is only where the phonograph was a century ago. In the future, mastery of the Internet may matter most in the election of a president, and the candidate who is a true master of that medium may be the winner.

4 The Speechwriters

As everyone knows, most of what presidents nowadays say is written for them, and their chief job is to read it as if they themselves wrote it and actually believed it.

—Joseph Epstein in *The Vocabula Review*, March 2001

Did the orations and communications celebrated in the two previous chapters reflect the real voices of the presidents? Weren't their speeches and remarks, even their jokes and quips, scripted by their speechwriters?

That could indeed be a serious problem. Consider, for example, how one of the most famous presidential addresses of all time came into being:

The president met with an aide and discussed the topics he wanted to cover. The aide took notes and wrote a draft. The president looked the draft over and then, some time later, gave it to another aide for revision. This second aide and the president exchanged revisions of the draft over the course of several months. Eventually the second aide called on a third aide for advice, reading the draft aloud to the third aide and discussing and refining each paragraph. The draft resulting from this conversation was then returned to the president for one final reworking before being presented to the public.

Yes, the address came from the president and reflected his views. But his views were articulated and phrased, for the most part, by others.

That kind of close interaction between the president and those who advise and write for him seems typical for the present day. But the president in this example was not George W. Bush. Nor was it Clinton, or Reagan, or one of the Roosevelts, or indeed anyone else from the twentieth or even the nineteenth century. No, this example goes back to the very beginning. The president was George Washington himself; the three aides were James Madison, Alexander Hamilton, and John Jay.

The document that resulted from their extensive collaboration was none other than Washington's Farewell Address, written for the occasion of his finishing his second term in 1796. That famous address begins with praise for the newly formed union of states—from our present-day perspective something that would hardly require mention, but an event still needing affirmation less than a decade after the Constitutional Convention:

> It is of infinite moment that you should properly estimate the immense value of your national union to your collective and individual happiness.

He then issued a still-famous warning against political parties:

> I have already intimated to you the danger of parties in the State, with particular reference to the founding of them on geographical discriminations. Let me now take a more comprehensive view, and warn you in the most solemn manner against the baneful effects of the spirit of party generally.

From our present-day perspective that too would hardly be mentioned, but for the opposite reason: The triumph of partisan politics has been complete. Win one, lose one. Washington's address then continued with an even more famous warning against entangling alliances:

> Observe good faith and justice towards all nations; cultivate peace and harmony with all. . . . Why, by interweaving our destiny with that of any part of Europe, entangle our peace and prosperity in the toils of European ambition, rivalship, interest, humor or caprice?

On this, the jury nowadays is still out. Sometimes we entangle our destiny with Europe and the rest of the world, sometimes we pull back.

Are these famous statements truly in Washington's own words? In a narrow sense, we don't know. Most likely Washington and his three aides didn't know either, after the draft had circulated and recirculated so many times. But in a larger sense, who first brought forth a word or phrase, or even an idea, doesn't matter. If Washington wasn't their biological father, he was their adoptive one. The very same words delivered by one of his aides would have had much less moment. Adopted by Washington, they became his, and thereby presidential, whatever their origin.

Such collaboration was typical for Washington. Almost all of his speeches and declarations had the assistance of perhaps the most brilliant group of speechwriters ever assembled, one of whom, of course, later became president in his own right. That Madison later became president doesn't change the situation, however. Madison-as-Washington has a different effect than Madison-as-Madison. (Incidentally, the Farewell Address was given to a newspaper to print rather than being read aloud by the president. It's over 6000 words, twice as long as the longest speech false-toothed Washington actually gave. Neither he nor his advisers would have had him actually speak it.)

Self-Writing Presidents

Admittedly, aside from Washington, the founding fathers who became president tended to compose their speeches themselves. John Adams, the great orator; Thomas Jefferson, no orator at all but a great writer; James Madison, even less of an orator but good enough as a writer to be "the father of the Constitution," all did their own speechwriting. But James Monroe got plenty of help from his brilliant and pedigreed secretary of state, John Quincy Adams, soon to assume the presidency himself. The Monroe Doctrine of 1823, for example, was largely Quincy's work.

Andrew Jackson, the first of the log-cabin presidents, was no mean speaker in his own right, but he too had lots of help: from his vice president John C. Calhoun for his first inaugural address, for example, and from his secretary of state Edward Livingston for his famous Nullification

Proclamation of 1832, which told South Carolina that it could not ignore federal law.

As late as Woodrow Wilson, American presidents generally took a large part in composing their own remarks. Even so, the earlier presidents had plenty of help.

Lincoln's Mystic Chords

The most memorable speeches in American history came from Abraham Lincoln. And they were written by him, too. During many pre-presidential years of courtroom practice and political debate, he was used to and experienced in preparing his own remarks. As president, he gave relatively few speeches, and those he wrote himself.

But Lincoln too got some help. For example, for the conclusion of his otherwise unexceptional first inaugural address, it was his secretary of state-elect William Seward who came up with the poetic phrase "mystic chords." Seward proposed this ending for the speech:

> *The mystic chords which proceeding from so many battlefields and so many patriot graves pass through all the hearts and all the hearths in this broad continent of ours will yet again harmonize in their ancient music when breathed upon by the guardian angel of the nation.*

Whew! A little rich! Lincoln liked the idea and the wording but whittled it a little to give it more tautness of expression:

> *The mystic chords of memory stretching from every battlefield and patriot grave to every living heart and hearthstone all over this broad land will yet swell the chorus of the Union, when again touched, as surely they will be, by the better angels of our nature.*

At first sight there is little difference between the two versions. Seward's has 47 words, Lincoln's 46. In both, words of one syllable predominate. But Seward has 9 words of two syllables and 6 of three; the three-syllable words are spread throughout the paragraph. Lincoln has

14 two-syllable words but only 3 of three syllables, and all the words of three syllables come within the first 11 words. Lincoln's version is more brisk and rhythmic. It's reminiscent of Shakespeare's reworking of the historian Holinshed: practically the same words as the source, but invigorated. Lincoln was wholly indebted to Seward, and yet he made the passage wholly his own.

Five Sons and a Ghostwriter

Lincoln offers us another speechwriting—or ghostwriting—example of a quite different sort. It's his famous letter to Lydia Bixby, the Boston widow who supposedly had lost her five sons fighting for the Union. This letter, so moving and full of compassion, is featured in the movie *Saving Private Ryan* and serves as motivation for its plot.

Executive Mansion,
Washington, Nov. 21, 1864.

Dear Madam,
    I have been shown in the files of the War Department a statement of the Adjutant General of Massachusetts that you are the mother of five sons who have died gloriously on the field of battle.
    I feel how weak and fruitless must be any word of mine which should attempt to beguile you from the grief of a loss so overwhelming. But I cannot refrain from tendering you the consolation that may be found in the thanks of the Republic they died to save.
    I pray that our Heavenly Father may assuage the anguish of your bereavement, and leave you only the cherished memory of the loved and lost, and the solemn pride that must be yours to have laid so costly a sacrifice upon the altar of freedom.
    Yours, very sincerely and respectfully,
    A. Lincoln

That Mrs. Bixby in actuality lost only two of her five sons does not detract from the poignancy of the letter. Nor does it that one of her other sons joined the Confederate army, that she herself sympathized with the Confederacy, that she ran a house of prostitution, or that she angrily destroyed Lincoln's letter.

None of that takes anything away from the noble sentiment of the letter. But does it detract from it to learn that Lincoln had no part in writing this letter except adding his signature? We now know that it was written not by Lincoln but by his assistant secretary, John Hay (later secretary of state for McKinley and Theodore Roosevelt). Furthermore, as historian Michael Burlingame has shown, the Bixby letter uses language typical not of Lincoln but of Hay: "gloriously," "beguile," "I cannot refrain from tendering

John Hay served as Abraham Lincoln's private secretary between 1861–1865. He was also Secretary of State under presidents William McKinley and Theodore Roosevelt.

you," "I pray that our Heavenly Father," and "cherished" all occur frequently in Hay's other writings, but rarely or never in Lincoln's.

So that's how one of the most famous presidential statements of all time came into being. Very simply, it was written by the president's secretary and then presented to the president for his signature.

Does it make a difference that the letter bore Lincoln's signature rather than Hay's? Absolutely. Imagine if it had begun, "President Lincoln has been shown in the files of the War Department a statement. . . . The President has asked me to convey his sincere condolences. I am happy to do so. . . ." No, that wouldn't do at all, a condolence note from an assistant secretary. Let it carry the transforming weight of presidential authorization and approval.

The Office of Speechwriter

Until recently, the polite fiction was maintained that presidents, and indeed other persons in authority, were the sole authors of the utterances that were made in their names. Or perhaps it wasn't a fiction but a convention. The assistance that Washington, Monroe, Jackson, and Lincoln had in their day was no state secret; it simply wasn't the custom to credit speechwriters. The collective voice was customarily attributed to a single person.

This convention persisted until recently, and not just for presidents and speeches. Thomas Edison took credit for all the inventions at Menlo Park; Walt Disney was the only credited creator of his movies and comics. Until not long ago, publications like *Time* and the *Times Literary Supplement* had a proud tradition of anonymity for their authors.

We're in a very different era now, where even the caterer's assistants get named in the credits that follow movies, and where *Time* carefully specifies exactly who wrote each article as well as who reported it and from where. This coincides with growing openness about presidential speechwriters. Where formerly they were expected to keep modestly to the background, now the exact authorship of a presidential speech is often declared as soon as it is made.

This changing attitude is reflected in the use of the word *speechwriter* itself. Back in Washington's day, and in Lincoln's, those who helped the president write speeches were not called speechwriters and did not function primarily as such; they were advisers, aides, officers in the government with duties involving the making of policy as well as the making of speeches. The very word *speechwriter* did not exist until the nineteenth century—the earliest evidence the *Oxford English Dictionary* can find for the word is in 1834, by the British author John Stuart Mill—and no president had a staff member with the title "speechwriter" until well into the twentieth.

New York Times columnist and former Nixon speechwriter William Safire, who ought to know, says that a certain Judson Welliver was the first person hired full-time specifically to write presidential speeches. Welliver wrote for Harding and Coolidge. About sixty years later, Safire created an association of former presidential speechwriters and named it the Judson Welliver Society in his honor. But even Welliver didn't have the title of speechwriter; he was a "literary clerk." It was during the 1970s that the White House began hiring persons with the specific title of speechwriter.

Today, speechwriters are anything but hidden. Instead of laboring in obscurity, they hold positions of high prestige. We think we know how glamorous it is to be a present-day presidential speechwriter, thanks to the inside glimpse provided on television by the episodes of *The West Wing*. If you're a speechwriter for President Bartlet, you're brilliant. You're quick-witted. You're tireless. You're a master of spoken and written language. You have a profound understanding of your president's ideas and way of speaking. You're obsequious, but also arrogant. How could you not be? You . . . make . . . history.

And, at least according to *The West Wing*, you're very special; you are one of the very few people in the country, indeed in the whole world, talented enough to discern your president's thinking and embody it in words—words that the president would craft if only he were as gifted as you. Why, you might even be as talented as the creator and writer of the show, Aaron Sorkin.

Famous Speechwritten Remarks

Whether acknowledged at the time or not, there are many more examples of famous presidential remarks that originate with speechwriters or advisers rather than with the president. When a modern president actually writes the words of a major statement like an inaugural or a State of the Union address, it is so rare that it earns notice, at least from insiders. For example, Safire in his *New Political Dictionary* makes a point of telling how Franklin D. Roosevelt came up with the Four Freedoms (of speech and religion, from want and from fear) of his 1941 State of the Union message on his own.

Roosevelt, however, did have help with the rest of that speech, as with many others. For his first inaugural address in 1932, to take another example, speechwriter Louis Howe added the famous declaration: "the only thing we have to fear is fear itself." In contrast, we know that Roosevelt wrote his Pearl Harbor address to Congress himself. But the knowledge of that difference doesn't change the importance of either speech. They both were delivered by him and in his name.

Here are a few additional examples:

—President Eisenhower's farewell address warning of the "military-industrial complex" was the work of Malcolm Moos, later president of the University of Minnesota.

Special Counsel Theodore Sorenson (right) meeting with John F. Kennedy in the Oval Office of the White House in 1961.

—Richard Goodwin coined the phrase "Alliance for Progress" and wrote Lyndon Johnson's "Great Society" and "War on Poverty" speeches.

—Bob Orben had the assignment of putting humorous remarks in Gerald Ford's speeches. After Ford's speech at Tulane University in April 1975, Orben complained about lack of recognition in official transcripts: "At one point the president brought down the house but the transcript doesn't show it. [The stenographers are] supposed to note 'laughter' in parentheses."

—John F. Kennedy's famous inaugural phrases, "Ask not what your country can do for you, ask what you can do for your country" and "Let us never negotiate out of fear, but let us never fear to negotiate" come from speechwriter Theodore Sorenson, with his distinctive use of the figure of speech known as chiasmus.

Axis of Authorship

When George W. Bush characterized Iraq, Libya, and North Korea as an "axis of evil" during his 2002 State of the Union address, it was common knowledge that the phrase was not entirely his own invention. One speechwriter had come up with the phrase *axis of hatred*; another changed *hatred* to *evil*. The president liked the latter and thus used *axis of evil* in his speech. Was it his? Can we count it as a George W. Bush coinage? Does it matter?

It's clear that it's not as much of a George W. original as *women of cover*, for example, his term for Islamic women, uttered spontaneously at a speech to State Department employees on October 4, 2001, and several times after that. And it's not one of the many "Bushisms," his disingenuous malapropositional inventions like *misunderestimate* or *arbo-tree-ist* or *embetterment*. But Bush adopted *axis of evil* as his own, and to the extent that the term goes down in history, it will be associated with his name.

We can deplore the inauthenticity of presidential discourse in modern times, depending as it so often does on the words of others rather than those that originate with the president. But if we do, we have to extend modern times back to the very first presidency. The presidency is a construction, a conglomerate, personified by one person but having plural resources.

It can safely be argued that a speechwriter's words, even if unaltered by the president who uses them, acquire presidential gravitas through being uttered by the president. They appear on center stage; they go under the microscope; they become the subject of discussion and minute scrutiny, as they would not if they remained only the words of someone less in the spotlight than the president.

5 The Down-to-Earth President

Even if George Washington had not set the example to begin with, it is clear that the presidency would require some formality in public statements. The words of the president tend to be weighty because the declarations of the president have a weighty effect. The burden weighs lightly on presidents who have been accustomed to weighty responsibilities from childhood, but it can weigh heavily on others who have not had the experience of growing up in such circumstances. In either case, until recently it has meant that almost all utterances by all presidents have had a certain solemnity. It took more than a century and a half to produce a truly down-to-earth president.

Because of the solemnity involved, if you want to be president, it helps to come from a "good family." George Washington set the pattern for that, as for so many other things. A good family means one that offers opportunity for cultivation: a good education, travel, diplomacy, and firsthand experience in matters of state and government. It allows the opportunity, for example, to become the best horseman on the continent, or to pursue a political career. Our first six presidents, from Washington to John Quincy Adams, all came from very good families. That seemed to be the standard.

But then came Andrew Jackson, whose upbringing was the very opposite. He was born in a log cabin to dirt-poor Irish immigrant parents. Instead of hurting his chances to be president, however, his down-to-earth background helped. After all, the American republic was grounded in the Enlightenment view that "all men are created equal," with the logical consequence of equal opportunity for anyone, of any background, to become president.

So a second presidential model emerged, the down-to-earth president: a man of the people, not above them. That democratic notion of allowing anyone to rise to the highest office became so popular that for the rest of the nineteenth century seven more presidents proudly claimed to have been born in a log cabin. Abraham Lincoln was just one of those who benefited from Jackson's example. And though no presidents of the twentieth or twenty-first centuries have dared to claim log cabin birth, they still make political profit from claiming ordinary origins. Take the election of 2000, for example, in which two men with excellent family connections in Washington, one the son of a U.S. senator and the other the grandson of a senator and son of a president, posed as ordinary people from Tennessee and Texas.

An 1830 lithographic portrait of Andrew Jackson after a painting by William James Hubard (1807–1862).

Nevertheless, Washington's aristocratic influence on the presidency was hardly diminished. To be born in a log cabin, to need to educate oneself, and to have to ascend from obscurity without assistance only made the achievement of greatness and good manners the more impressive. The end result was the same: a cultivated, dignified president. To a man, the log-cabin presidents of the nineteenth century aimed in their presidential utterances for as much dignity as had the founding fathers.

Down-to-Earth, but Cultivated

So it happens that likely candidates for down-to-earthness in speaking turn out to be otherwise. Jackson, for example, at least by the time he became president, was known for his charm and good manners, and there was not a hint of rusticity in his addresses and messages to

Congress. Or take Andrew Johnson, Lincoln's successor, who came from a background as humble as Jackson's, and who didn't even learn to read until he was nearly in his teens. We might expect him to talk the way he supposedly did after having a few drinks on the occasion of his inauguration as vice president:

> I'm a-goin' for to tell you here today. Yes, I'm a-goin' for to tell you all, that I'm a plebeian. I glory in it. The people, yes, the people have made me what I am. And I am a-goin' for to tell you here today, yes, today, in this place, that the people are everything.

But even if that report of his remarks is true, there is no doubt that as senator and then president he was generally eloquent. Just a little extreme. In an extemporaneous speech in Cleveland on September 3, 1866, for example, he reached this height of denunciation:

> Let me say to you of the threats from your Stevenses, Sumners, Phillipses [his political opponents] and all that class, I care not for them. As they once talked about forming a league with hell and a covenant with the devil, I tell you, my countrymen, here tonight, though the power of hell, death and Stevens with all his powers combined, there is no power that can control me save you the people and the God that spoke me into existence.

And so it has been with all the presidents. Some have been less than 100 percent couth behind closed doors, but they have done their best to don dignity in public. In our more intrusive times, we have learned that Lyndon Johnson, for example, and Nixon used profanity in private— and we have been shocked, and we have not wanted to hear about it. In public, those two presidents of polar opposite character had one thing in common: they did their best to keep their dignity.

Cultivated, but Plainspoken

Dignity and cultivation do not necessarily mean ornate and obscure language, of course. Lots of presidents have declared or demonstrated their allegiance to a plain, down-to-earth speaking style as opposed to an elaborate, ornate one. Look to Washington, once again, for starting the trend. He exemplified it in his second inaugural, still by far the shortest on record and one of the plainest, beginning with the simple declaration, "I am again called upon by the voice of my country. . . ."

His successor, John Adams, declared his disdain for rhetorical elegance, professing to let the facts speak for themselves. But we saw in chapter 2 that to him plain speaking entailed considerable ornamentation. And Jefferson, the third president, was, at least in his own mind, even more a man of plain speaking, though the plainness of a cultivated Virginia gentleman could still involve long and elaborate statements. Here's the first sentence of Jefferson's first inaugural:

> *Called upon to undertake the duties of the first executive office of our country, I avail myself of the presence of that portion of my fellow-citizens which is here assembled to express my grateful thanks for the favor with which they have been pleased to look toward me, to declare a sincere consciousness that the task is above my talents, and that I approach it with those anxious and awful presentiments which the greatness of the charge and the weakness of my powers so justly inspire.*

Words of one syllable, by and large, but rather intricately put together. Still, Jefferson was an outspoken advocate of plain speaking. He preferred, as he wrote in his 1821 autobiography, "logical reasoning, and chaste eloquence, disfigured by no gaudy tinsel of rhetoric or declamation." A speech that Jefferson particularly admired was one of great simplicity. It's the well-known speech of Logan, a Mingo chief, to the governor of Virginia. Jefferson presents it in his *Notes on the State of Virginia* as equal to anything in "the whole orations of Demosthenes and Cicero." This is the simple style Jefferson applauds:

> *I appeal to any white man to say, if ever he entered Logan's cabin hungry, and he gave him not meat; if ever he came cold and naked, and he clothed him not. During the course of the last long and bloody war, Logan remained idle in his cabin, an advocate for peace. Such was my love for the whites, that my countrymen pointed as they passed, and said, "Logan is the friend of white men." I had even*

thought to have lived with you, but for the injuries of one man.
Col. Cresap, the last spring, in cold blood, and unprovoked, murdered
all the relations of Logan, not sparing even my women and children.
There runs not a drop of my blood in the veins of any living creature.
This called on me for revenge. I have sought it: I have killed many: I
have fully glutted my vengeance. For my country, I rejoice at the
beams of peace. But do not harbour a thought that mine is the joy of
fear. Logan never felt fear. He will not turn on his heel to save his
life. Who is there to mourn for Logan?—Not one.

Jefferson's own public statements never attained such simplicity, but now and then in his writing he attained a powerful plainness: "We hold these truths to be self-evident, that all men are created equal; that they are endowed by their Creator with certain inalienable rights; that among these rights are life, liberty, and the pursuit of happiness."

Another advocate of plain speaking was one of the most scholarly presidents, a former professor of classics and college president, one who was said to amuse himself by writing Greek with one hand and Latin with another. Known for his oratory, James A. Garfield nevertheless declared, "The age of oratory has passed. The newspaper, the pamphlet, the book have abolished it. Only plain speaking—argument and fact that may be printed—are of any great value now." His inaugural address in 1881 begins more plainly than Jefferson's but still partakes of formal rhetoric:

We stand today upon an eminence which overlooks a hundred
years of national life—a century crowded with perils, but crowned
with the triumphs of liberty and law. Before continuing the onward
march let us pause on this height for a moment to strengthen our
faith and renew our hope by a glance at the pathway along which our
people have traveled. . . .

The Bully President

It could be argued that Teddy Roosevelt was a genuinely plainspoken president—our first, really. After all, he had left his cultivated Eastern upbringing behind and turned to the rough, democratic wilderness of the West for his greatest pleasure and inspiration. And his favorite word seemed to be the slang expression *bully*. He went so far as to use *ain't* in private conversation, though that has sometimes been the prerogative of those with the highest level of cultivation as well as those with the lowest: "By George! Look at it! Ain't that *bully?*"

Even in formal moments Teddy was relatively plain and direct. Here's how his 1905 inaugural address started:

> No people on earth have more cause to be thankful than ours, and this is said reverently, in no spirit of boastfulness in our own strength, but with gratitude to the Giver of Good who has blessed us with the conditions which have enabled us to achieve so large a measure of well-being and of happiness. To us as a people it has been granted to lay the foundations of our national life in a new continent. We are the heirs of the ages, and yet we have had to pay few of the penalties which in old countries are exacted by the dead hand of a bygone civilization. . . .

But it's hard to remove all the elegance from a patrician upbringing in New York City with private tutors, finished with an undergraduate education at Harvard. That combined with his roughing-it and democratic enthusiasm made Roosevelt a great speaker, just not always a completely down-to-earth one. So we get speeches with passages of some eloquence like this:

> In Pilgrim's Progress *the Man with the Muck Rake is set forth as the example of him whose vision is fixed on carnal instead of spiritual things. Yet he also typifies the man who in this life consistently refuses to see aught that is lofty, and fixes his eyes with solemn intentness only on that which is vile and debasing.*

"Him whose vision is fixed on carnal instead of spiritual things" includes a delicately balanced relative clause; "aught that is lofty" includes a lofty word; and "vile and debasing" is the opposite of debasing in its vocabulary. Nonetheless—or therefore—it's a grand and memorable speech.

Give 'em Hell

So it comes down to this: Of all the presidents from George Washington to George W. Bush, only one has been admired specifically for his down-to-earth language. This, of course, is none other than Harry S. Truman. Shall we say it? He's the only one who has been a true man of the people in the way he speaks.

Like the log-cabin presidents of the nineteenth century, he had the right background for being down-to-earth. Well, perhaps as close as you can reasonably come in the twentieth century. He grew up on a farm in plainspoken western Missouri. But his family wasn't dirt-poor, and he did, after all, finish high school. Still, he was the only twentieth-century president not to have had a college education.

After escaping the farm, becoming a war hero, and failing in business, Truman took to politics. He was increasingly successful in his hometown of Independence, Missouri, and in nearby Kansas City, and was elected to the U.S. Senate as a Roosevelt Democrat. His plain speaking had helped his political career; already by the 1930s he was known as "Give 'em hell Harry." Truman's association with that phrase is so strong that a current collection of books about him is known as the "Give 'em Hell Harry Series." It's also the

Presidential candidate Harry S. Truman (right) delivered speeches in several cities throughout Pennsylvania and New Jersey on October 7, 1948.

title of a popular one-man show about Truman, the 1975 film version of which earned James Whitmore an Academy Award nomination.

Though it had served him well earlier, neither Truman nor his advisers envisioned that the down-to-earth style would be appropriate for him after he became president in 1945. Consequently, he was given dignified speeches to read, which he read awkwardly. A speech tutor was engaged to no avail.

It was not until the election campaign of 1948, when he had been struggling with elevated language for some time, that he and his advisers realized that the down-to-earth style would succeed. He hit his plainspoken stride during his whistle-stop campaign, badgering the Republicans with remarks like this in Fresno, California:

> *You have got a terrible congressman here in this district. He is one of the worst. He is one of the worst obstructionists in the Congress. He has done everything he possibly could to cut the throats of the farmer and the laboring man. If you send him back, that will be your fault if you get your own throat cut. I am speaking plainly these days. I am telling you the facts.*

In Rittman, Ohio, a gift of salt and bacon prompted him to these remarks:

> *I understand that this is a sample of the salt of this great community, and don't you think I'm not going to put it on the tail of the opposition. The President Truman brand of salt. I'm sure going to sprinkle that around where it will do the most good.*
>
> *Bacon in there, too! That means we're going to bring home the bacon.*
>
> *Everywhere I go, it's just like this. Everybody is interested, and I'm glad of it. I want you to know the facts, and then use your judgment.*

And he could get earthier than that, although not in public while running for election. But he was known for his public utterance of words and expressions not customary to polite society. Columnist Westbrook Pegler, no fan of Truman, complained in a column of November 16, 1953, that

Truman often resorts wantonly to vulgarity. In this case he snarled that the charge he promoted a Russian spy to yet higher rank in the Truman administration after he was warned of the spy's treason, was "snollygosterish."

Then, for lagniappe, he told the reporters that this was "a southern word meaning a man born out of wedlock."

It doesn't, of course. Pegler quoted an 1895 editor who defined *snollygoster* as "a fellow who wins by sheer talk-nothical assumacy." And Pegler added:

Truman as President applied the term "s.o.b." to Drew Pearson for publication, the first president, as far as most of us know, who ever used this expression outside his privacy. For that matter he may have used the actual phrase for which these initials stand, but, if so, the press gave us the slightly less indecent version.

Truman's grossness shows up in the fact that he took pains to tell the reporters what he meant, adding a fillip which was not volunteered when he used the word "snollygoster" in speech in 1952.

As ex-president, Truman felt free to express his animosity to Richard Nixon in the strongest terms. During the 1960 campaign, in a speech in San Antonio, Texas, he declared that "any Democrat who votes for Nixon ought to go to hell." Reactions to that were mixed. The president of the Southern Baptist Convention promptly proposed that Truman be dropped from membership. John Kennedy, on the other hand, whose Catholicism had been an issue in the campaign, took the opportunity to spin it in a message to Truman: "I have noted with interest your suggestion as to where those who vote for my opponent should go. While I understand and sympathize with your deep motivation, I think that our side should try to refrain from raising the religious issue."

Nixon may have seemed finished after the 1960 election, but he wasn't, and Truman wasn't either. When Nixon ran for president again in 1968, Truman declared, "Nixon is a shifty-eyed goddamn liar, and people know it. He's one of the few in the history of this country to run for high office talking out of both sides of his mouth at the same time and lying out of both sides." Truman's post-1948 attitude about his down-to-earth style comes through clearly in a handwritten letter to Kennedy in 1962:

> *Dear Mr. President:*
>
> *Don't let these damned columnists and editorial writers discourage you. In my opinion you are on the right track. The president is just as great as the Congress and really greater when he exercises his Constitutional prerogatives. You are going through the same situations and troubles that Franklin Roosevelt, Abraham Lincoln and I had to meet. I don't like to put myself in that high class, but I had a hell of a time. You meet 'em. Cuss 'em and give 'em hell and you'll win in 1964.*

It is more than a shame that Kennedy never had the opportunity to follow Truman's advice in the 1964 election. But he wouldn't have, in any event. There has never been, before or since, a president whose language was so essentially down-to-earth. As such, it seems completely free of guile or misdirection. Truman famously said, with regard not just to the Republican Congress: "I never did give anybody hell. I just told the truth, and they thought it was hell." No wonder that, after the passage of several decades, even Republicans could enjoy his style and invoke him as a muse for their supposed plain speaking.

Earthiness Since Truman

Truman's success in being down-to-earth has tempted some presidents since to try their own brand of earthiness. For the most part, the attempts have failed. For example, it hasn't raised the stature of either Lyndon Johnson or Richard Nixon to have it known that they used salty language in private, though it was more of a shock to learn this about the publicly prudish Nixon.

Ronald Reagan, as befits his skill as a communicator, knew to toss in a down-to-earth line at a key moment. But he was too polished a speaker to use it without a certain amount of hemming and hawing. At his reelection celebration in Los Angeles on November 6, 1984, he ad-libbed this conclusion:

America's best days lie ahead. And you know—you'll forgive me, I've got—I'm gonna do it just one more time—You ain't seen nothin' yet.

And what about George W. Bush? Doesn't he speak plainly too, and speak his mind, with a down-to-earth West Texas accent? Indeed he does, but the problem is that his speech is too contaminated with the vocabulary he acquired in his Eastern education. The words he mangles in his remarks aren't plain. They are well-educated, or nearly so: *malfeance* for *malfeasance, admissions* for *emissions.* So are many of the words he uses correctly, like *paradigm.* Too much education has spoiled a natural talent.

6 The Blunderers

A mong more than forty presidents, none of them chosen for speaking ability alone, we can expect to find a number who blunder when they speak. In fact, we can expect to find many. A president comes under close scrutiny every time he opens his mouth, and who among us speaks fluently on all occasions? Every president has had enemies, and the enemies have been all too ready to pounce on a grammatical mistake or slip of the tongue.

Considering this intense scrutiny, however, it's remarkable how few presidents have blundered. Making proper allowance for the partisan nature of attacks on their language, we find that most presidents are guilty of nothing more than being human in their occasional lapses. Before we get to the few genuine blunderers, then, we need to allow other candidates for blunderacy to acquit themselves. They aren't as bad as their opponents say they are.

Old Hickory, the Hick

The first president not born with a golden spoon in his mouth, the first born in a log cabin to a dirt-poor family, was Andrew Jackson, hero of the Battle of New Orleans. His highly educated predecessor and opponent in the 1828 election, John Quincy Adams, wasn't the only one who considered Jackson practically illiterate. A curious aspect of that campaign was a furious argument about whether Jackson could spell. His enemies found letters of his with such misspellings as *solem* for *solemn, goverment* without an *n, sweepe* for *sweep, reguard* for *regard,* and *Canaday* for *Canada*. His friends found other letters with "fastidiously correct" orthography. All of which prompted a reporter for a pro-Jackson newspaper to tell the story of an "exact orthographer" who tried to persuade a farmer to support Adams over Jackson by explaining that Adams was "the best dictionary man."

> *"I am satisfied," said the farmer, "I know something how to vote now." "Adams is the man," said the orthographer. "Not exactly," said the farmer. "I never found a dictionary man that was not half a fool. I'm for Hickory, I believe."*

And however uncouth his language—he was said to have an Irish accent, having grown up in a community of Irish immigrants on the border between North and South Carolina—he had refined it to a charming manner by the time he became president. He began his first term with "the people's inaugural," a wild affair at the White House open to the public. But no populism peeks through the formality of his first inaugural address:

> *About to undertake the arduous duties that I have been appointed to perform by the choice of a free people, I avail myself of this customary and solemn occasion to express the gratitude which their confidence inspires and to acknowledge the accountability which my situation enjoins. While the magnitude of their interests convinces me that no thanks can be adequate to the honor they have conferred, it admonishes me that the best return I can make is the zealous dedication of my humble abilities to their service and their good.*
>
> *As the instrument of the Federal Constitution it will devolve on me for a stated period to execute the laws of the United States, to superintend their foreign and their confederate relations, to manage their revenue, to command their forces, and, by communications to the Legislature, to watch over and to promote their interests generally. And the principles of action by which I shall endeavor to accomplish this circle of duties it is now proper for me briefly to explain. . . .*

Even the backwoods Irishman felt the need for formal rhetoric before the wild party began.

Once More the Bloviator

Search as you will among the other presidents of the nineteenth century, you won't find much in the way of blunderers. Some were hard to hear and understand, like Madison; some were long-winded, like Harrison; some were pedantic, like Garfield. But they all demonstrated fluency in their use of the language, even unlikely presidents like Lincoln's successor, Andrew Johnson, whose language as a young man was reported to have been most uncouth. It is not until the twentieth century that we encounter another serious candidate for blunderer: Warren G. Harding, whom we met at the tail end of the chapter on great presidential orators.

Like George W. Bush in the twenty-first century, Harding seemed to be self-parodying; if there had been a *Saturday Night Live* in the 1920s, a sketch would have been an uproarious success with a Harding speech given straight up. Harding's style, as we saw, set H. L. Mencken's teeth on edge and inspired one of his greatest rants. The poet e.e. cummings (a Harvard-educated rebel sometimes referred to as a lowercase highbrow) sneered that Harding was "the only man woman or child who wrote / a simple declarative sentence with seven grammatical / errors."

Harsh criticism indeed. But puzzling. Unless cummings meant something other than grammatical when he wrote "grammatical," he was off his rocker. If anything, Harding's remarks had too little ungrammaticality. They flowed on and on, uninterrupted by pauses for thought. His celebrated inaugural address had passages like this:

> *Our eyes never will be blind to a developing menace, our ears never deaf to the call of civilization. We recognize the new order in the world, with the closer contacts which progress has wrought. We sense the call of the human heart for fellowship, fraternity, and cooperation. We crave friendship and harbor no hate. But America, our America, the America builded on the foundation laid by the inspired fathers, can be a party to no permanent military alliance. It can enter into no political commitments, nor assume any economic obligations which will subject our decisions to any other than our own authority.*

A more accurate characterization of Harding's speeches was made by prominent Democrat William G. McAdoo: "an army of pompous phrases moving across the landscape in search of an idea." Bloviator he was, blunderer he was not.

The Fumbling General

During Dwight D. Eisenhower's presidency it was widely believed, especially by fans of Eisenhower's elegantly eloquent opponent Adlai E. Stevenson, that Ike had an awkward, ungrammatical way of speaking. At the start of Eisenhower's second term, chief Washington correspondent for the *New York Times* Arthur Krock gave a kindly yet condescending explanation:

> *His fumbles at news conferences, remarkably few in a record so outgiving, are traceable, I think, to his efforts at times to speak personally and not to be President. And that, of course, is impossible.*

As Krock indicates, it was in Eisenhower's press conferences that he gave the impression of fumbling. The verbatim transcripts of those conferences, duly printed the next day in the *Times*, were sufficient evidence. Here's an example from a memorable press conference on August 24, 1960:

David P. Sentner of The Hearst Newspapers: *Mr. President, would you please give us your latest opinion as to the major issues in the campaign?*

[Eisenhower]: *Well, I think that we have always agreed that politics ends at the water's edge. But the conduct apparently of foreign affairs is going to be a very important issue, whether or not I would believe it should be—it apparently is going to be, because it has been talked so much.*

At home I would say that the basic material question would be the farm, and of course I think we will make, most certainly, sound money or—not sound money—but preventing the debasement of our currency, and with fiscal responsibility.

So I think things of that kind are going to be probably debated more than anything else in the campaign.

Despite the most ingenious punctuation an editor could devise, including liberal use of dashes, the transcript shows glaring lapses in grammar. In the brief space of that answer, Eisenhower managed to put *apparently* in an odd place in the first sentence and *probably* in an odd place in the last, omitted *about* after *talked*, and changed his mind twice in the third sentence and then inserted a preposition (*with*) that didn't fit.

That's just one example. Here's another, from later in the same press conference. Asked by Rutherford M. Poats of United Press International about the role of foreign affairs in the Nixon-Kennedy presidential campaign, Eisenhower said, in part:

> *Now it is in this kind—with this kind of a background that I would have hoped that our foreign affairs could be truly and as a matter of tradition almost conducted in a bipartisan spirit, and true bipartisan action.*
>
> *If we are going to make these things such an important part of political, or parties in debate, I think it is a little bit too bad.*

The closer you look at this excerpt, the more puzzling it gets. What he's trying to say is clear enough: foreign affairs should be bipartisan and above politics. But what is the grammar of "truly and as a matter of tradition almost conducted in a bipartisan spirit, and true bipartisan action"? Or of "political, or parties in debate"? What was the president thinking?

Ike the Plain Speaker

Well, as it turned out, what seemed awkward and ineffective in cold print made a different impression in person. I happened to have attended that conference, as a summer intern with the *Wall Street Journal,* and I came away realizing (as I noted at the time) why the transcripts of his press conferences make him seem so ridiculous: "He apparently considers himself to be amid a small gathering of friends, helping them with information on things they're curious about. He speaks softly and very informally; apparently he has no concern about making eloquent statements that will look good in print."

No highfalutin bloviation for him, just plain down-to-earth man-to-man (and a few women) talk. He wasn't being awkward, he was treating the press corps like his confidantes—though a word like "confidante" wouldn't have been appropriate for his conversational style that morning.

And even in that informal atmosphere, Eisenhower was sometimes stirred in the direction of formal eloquence. For example, there was his defense of Ezra Taft Benson when Felix Belair (yes, they used to have names like that!) of the *New York Times* asked the president's judgment on his secretary of agriculture:

> *Well, I think I did that a couple of weeks ago, when I said that I have never known a man who was more honest, more dedicated, and more informed in his particular work. He is, moreover, a courageous man in presenting the views of the Administration, and with his work I have not only had the greatest sympathy, but whatever I could possibly find a way to do it, I have supported exactly what he has been trying to do.*
>
> *Now, I don't know about anything—anything about the effects in the Farm Belt at this moment, for the simple reason I haven't had any recent reports of opinion there. I do know this: In the long run, people respect honesty and courage and selflessness in the Governmental service. And I don't believe that any of us should be so free as to crucify Secretary Benson. I think he has done a wonderful service.*

A nitpicker reading this could find fault with "whatever" where he should have said "whenever," and with the slightly opaque grammar at the end of the second sentence, but Eisenhower's graceful use of parallel and contrasting phrasing in that tribute makes such quibbling seem petty.

And then there was his response to Sarah McClendon of the *El Paso Times* when she asked him to "tell us some of the big decisions that Mr. Nixon has participated in since you have been in the White House and he, as Vice President, has been helping you." Ike was emphatic in his reply:

> *Well, Miss McClendon, no one participates in the decisions. Now we just—I don't see why people can't understand this. No one can make a decision except me, if it is in the national executive area.*
>
> *I have all sorts of advisers, and one of the principal ones is Mr. Nixon. But any Vice President that I should have, even if I did*

not admire and respect Mr. Nixon as I do, would still keep him close in all these things, because I think any president owes it to the country to have the next individual in line of succession completely aware of what is going on. Otherwise, you have a break that is unconscionable and unnecessary.

Now, just—when you talk about other people sharing a decision, how can they? No one can, because then who is going to be responsible? And because I have been raised as an Army individual, and have used staffs, I think you will find no staff has ever thought that they made a decision as to what should be done or should not be done when I was a commander. And I don't think anyone in the government will find—or you can find anyone that would say differently.

In the heat of his reply, he made a few false starts, but otherwise the grammaticality of his sentences was well under control, and there were rhetorical flourishes like "unconscionable and unnecessary."

A certain formality marked the occasion of a presidential press conference in those days, and if the president himself generally eschewed formality, the reporters kept to it. The extreme in stiffness came not in a remark by the president, but in a question from a science reporter, so lengthy and convoluted that it drew laughs.

Lillian Levy of Science Service: *Mr. President, on May 13 you signed an executive order which allows each interested Federal agency to fix its own radiation safety standards and to exceed, if it deems necessary, the standards recommended by the Federal Radiation Council. Is there any reason why the executive order did not provide that any standards set by the individual agency which would exceed the radiation safety levels recommended by your council be subject to review and approval by the Federal Radiation Council which originally was established, I believe, for the purpose of recommending radiation safety standards for all agencies, so that the confusion and conflict* [laughter] *within an agency between keeping to standards of safety on the one hand, and performing its functions in developing nuclear energy on the other, might be eliminated?* [Laughter]

With appropriate presidential dignity, Eisenhower ignored the laughter, listening patiently and responding plainly and directly. Against the overelaborateness of the question, Eisenhower's plain style showed to advantage:

> *Well, as a matter of fact, the question is sensible, because I assume, from the way you have read it, that there could be some confusion here if any excess radiation were allowed to escape and were not reported to the proper people. If the order is defective, I will try to find out about it.*

Ike the Fox

So was Eisenhower eloquent or tongue-tied? Clueless or clever, or both? Arthur Krock, senior Washington columnist for the *New York Times*, gave a contemporary interpretation of the Eisenhower press-conference phenomenon in a 1957 article in the *Times* Sunday magazine. While asserting that "the President's mental process is penetrating and alert," he added, "This quality is often obscured by the prolixity of his replies, in which numbers and genders collide, participles hang helplessly and syntax is lost forever." No matter, though; "these flaws invest the diction of most Americans who like to talk—which the President very much does."

The luxury of hindsight allows us to see that even when he lapsed from plain speaking, Eisenhower's language was deliberate and effective. Instead of a curt "No comment" when asked a touchy question, Eisenhower's tactic was to let loose a flood of words. In 1955, for example, anticipating a question on whether he would use atomic weapons to

Dwight D. Eisenhower held the first televised presidential press conference from the Indian Treaty Room in the Old Executive Office Building on January 19, 1955.

defend the offshore islands of Quemoy and Matsu against an attack by mainland China, Eisenhower told his press secretary: "Don't worry, Jim. If that question comes up, I'll just confuse them."

Similarly, most likely, with his remarks about Vice President Nixon in that press conference of August 24, 1960, at the height of the Nixon-Kennedy presidential campaign. His reply to Sarah McClendon of the *El Paso Times* diverted the question from Nixon's role in making policy to his own. At the end of that press conference, Charles H. Mohr of *Time* tried again, asking whether Nixon "has been primarily an observer and not a participant in the executive branch of the government." Once again, Eisenhower evaded the question by talking all around it. In the manner of a magician announcing that he is going to show how an illusion is performed but then making magic all the same, he began his answer by declaring:

Well, it seems to me that there is some confusion here, haziness, that possibly needs a lot of clarification.

And after a detailed discussion of his "consultative conferences with his principal subordinates," one of whom was Nixon, the president came to this noncommittal summation:

So Mr. Nixon has taken a full part in every principal discussion.

It seemed evident at the time, as it does from today's perspective, that Eisenhower was less than enthusiastic about the man he should have been endorsing, his vice president. Not that he favored Kennedy over Nixon; he simply didn't relish the thought of either of them taking his place. This was even more evident when the *Time* reporter tried once more:

We understand that the power of decision is entirely yours, Mr. President. I just wondered if you could give us an example of a major idea of his that you had adopted in that role, as the decider and final—

To which Eisenhower replied:

If you give me a week, I might think of one. I don't remember.

No grammatical problems with that.

A Ford, Not a Lincoln

Poor Gerald Ford, decent honest congressman from Michigan. He was the only president never to have been elected at least vice president, if not president. When silver-tongued ("hopeless, hysterical hypochondriacs of history" and "nattering nabobs of negativism," courtesy of speechwriter William Safire), scandal-ridden Spiro Agnew resigned as vice president, Nixon chose Ford to fill out the term; when Nixon resigned, there was Ford as president, pardoning Nixon; when Ford ran for president in his own right, he was defeated by Jimmy Carter. Even in high school, he had lost an election for class president.

His failure as a speaker wasn't as perversely hypnotic as Warren G. Harding's or as spectacular as George W. Bush's. He just stumbled along, committing the sorts of blunders that would have earned him a C rather than an A, but also not an F, in a public-speaking class.

His delivery was flat and monotonous, like Herbert Hoover's. Unlike Hoover, however, he stumbled over big words. One of his pet projects was geothermal energy, but he stumbled over the very word *geothermal* several times in a 1975 speech on the subject. (He finally had it learned by the time he mentioned it in his 1977 State of the Union address.) For him, also, *judgment* was always a three-syllable word (with an extra syllable in the middle). And *children* was pronounced *childern*.

He couldn't resist embellishing routine phrases: "I hope" in the prepared text of a speech would become "I honestly and sincerely hope," "I commend" would become "I strongly commend," "the House and Senate" would become "the House as well as the Senate."

Worse, he had what one speechwriter called "swimmer's breath": "the inability to go through a long sentence without having to draw a shuddering gasp of breath somewhere in the middle." The breaths sometimes came in strange places, as in his August 9, 1974, speech on being sworn in as president:

Mr. Chief Justice, | my dear friends, | my fellow Americans:
The oath that I have taken | is the same oath that was taken by |
George Washington | and by every President under the Constitution. |
But I assume the | Presidency under extraordinary circumstances |

never before experienced by Americans. | This is an hour | of history |
that troubles our minds | and hurts our hearts.

Not only did his speech come with frequent pauses, but the pauses came at inappropriate places, as after *by* and *the* above. He continued:

Therefore, I feel it is my first duty | to make an unprecedented com-
pact | with my countrymen. | Not an inaugural address, | not a fire-
side chat, | not a campaign speech |—just a little straight talk |
among friends. | And I intend it to be | the first of many.

I am acutely aware | that you have not elected me | as your
President | by your ballots, | so I ask you to | confirm me | as your
President | with your prayers. | And I hope that such prayers will |
also be the first of many.

Later in that speech he had similar odd pauses for breath:

. . . I expect to follow my | instincts of openness and candor. . . .
. . . a higher power | by whatever name | we honor him. . . .

Not that the speech itself was bad. It uses plain, straightforward language and many nice parallel phrases ("Not an inaugural address, not a fireside chat, not a campaign speech"; "the first of many," repeated; "I am indebted to no man, and to only one woman—my dear wife"; "I have not sought this enormous responsibility, but I will not shirk it.") It wasn't written by Ford, of course, but by his speechwriters. His chief assistant, Robert Hartmann, then put the final touches on it.

Ford had no illusions of being a great speaker. As he said in his inaugural address as vice president, some eight months before he became president, "I am a Ford, not a Lincoln. My addresses will never be as eloquent as Mr. Lincoln's. But I will do my very best to equal his brevity and his plain speaking."

He spoke all too plainly in his third debate against Jimmy Carter in the presidential campaign of 1976. In response to a reporter's question, he declared,

There is no Soviet domination of Eastern Europe and there never
will be under a Ford administration. . . .

I don't believe, Mr. Frankel, that the Yugoslavians consider themselves dominated by the Soviet Union. I don't believe that the Rumanians consider themselves dominated by the Soviet Union. I don't believe that the Poles consider themselves dominated by the Soviet Union. Each of those countries is independent, autonomous; it has its own territorial integrity. And the United States does not concede that those countries are under the domination of the Soviet Union. As a matter of fact, I visited Poland, Yugoslavia and Rumania to make certain that the people of those countries understood that the President of the United States and the people of the United States are dedicated to their independence, their autonomy and their freedom.

That was fish in a barrel for Carter, who lightly responded,

I would like to see Mr. Ford convince the Polish-Americans and the Czech-Americans and the Hungarian-Americans in this country that those countries don't live under the domination and supervision of the Soviet Union behind the Iron Curtain.

It ranks among the most wrong-headed remarks ever made by a president, and it alone probably cost him the election.

Blunderer-in-Chief

Listen, presidents, whether things are good or bad, get the blame. I understand that. (George W. Bush, press conference, May 11, 2001)

I know what I believe. I will continue to articulate what I believe and what I believe. I believe what I believe is right. (Rome, July 22, 2001)

Far above all 41 presidents before him, George W. Bush stands out as a blunderer of heroic stature. The editor of the series that includes *Bushisms*, *More Bushisms*, and *Still More Bushisms* has had to publish a book a year just to keep up. For example:

And, you know, it'll take time to restore chaos and order—order out of chaos. (Washington, D.C., April 13, 2003)

Bush: *I talked to my little brother, Jeb. I haven't told this to many people. But he's the governor of—I shouldn't call him my little brother—my brother, Jeb, the great governor of Texas.*
Jim Lehrer: *Florida.*
Bush: *Florida. The state of the Florida.*

—(April 27, 2000, NewsHour with Jim Lehrer)

And so, in my State of the—my State of the Union—or state—my speech to the nation, whatever you want to call it, speech to the nation—I asked Americans to give 4,000 years—4,000 hours over the next—the rest of your life—of service to America. That's what I asked—4,000 hours. (Bridgeport, Connecticut, April 9, 2002)

This is a chance for the Security Council to show its relevance. And I believe the Security Council, will show its revalence—relevance. (Press conference with Spanish prime minister José María Aznar, Crawford, Texas, February 22, 2003)

Bush's spectacular bumbling is multifaceted. There are the simple misstatements and tautologies:

Pictured with Spanish Prime Minister José María Aznar, George Bush (right) speaks at a press conference from his Crawford, Texas ranch on February 22, 2003.

There's an old saying in Tennessee—I know it's in Texas, probably in Tennessee—that says, fool me once, shame on—shame on you. Fool me— you can't get fooled again. (Nashville, Tennessee, September 17, 2002)

Security is the essential roadblock to achieving the roadmap to peace. (Washington, D.C., July 25, 2003)

There's no bigger task than protecting the homeland of our country. (August 23, 2002)

We ended the rule of one of history's worst tyrants [Saddam Hussein], *and in so doing, we not only freed the American people, we made our own people more secure.* (Crawford, Texas, May 3, 2003)

I am determined to keep the process on the road to peace. (Washington, D.C., June 10, 2003)

There are the malapropisms, the wrong words in the right places:

I do not agree with this notion that somehow if I go to try to attract votes and to lead people toward a better tomorrow, somehow I get **subscribed** *to some—some doctrine gets* **subscribed** *to me.* (*Meet the Press,* February 13, 2000)

There was no **malfeance** *involved. This was an honest disagreement about accounting procedures. . . . There was no* **malfeance**, *no attempt to hide anything.* (Press conference, Washington, D.C., July 8, 2002)

The law I sign today directs new funds and new focus to the task of collecting vital intelligence on terrorist threats and on weapons of mass **production**. (November 27, 2002)

Hydrogen power will dramatically reduce greenhouse gas **admissions**. (February 6, 2003)

Oftentimes, we live in a **processed** *world—you know, people focus on the process and not results.* (Washington, D.C., May 29, 2003)

A free, peaceful Zimbabwe has got the capacity to deliver a lot of goods and services which are needed on this continent in order to help **aleve** *suffering.* (Pretoria, South Africa, July 9, 2003)

And the other lesson is that there are people who can't stand what America stands for, and desire to conflict *great harm on the American people.* (Pittsburgh, July 28, 2003)

We're conscience *of folks flying—and getting lists of people flying into our country and matching them now with a much improved database.* (Washington, D.C., July 30, 2003)

Remarks like these exemplify the ruinous effect of a high-class education. Though he grew up in Midland, Texas, George W. was sent to the finest of Eastern schools: Phillips Academy, Yale University, Harvard Business School. His mother, Barbara, former first lady, said in a *Washington Post* interview, "Harvard was a great turning point for him. I think he learned—what is that word? Structure."

Clearly he learned many other words too—big words, academic words—that he earnestly tries to use and half remembers. Sometimes he will properly employ learned words like *effect* as a verb, and *paradigm*:

You've also got to measure in order to begin to effect *change that's just more—when there's more than talk, there's just actual—a* **paradigm** *shift.* (Washington, D.C., July 1, 2003)

But he can also tangle himself up in modesty:

Well, **all due in modesty,** *I thought I did a pretty good job myself of making it clear that he's* [Saddam Hussein is] *not disarming and why he should disarm.* (Washington, D.C., January 31, 2003)

And then there are Bush's plain ungrammaticalities:

For years the **freedom** *of our people* were *really never in doubt.* (FBI Headquarters, February 14, 2003)

There **was wars** *on other continents, but we were safe.* (Washington, D.C., February 10, 2003)

I know there's a lot of young ladies who are growing up wondering whether or not they can be champs. And they see the championship teams from USC and University of Portland here, girls who worked hard to get to where they are, and they're wondering about the example they're setting. What is *life* choices *about?* (Washington, D.C., February 24, 2003)

I went down to Mississippi, met a man who had moved to Mississippi to provide health care for some of our most neediest *citizens.* (Washington, D.C., March 4, 2003)

Hopefully, this can be done peacefully. Hopefully, that *as a result of the pressure that we have placed, and others have placed,* that *Saddam will disarm and/or leave the country.* (Washington, D.C., March 6, 2003)

Like his mistakes in vocabulary, his ungrammaticality emerges on high levels as well as low ones. He is so polite that he uses *he* where he should use *him*:

Laura and I are looking forward to having a private dinner with he *and Mrs. Blair Friday night.* (Press conference, Washington, D.C., February 22, 2001)

although he also goes the other way, using *her* for *she*:

You teach a child to read, and he or her *will be able to pass a literacy test.* (Townsend, Tennessee, February 21, 2001)

Although Bush's bumbling is the opposite of Warren G. Harding's glibness, the two are alike in relishing their speaking styles rather than being embarrassed by criticism. Does Bush seem like a *Saturday Night Live* caricature of himself? Very well then, he happily adopts that role. A noted *SNL* sketch just before the 2000 election parodied the Bush-Gore television debate and had the pseudo-Bush sum up his candidacy in a single word: *strategery.* Bush himself hadn't used that word, but by next spring there was a "Strategery Group" of Bush's advisers in the White House. And Bush himself happily continued with his misstatements as well as his fresh coinages, which will get their due respect in the next chapter.

Nucular Presidents

No chapter on presidential blunderers would be complete without a nuclear explosion. The explosion is the wrath of language purists who point out that the spelling *nuclear* should guide the pronunciation. That is, there should be nothing between the *c* and the *l*. When the *c* and the *l* are pushed apart to make the pronunciation "noo-kyu-lar," the purists hear an abomination.

President G.W. Bush goes *nucular*, of course. But he happens to come from a distinguished line of *nucular* presidents, starting with Eisenhower in the 1950s, not long after nuclear reactions first became topics for presidential discussion.

Most presidents between Eisenhower and Bush the Younger have used the standard *nuclear* pronunciation. Gerald Ford, however, mangled the word, adding an extra syllable. And Jimmy Carter said it with his Georgia accent as "noo-kee-uh."

The situation with *nuclear*, however, is more complicated than simple right and wrong. When G.W. Bush says *remenants* for *remnants*, he's using a pronunciation that educated people avoid. But when he says *nucular*, he's aligning himself not only with Eisenhower, but with military usage in general. Hardly surprising for a military man like Eisenhower or a would-be military man like Bush.

Indeed, there are people today who consciously or unconsciously use the two pronunciations to distinguish between two kinds of nuclear: *nucular* weapons, for military use, and *nuclear* for nonmilitary purposes like nuclear medicine. Saying *nucular* weapons rather than *nuclear* weapons therefore puts Dubya on the side of the warriors. Which may be no accident.

7 Presidents as Neologists

The top ten words invented or promoted by presidents, in presidential order:

administration (Washington)
caucus (John Adams)
lengthy (John Adams), lengthily (Jefferson)
belittle (Jefferson)
muckraker (Theodore Roosevelt)
lunatic fringe (Theodore Roosevelt)
bloviation (Harding)
normalcy (Harding)
misunderestimate (George W. Bush)
embetterment (George W. Bush)

A person who creates new words, or makes a point of using them, is a *neologist*. George W. Bush, who shares with Thomas Jefferson the distinction of being the greatest of presidential neologists, might describe such a person as a *neo-word-ist*, as he did when trying to remember the term *arborist* for "somebody who knows about trees" and came up with *arbo-tree-ist*. But whichever term you'd use, some of the presidents have been instrumental in bringing new or newly refurbished words into wide circulation.

And Tom and Dubya top the list: Tom because he advocated neology—the coining of new words—as well as practiced it; Dubya because—well, it's hard to misunderestimate his contributions to the English language.

The Advocate of Neology

Thomas Jefferson had informed and thoughtful opinions on language, as he did on almost every other field of knowledge in his day. Many people object to the introduction of new words and meanings, but Jefferson thought it was not only necessary (since new objects and ideas continually come our way), but desirable. In an 1820 letter to his old friend John Adams he wrote,

Portrait of Thomas Jefferson attributed to Thomas Sully (1783–1872).

> *I am a friend to neology. It is the only way to give to a language copiousness and euphony. Without it we should still be held to the vocabulary of Alfred or of Ulphilas* [nearly a thousand years earlier]*; and held to their state of science also: for I am sure they had no words which could have conveyed the ideas of oxygen, cotyledons, zoophytes, magnetism, electricity, hyaline, and thousands of others expressing ideas not then existing, nor of possible communication in the state of their language. What a language has the French become since the date of their revolution, by the free introduction of new words! The most copious and eloquent in the living world; and equal to the Greek, had not that been regularly modifiable almost ad infinitum. . . .*
>
> *Dictionaries are but the depositories of words already legitimated by usage. Society is the workshop in which new ones are elaborated. When an individual uses a new word, if ill-formed it is rejected in society, if well-formed, adopted, and, after due time, laid up in the depository of dictionaries. And if, in this process of sound neologisation, our transatlantic brethren shall not choose to accompany us, we may furnish, after the Ionians, a second example of a colonial dialect improving on its primitive.*

These observations show Jefferson to have been as expert in linguistics as he was in other scientific fields. He understood the function of dictionaries, was familiar with scientific terminology, and saw the likelihood of some drifting apart of British and American English, in part driven by American coinage of new words—as of course has happened.

Accidental Neologists

But whether or not we think about neology or approve of it, we are all accidental neologists. We couldn't not be, even if we tried. The nature of language invites us to create new words by such means as adding prefixes and suffixes—to add *ism* to a president's name to mean a word created or typically used by that president, for example. That's where *Bushism*, meaning a word created by G.W. Bush, came from.

And it also means that most neologisms are boring. They are such natural extensions of the language that they don't get noticed, and if they do, the natural reaction is, So what? Yet they are significant. Take the example of *lengthy* and *lengthily* on the top-ten presidential list. No question that these are familiar and useful terms nowadays. A recent Google search turned up nearly a million hits for *lengthy* and nearly five thousand for the rarer but still well established *lengthily*. To the best of our knowledge, the earliest users of these words were John Adams and Thomas Jefferson, respectively, in their pre-presidential years.

These words go back to the adjective *long*, which has long belonged to the English language—for more than a thousand years, in fact. Several centuries later the familiar suffix *th* (as in *strength*) was added to create the related noun *length*. From that, adding a *y*, you get the adjective *lengthy*. It's commonplace now, but the earliest evidence for it discovered so far is in John Adams's diary for 1759. To *lengthy* add *ly*, and you get the adverb *lengthily*. The first evidence for its use is in a 1787 letter by Thomas Jefferson.

In neither case does this mean that the future presidents actually invented those words. The inventions are so natural that they may well have been invented and used by others around the same time. But it does mean that Adams and Jefferson were neologists in that they used newly created words rather than shying away from them. And because the men were prominent then and became even more prominent as presidents, their words became prominent too and helped spread the neologisms.

Presidential Neologists: A Quick Overview

Many presidents have introduced new words and phrases into our language, or reintroduced and revitalized old ones. George Washington gives us the earliest evidence for *corn row* (a row of corn), *hatchetman*, *to average, indoors, rehire, bakery*, and *tin can*, as well as the designation *administration* for his government. John Adams appears to have been responsible not only for *lengthy*, but for *social science, Quixotic, caucus*, and *hustling*. Thomas Jefferson put into play everything from *lengthily, belittle*, and *bid* (the noun) to *public relations, electioneering*, and *Anglomania* and *Anglophobia*, as well as *authentication, countervailing, indecipherable*, and *millionaire*.

James Madison is credited with *caption, amenability*, and *squatter.* Andrew Jackson gets some credit for spreading the word about *dead duck*, though he wasn't the first to use it. Franklin Pierce has the honor, such as it is, of introducing *violative.* Abraham Lincoln is credited with *relocate* and *relocation, wooling*, meaning pulling someone's hair, and *change horses in midstream*, not to mention *Michigander*, meaning a resident of Michigan.

Andrew Johnson, Lincoln's successor, is the originator of *discriminate* and *discrimination* in reference to civil rights. U. S. Grant used *bring up* in reference to troops and *points* in reference to destinations. James A. Garfield used *misadjustment* as a euphemism for "disagreement." Grover Cleveland used *extensory* to describe extending an arrangement. Benjamin Harrison is noted for an early use of *Latin American* instead of *Spanish American.*

Not to be overlooked in this regard is Theodore Roosevelt, who named the *lunatic fringe* and invented a new meaning for *muckraker*, not to mention having inspired the *teddy bear.* Like no president before or since, he peppered his utterances with the bully adjective *bully.* "Speak softly and carry a big stick," he famously declared. To announce

Painted glass in a walnut base, this "The Buck Stops Here" sign was made in the Federal Reformatory at El Reno, Oklahoma and presented to Harry S. Truman by his friend Fred M. Canfil, a U.S. Marshal.

his campaign for the Republican nomination in 1912, he borrowed a phrase from boxing, "My hat's in the ring," and declared, "I'm as fit as a bull moose." That remark led to the nickname Bull Moose for the breakaway Progressive Party he founded after being denied the Republican nomination. He also seems to have invented the expression *nail jelly to the wall.*

Woodrow Wilson is among the first to have used *capitalistically* and, more significantly, the slogan *America First.* He also gave his *okeh* to *OK.* President Harding enjoyed *bloviation,* revived *normalcy,* and promoted *hospitalization,* much to the displeasure of purists. President Hoover was noted not only for *rugged individualism,* but for the *good neighbor* policy towards Latin America. Franklin D. Roosevelt inaugurated *pump-priming* and the figurative use of *scoreboard* ("the national scoreboard"), and even provided the first instance of *cheerleader,* from a letter he wrote while in college.

President Truman turned our attention to *whistlestops* and made famous the slogan *The buck stops here.* President Eisenhower not only provided early examples of *counter-productive* and the *domino theory,* but also invented the *military-industrial complex.* President Kennedy won election with the help of the *missile gap* and provided an early example of *megatonnage.* President Nixon provided the earliest evidence for *fast track* beyond its usual reference to horse racing. And don't *misunderestimate* President No. 43, George W. Bush, in his quest for *the embetterment of mankind.*

That's a quick tour of the lexical contributions from those in a position to be heard and heeded by virtue of occupying the *bully pulpit* of the presidency, to use Teddy Roosevelt's term. Of all our presidents, Jefferson made by far the greatest contribution to the permanent vocabulary of our language. As we have seen, it was no accident; he was an enthusiastic advocate of neology, which, by the way, was a new word itself in Jefferson's day. All told, Jefferson accounts for well over a hundred first instances of words and phrases. His predecessors,

George Washington and John Adams, get credit for about thirty each, while the other later presidents have far fewer still.

As Seen in the Oxford English Dictionary

How do we know all this? For the most part, it is thanks to that full and faithful compendium of the vocabulary of the English language, the *Oxford English Dictionary*. That twenty-volume dictionary, abbreviated *OED*, not only has the most copious and complete collection of English words, but also gives their history, illustrating the development of each word from its earliest known use to the present day with quotations from various sources. For each word, the first quotation recorded in the *OED* is the earliest evidence they have for its use. Those are the "first instances" mentioned above. To say that Jefferson accounts for well over a hundred first instances of words and phrases means that the *OED* presents a quotation from Jefferson as the earliest evidence for each of these.

Though it had a strongly British bias till its current incarnation in a third edition, now under construction online, the *OED* from its beginnings in the mid-nineteenth century took notice of the American presidents and their contributions to the language. The process of reading to collect examples for the *OED* began in 1857, and the first of its 128 parts was published in 1884, so works that were published before then had an advantage for inclusion. Perhaps it is not a coincidence that the three presidents whose collected writings had been published by the 1850s—Washington, John Adams, and Jefferson—are still the three best represented in the *OED*.

What It Means to Be First in the OED

In most cases, for Jefferson as well as for all other authors quoted in the *OED*, earliest evidence is not the same as invention. The provider of the first quotation in an *OED* entry may have had an important part in propagating the word, but that doesn't mean that person necessarily was its creator.

Words such as Washington's *indoors*, Jefferson's *belittle*, and John Adams's *lengthy* are like *embetterment*—natural enough that they probably had been spontaneously invented over and over before the instance of their use in print that caught the attention of the *OED*. Still, a president's using such a word would help it move from the fringe of the language towards its heart. The presidency may give legitimacy to spontaneous creations that otherwise would be discredited.

Even a word that must have had just one inventor may not be credited to the inventor in the *OED*; not because the *OED* deliberately overlooks the inventor, but because the inventor didn't write something about it that the *OED* editors could find. The word *odometer*, for example, is first attested in the *OED* in a quote from Jefferson. But though Jefferson was an inventor, we know he didn't invent the odometer. That's because the item from Jefferson's notebook for September 2, 1791, quoted as the first example in the *OED* indicates that he bought one in Philadelphia from a certain Leslie: "pd Leslie for an odometer 10 D[ollars]." He then set out on a journey to his Virginia home, Monticello, keeping track of the distances from place to place as measured by the odometer attached to his phaeton.

All we can say for certain about most of the words and phrases credited to presidents in the *OED* is not that the presidents invented them, but that owing to the prominence and prestige of the office, the presidents gave them fame and fortune. And that can be considered a more important contribution to the viability of a word than the invention of it.

An example of this principle is the word *caucus*. The diary of the young John Adams, future president, provides the *OED*'s first example of that word, dated 1763. But in his diary Adams writes about going to a meeting of the *Caucus Club*, the group that is the source of the name. Clearly Adams did not invent the name, and clearly his diary didn't do much to publicize the word, as the diary wasn't published until the middle of the nineteenth century, nearly a hundred years later. Nevertheless, Adams surely used *caucus* in speaking, and as an increasingly prominent politician and then president, he was in a position to give the word wide recognition.

One further caution about the *OED*. Its sources for quotations are anything but a random sample. For example, the third-most-quoted White House occupant in the *OED*, right after Jefferson and John Adams, is none other than *Mrs.* Lyndon B. Johnson, wife of the 36th president. The *OED* quotes about 240 examples from her *White House Diary*, while her husband is quoted only twice.

Six Great Presidential Neologists

Washington: Farmer and Founding Father

George Washington, father of his country, enjoyed respect in Britain as well as in the United States. His writings were diligently read for the *Oxford English Dictionary* and provide evidence that he fathered, or stepfathered, some thirty new words. Many are connected with home and farm, and some are as simple as *indoors*. He wrote in 1799, near the end of his life: "There are many sorts of **indoors** work, which can be executed in Hail, Rain, or Snow, as well as in sunshine."

Washington also provides the earliest evidence for *average* as a verb. The noun *average* was just coming into being at this time with the modern meaning of the arithmetical mean. In his diary for 1769, Washington wrote that a "fat wether . . . would **average** the above weight."

Other words from home, farm, and nature for which Washington's writing appears first in the *OED* include:

hatchetmen (those who work with hatchets, 1755)
rider (verb, to put "riders" on top of a rail fence, 1760)
tinings (tines on a harrow, 1760)
New Town Pippin (apple, 1760)
magnum bonum plum (1764)
cradlers (persons who reap with a cradle scythe, 1766)
corn rows (1769)
tin can (1770)
bakery (1780)
ravine (1781)
logged (house made of logs, 1784)
magotty bay bean (1786)
shockers (persons who put grain in shocks, 1786)
baking (very hot, 1786)
towpath (alongside a canal, 1788)
plateau (elegant plate, 1791)
rehire (noun, 1793)
gullied (land, 1794)
rare-ripe (early ripe, 1799)

At the time he died, George Washington (second from the right) owned almost 8,000 acres of land comprising five working farms.

The exact role Washington played in any of these remains to be determined. *Bakery,* for example, appears in a letter dated May 24, 1780, signed by Washington—but in the handwriting of his secretary Alexander Hamilton. Hamilton could have been the one to write *bakery* instead of the more common *bake house* when the general dictated the letter. Nevertheless, as far as we know now, in the words of researcher Fred Shapiro who discovered this usage, Washington "remains first in war, first in peace, first in the hearts of his countrymen, and first in using the word *bakery.*"

Presidential use doesn't guarantee the success of a word. The *OED* gives Washington first place in the examples of *jabble,* to mix together, which he used in 1760: "All . . . mix'd . . . by **jabling** them well together in a Cloth." We just don't jabble much nowadays.

Not all of Washington's firsts are so domestic. As might be expected, some have to do with government and the military life. His was the first presidential *administration,* and he was the first to use that term for it in 1796: "In reviewing the incidents of my **administration,** I am unconscious of intentional error." Washington also provides the first *OED* evidence for *unconstitutionality* (1795). And in a letter of 1798, Washington provides the first example of *infract* meaning to "break" or "violate": "I think every nation has a right to establish that form of government, under which it conceives it shall live most happy; provided it **infracts** no right, or is not dangerous to others." His is the first *OED* example of *outpost* (1757) designating a military unit at a distance from others. He used *non-effective* (1756) in reference to soldiers unfit for combat. He used *reconnoiter* as a noun (1799): "Your **Reconnoitre** of the seaboard to St. Mary's."

Other words he invented, or appropriated for his use, include *exchangeability* (1778) and *rallying*, in the phrase *rallying point* (1799): "It would be a **rallying-point** for the timid." Also in 1799, Washington came up with the coinage *objectioner*, meaning someone who objects: "The testimony of Generals Lincoln, Knox, Brooks, Jackson, and others . . . would be a counterpoise to the **objectioners**." It's the only *OED* example for this rare word. Evidently others didn't take him up on this example.

He used his knowledge of geography, or perhaps of word origins, for a unique coinage that means "boasting": "The summons is so insolent, and savours so much of **gascoigny**, . . . " he wrote in a 1754 letter. *Gascoigny* refers to *gasconade*, a word for boastfulness that was associated with Gascony (to use the modern spelling) in southwestern France. Washington's is apparently the only example of this twist on a better-known word.

The *OED* uses Washington's writings as first evidence for a number of names. He was a Virginian, but he has the first example of *New Yorker* in a 1756 letter: "The Jerseys and **New Yorkers**, I do not remember what it is they give." He also has the first examples for *Chippewa* (which he spells *Chippoway*) and for *Dunkers*, a group of German Baptists.

In 1798, his is the first evidence for referring to members of the Democratic or Anti-Federalist Party as *Democrats*, though members of that party would surely have previously invented that term.

Adams the First: Lengthy Contributions

"I grow too minute and **lengthy**," John Adams wrote in his diary for January 3, 1759. Appropriately for the man who provides that first evidence for the word, John Adams has a lengthy list of firsts in the *OED*, second only to Jefferson among U.S. presidents. With a wide range of Adams's interests reflected in his neologisms, we notice one area notably missing: farming and managing an estate. Adams grew up on a farm, but evidently his interests lay elsewhere.

Adams provides the first *OED* evidence for *social science*, not as a founder of that science but as a forebear, an inspirer perhaps of a field of study that would begin a century later. He wrote in a 1785 letter, "The **social science** will never be much improved, until the people unanimously know and consider themselves as the fountain of power."

He is also the first to use *to net* in a common modern meaning, writing in his diary about someone who sells sugar and other goods to "**net** a few shillings profit."

In a 1777 letter to his wife, he provides the first evidence for converting the noun *maneuver* to a verb: "Mr. Howe, by the latest advices, was **manuvring** his fleet and army in such a manner as to give us expectations of an expedition somewhere."

He didn't invent *depreciate*, a verb that had been around for a century, but he did provide the first example of the adjective *depreciating* (1777): "There is so much injustice in carrying on a war with **depreciating** currency that we can hardly pray with confidence for success."

Adams was the first to call lack of discipline *indiscipline* (1783): "To venture upon a piece of **indiscipline**, in order to secure a tolerable peace."

He is the first on record with the abbreviation *spec* for *speculation* (1794): "Many merchants have already made a noble **spec.** of the embargo by raising their prices."

His taste in reading resulted in the earliest *OED* example of turning the name of the character Don Quixote into the vivid adjective *Quixotic* to characterize unrealistic schemes. In 1815 he wrote, "I considered Miranda as a vagrant, a vagabond, a **Quixotic** adventurer." His erudition also shows in his use of John Milton's poem "Il Penseroso" to describe a melancholy person, writing in his diary in 1765: "The **Il Penseroso**, however, is discernible on the faces of all four." And he shows his knowledge of classical Greece and Rome by referring in a letter of 1776 to the *pileus*, a round skullcap worn in ancient times: "For the seal, he proposes . . . on one side . . . Liberty with her **pileus**."

Hustling and Foppling It appears that the young Adams enjoyed *hustling*, whatever that might be. His diary has an instance of that word dated June 2, 1760, when he wasn't able to hustle: "I had no . . . companions for pleasure, either in walking, riding, drinking, **hustling,** or any thing else." What exactly he meant by *hustling* in that passage the *OED* doesn't say, merely putting that quotation first under the vague definition "The action of the verb HUSTLE in various senses."

In his diary for March 15, 1756, young Adams uses the word *fopple* in an uncomplimentary way: "At one table sits Mr. Insipid, **foppling** and fluttering." The *OED* gives just this one quotation for *fopple* and labels the word "obsolete and rare." The dictionary doesn't provide a definition for this word, so we have to guess at its meaning from the context, which isn't much help. Apparently not many others took up *foppling,* and the word died along with the custom.

He rode in a *scow,* a flat-bottomed boat, in 1775, and his statement about it became the earliest *OED* quotation for that term: "Father Smith prayed for our **scow** crew, I doubt not."

Unlike Washington, Adams didn't have a plantation to take care of, and he doesn't get much credit in the *OED* for words designating things in the natural world. He does have the first example of *bobolink,* but he uses it in reference to a human companion in his diary for October 24, 1774: "Young Ned Rutledge is a perfect **Bob-o-Lincoln.**"

Adams also provides the first evidence for *mussel-mud* (1774), a down-to-earth word for mud containing mussels to be used for fertilizer.

Politician and Diplomat But it is in the thick of politics and diplomacy that Adams's contributions are most notable. As mentioned earlier, it is in his diary for 1763 that we find first mention of that great American political institution, the *caucus:* "This day learned that the **caucus** club meets, at certain times, in the garret of Tom Dawes."

Not quite so well known, to say the least, is *imborsation,* an Italian method of electing by drawing names from a bag. He wrote about it in 1787: "The **imborsations** are made, and eight hundred names are put in the purses." As the *OED* says, that word is rare. In fact, the Adams quotation is the only illustration in the dictionary for that word.

Adams could not have been the first to refer to England as *John Bull,* but his is the first *OED* example of it as a symbol of England in a 1778 letter: "France . . . assisted the American cause, for which **John Bull** abused and fought her. But John will come off wretchedly."

Adams accounts for the first instances of several technical diplomatic terms. One is *casus foederis* (1780), explained by the *OED* as a situation covered by a treaty and thus requiring the parties to act accordingly: "These powers will not be duped by the artifice of the British Court, and adjudge this war not a **casus foederis**."

He also provides the earliest example of the term *ad referendum*, explained by the *OED* as "acceptance of proposals by representatives subject to the assent of their principals." Adams wrote in a 1781 statement: "They will take the proposition **ad referendum** immediately."

French Accent Between the signing of the Declaration of Independence in 1776 and the ratification of the Constitution in 1789, Adams spent a crucial decade in Europe, mainly in France, representing the new government. He became fluent in French and fond of French ways, as evidenced in some of the entries in the *OED* for which he provides earliest evidence:

mal de mer (seasickness, 1778)
Tiers Etat (third estate, the common people, 1783)
égalité (1794)

In a letter in 1819 Adams gave the earliest *OED* example of the recent French term *noyade*, meaning execution by drowning. He gave it a more playful meaning in a reference to participants in the Boston Tea

Lithograph entitled The Destruction of Tea at Boston Harbor.

Party of long ago: "The Mohawks, who were concerned in the **noyade** of the tea in Boston harbor."

His interests were diverse. Adams provides first evidence for *Bermudian* (1777): "Many french Vessells have arrived there, some **Bermudians**, and some of their own." And he was familiar with the *pistareen*, a small Spanish silver coin. In a 1774 letter he wrote: "I gave **pistareens** enough among the children to have paid twice for my entertainment."

Obscure Innovations Not all of his innovations that the *OED* respectfully records have had success. Half a dozen of the words for which Adams provides first instances remain largely on the sidelines today.

For example, Adams is first, but also one of the last, on record there to use *nameable* to mean "memorable." In a letter of 1780 he wrote, "no person, in America, is of so much influence, power, or credit, that his death, or corruption, by English money, could be of any **nameable** consequence."

For *complainer* he constructed the reciprocal term *complainee* (1779): "These might have determined whether the complainers or **complainees** have most to boast of."

Adams came up with *qualminess* for nausea, noted in his diary for 1778: "The smell of the ship . . . or any other offensive smell will increase the **qualminess**."

While others used plain *sexennial* for a word meaning "every six years," Adams in 1814 added an extra *t*. His is the only instance of this variant in the *OED*: "The legislatures of the several states are balanced against the senate by **sextennial** elections."

He wrote of *plagiat*, the kidnapping sailors for forced labor on other ships, in 1809. Civilians may have used the term, as he states, but there haven't been many English-speaking ones who did: "The impressment of seamen . . . is no better than what civilians call **plagiat**, a crime punishable with death by all civilized nations."

He used the term *proprietarian* in 1776 for—well, the *OED* guesses, with a question mark, that it means proponents of proprietary government; that is, government by those who own the territory. His is the only example in the *OED* for this obsolete word: "The quakers and **proprietarians** together have little weight."

BELITTLING JEFFERSON

One word attributed to Jefferson stirred up the first controversy about presidential language—or more accurately, would-be presidential language, because Jefferson would be president a dozen years later. The controversy was evoked by the publication in 1787 of Jefferson's *Notes on the State of Virginia*. In that book Jefferson indignantly responded to the insulting insinuations of a French zoologist, the Count de Buffon. As Jefferson explains:

> The opinion advanced by the Count de Buffon, is 1. That the animals common both to the old and new world, are smaller in the latter. 2. That those peculiar to the new, are on a smaller scale. 3. That those which have been domesticated in both, have degenerated in America: and 4. That on the whole it exhibits fewer species. And the reason, he thinks, is that the heats of America are less; that more waters are spread over its surface by nature, and fewer of these drained off by the hand of man. In other words, that heat is friendly, and moisture adverse to the production and development of large quadrupeds.

Jefferson replies lengthily to these charges with comparisons, species by species, of the weights of American and European animals, showing that the former are assuredly equal to, and often greater than, their European counterparts. And he concludes:

> So far the Count de Buffon has carried this new theory of the tendency of nature to **belittle** her productions on this side the Atlantic.

Jefferson's book made its way to a reviewer for the *European Magazine* in London, who commented in a footnote:

> Belittle!—What an expression!—It may be an elegant one in Virginia, and even perfectly intelligible; but for our part, all we can do is, to guess at its meaning.—For shame, Mr. Jefferson!— Why, after trampling upon the honour of our country, and representing it as little better than a land of barbarism—why, we say, perpetually trample also upon the very grammar of our ▶

language, and make that appear as Gothic as, from your de-
scription, our manners are rude?—Freely, good sir, will we for-
give all your attacks, impotent as they are illiberal, upon our
national character; *but for the future, spare—O spare, we be-*
seech you, our mother-tongue!"

A little later, the reviewer grumbled again about *belittle*: "A *new*, but *favourite* expression of our author."

That seems to be as far as the complaint went. There is no record of Jefferson, or anyone, discussing *belittle* further. Without objection, the word quietly continued insinuating its way into the English language, where it is freely used today, even by the English.

This first use of *belittle* had a more literal meaning than it does today. Jefferson literally meant "to make little." Not long after, though, in 1797, the *Independent Chronicle* of Boston used *belittle* in the modern sense, perhaps taking a hint from Jefferson's literal use: ". . . an honorable man . . . let the writers . . . endeavor to belittle him as much as they please."

Whether or not *belittle* was an original coinage of Jefferson's, he did not make much use of it, before or after the 1780s; we don't read in his most famous writing, the Declaration of Independence, that Americans were *belittled* by the king of Great Britain. In fact, *belittle* is absent from all of Jefferson's writings that are accessible electronically, with the sole exception of *Notes on the State of Virginia.* Not to belittle *belittle*, then, but it matters little to his stature as a neologist.

Hail to the Chief Neologist

Though Washington attained some recognition in the *OED*, and John Adams still more, they and all subsequent presidents are distant runners-up compared to Thomas Jefferson, who enjoyed creating new words even more, and much more systematically, than his epigone George W. Bush. More than a hundred entries in the *OED* give first place to Jefferson's writings.

As is the case with any other great promoter of new words, many of Jefferson's creations stayed on the fringe of the English vocabulary or never established themselves at all. That's not surprising. It is surprising that so many succeeded, because even the most noted of word creators fails more often than succeeds.

Jeffersonian Science Science, technology, and natural science are the areas where Jefferson saw the greatest need for neology, and where he made many contributions. He was fond of the *polygraph*, an instrument for making multiple copies of whatever one was writing. It was invented in France in the 1760s by a M. de Cotteneude, but Jefferson in 1805 provides the earliest *OED* evidence for the use of that name in English: "I have laid aside the copying press, for a twelvemonth past, and write always with the **polygraph**." Not content with what others had made, he invented improvements for that device.

There were other inventions that were clearly not his own but for which he stands first in the *OED*. Perhaps using a polygraph some two decades earlier, he wrote of a *lunarium*, an instrument representing the phases of the moon: "What is become of the **Lunarium** for the King?" That same year, 1786, he wrote of a *plexi-chronometer* (a kind of metronome): "They have ordered all music which shall be printed here, in future, to have the movements numbered in correspondence with the **plexichronometer**." And as mentioned above, Jefferson's notation of a purchase in 1791 is the first *OED* source for *odometer*.

He measured temperature not only in Fahrenheit but in *Réamur* (1782), a thermometer scale where zero degrees was freezing and 80 degrees the boiling point of water: "Late experiments shew that the human body will exist in rooms heated to 140° of **Reaumur**, equal to 347° of Fahrenheit."

As a scientist, Jefferson knew of the *catenary* curve formed by a rope or chain hanging from two posts (1788): "Every part of a **catenary** is in perfect equilibrium."

His is the first evidence for the name resulting from Charles Mason and Jeremiah Dixon's 1763–68 survey of the boundary between Pennsylvania and Maryland being *Mason and Dixon's line*. Jefferson referred to it in 1776 in regard to the ongoing boundary dispute between Pennsylvania and his Virginia: "I am indebted to you for a topic to deny to the Pennsylvania claim to a line 39 complete degrees from the equator. As an advocate I shall certainly insist on it; but I wish they would compromise by an extension of **Mason & Dixon's line**."

One word that was unquestionably Jefferson's own invention was a flop. In 1790, when the French were just beginning to devise what would become the modern metric system, Jefferson proposed a *meter* of his own in a report to Congress. This would be one-thousandth of a bushel, which he described as follows: "Let the bushel be divided into 10 pottles; each pottle into 10 demi-pints; each demi-pint into 10 **metres**, which will be of a cubic inch each."

Natural Wealth In proclaiming the natural wealth of the New World, Jefferson provided the earliest *OED* evidence of *mineralized* meaning "containing minerals." In his *Notes on the State of Virginia*, written from 1781 to 1782, he refers to certain medicinal springs on the Potomac that are "much more frequented than those of Augusta. Their powers, however, are less, the waters weakly **mineralized**, and scarcely warm."

In that same book, he provides the earliest example of using *mineral coal* for what we call simply *coal*: "The country on James river, from 15 to 20 miles above Richmond, and for several miles northward and southward, is replete with **mineral coal** of a very excellent quality."

Jefferson was acquainted with Linnaeus's classification system, and is recorded as first to refer to a flower commonly called *four-o'clock* or *pretty-by-night* (and also *umbrellawort, marvel-of-Peru, snotweed*, and *wishbone bush*) by its genus name, *Mirabilis* (1767): "**Mirabilis** just opened, very clever." He also first used *sulla*, a name for the French honeysuckle (1789).

He wrote about the ant bear, using its French name, *tamanoir*, in *Notes on the State of Virginia*, listing it as the sixth-largest animal native to America and not Europe.

Still other Jeffersonian neologisms reflect his interest in the fossil record of the New World and refer to two fossil sloths: *megalonyx* and *megatherium*. In 1797 he was installed as president of the American Philosophical Society, the scientific organization founded by Benjamin Franklin. That March he presented a paper before the Society in Philadelphia on "the **Megalonyx**, as we have named him."

Instructing Lewis and Clark in 1803 for their "voyage of discovery," he hoped to obtain more evidence of the other fossil sloth: "This voyage will procure us further information of the Mammoth, & of the **Megatherium**."

Jefferson at Home Jefferson helped with the introduction of homely words too. He provides the earliest *OED* evidence for calling the stuff of which bread is made (wheat or flour) *breadstuff* (1793): "France receives favorably our **bread stuff**, rice, wood, etc."

He was aware of the *doll-babies* from France that showed the latest fashions (1807), writing about "the dresses of the annual **doll-babies** from Paris."

He knew about *drayage*, the cost of conveyance by a dray, or cart, making a note in 1791: "Pd. Wm. Forbes freight, storage, **drayage** of 13 hhds. tobo."

A *post-note* was nothing like today's *Post-It Notes*. It was a banknote payable in the future. Jefferson's is the first attestation of the word, also in 1791: "Recd from bank a **post note** . . . for 116 D[ollars]."

Anglomania, Anglophobia, and Monocrats There is one area where Jefferson unquestionably did invent words rather than merely help them to greater notice. That area of his originality, not surprisingly, is politics. A strong partisan of the agrarian Republicans against the centralizing and pro-British Federalists, Jefferson coined *Angloman, Anglomania,* and *Anglophobia* in the 1780s. An *Angloman* was a man who took the side of the British. That disturbed Jefferson, as he wrote in 1787: "It will be of great consequence to France and England, to have America governed by a Galloman [who sides with the French] or **Angloman**." Again in 1795 he complained about "a treaty of alliance between England and the **Anglomen**, against the Legislature and people of the United States."

Along these lines, Jefferson invented the term *Anglomania*, which was (and still is) a predilection for things British. In 1787: "A little disposition to **Anglomania**." In 1805: "Till **Anglomany** . . . yields to Americanism."

The opposite attitude, *Anglophobia*, was also a Jefferson coinage, in 1793: "We are going on here in the same spirit still. The **Anglophobia** has seized violently on three members of our Council."

With similar inventiveness, he labeled his Federalist opponents *monocrats* because of their support for Britain and, implicitly, for monarchy. In a 1792 letter he fumed about "the doctrines of the **Monocrats**." In a 1793 letter he complained, "The war between France and England has brought forward the Republicans and **Monocrats** in every state."

War, Electioneering, and Public Relations Jefferson gives the earliest *OED* example of the term *war party* (1798) to designate those who favor war: "Parker has completely gone over to the **war party**."

Years later, in 1815, he appears to have been among the first to refer (negatively) to *Bonapartism*: " . . . disgraced by an association in opposition with the remains of **Bonaparteism**."

His is the first recorded reference to *electioneering* (1789): "All the world here is occupied in **electioneering**, in choosing or being chosen," and even that necessary aspect of electioneering, *public relations*. In his State of the Union message for 1807, a century before any other attestation of the term, Jefferson was on to it, though not exactly in a modern context. The budget surplus of the federal government, he said,

> . . . *may partly, indeed, be applied toward completing the defense of the exposed points of our country, on such a scale as shall be adapted to our principles and circumstances. . . . Whether what shall remain of this, with the future surpluses, may be usefully applied to purposes already authorized or more usefully to others requiring new authorities, or how otherwise they shall be disposed of, are questions calling for the notice of Congress, unless, indeed, they shall be superceded by a change in our* **public** *relations now awaiting the determination of others.*

By *public relations* in this context he may mean something like "relations with other countries" rather than "relations with the public."

In other government matters, Jefferson is the first cited for *municipally* (1818): ". . . the laws which regulate the intercourse of nations, those formed **municipally** for our own government."

He came up with both *non-exportation* (1774) and, 35 years later, *non-intercourse* (1809), both strictly legal terms: "The heavy injury that would arise to this country from an earlier adoption of the **non-exportation** plan . . ." for the former, and for the latter, "This view is derived from the former **non-intercourse** law only."

French and German Imports A man of the world, at least the European world, Jefferson provides the *OED*'s earliest evidence for certain foreign places and pleasures. He certainly did not invent any of these names, but his usage helped such words gain currency in English. They include:

Markebronn (a German wine, 1788)

mosseux (1788, a sparkling wine)

margravate (land ruled by a margrave, 1788)

metairie (French sharecropping system, 1788)

Barbaresques (natives of Barbary, North Africa, 1804)

Marsalla (wine, 1806)

Back in America, he had a role in calling the inhabitants of Indiana *Indianians*. This was in 1784, long before Indiana became a state in 1816: "Should . . . the **Indianians** and Kentuckians take themselves off. . . ."

French Millions Strongly influenced by French usage, Jefferson was the first noted in the *OED* to write of a *millionaire* (1786): "The poorest labourer stood on equal ground with the wealthiest **Millionary**." He also provides the earliest *OED* example of *milliard* for what we now call *billion*, that is, a thousand millions (1789): "Suppose that Louis XIV. and XV. had contracted debts in the name of the French nation to the amount of 10,000 **milliards** of livres. . . . The interest of this sum would be 500. **milliards**." And his 1821 autobiography provides the first example in the *OED* of an abbreviation for "millions": "The American war had cost them 1440. **millns**. (256. mils. of Dollars)."

Among other words from the French, Jefferson provides the earliest *OED* examples for:

Mme. (abbreviation for Madame, 1786)

retard (delay, 1788)

arrestation (stopping, 1793)

projet (proposal, 1808)

And Jefferson is credited with first importing *modus agendi* from Latin to English: "Nature has hidden from us her **modus agendi**," he wrote in *Notes on the State of Virginia*.

Everyday Jeffersonianisms Of all the words the *OED* attributes in the first instance to Jefferson, perhaps the most notable are those that escape notice because they are such everyday words. In addition to *lengthily* and *belittle*, already mentioned, Jefferson's are the earliest examples in the *OED* for half a dozen more. Writing to James Madison from Paris on July 31, 1788, Jefferson used *bid* as a noun:

> . . . *Littlepage who was here as a secret agent for the King of Poland rather overreached himself. He wanted more money. The King furnished it more than once. Still he wanted more, and thought to obtain a high* **bid** *by saying he was called for in America and asking leave to go there.*

Jefferson also has the first example of the verb *sanction* to mean *approve*, in a letter of 1778 regarding his draft of a bill: "In its style, I have aimed at accuracy, brevity, and simplicity, preserving, however, the very words of the established law, wherever their meaning had been **sanctioned** by judicial decisions, or rendered technical by usage."

He accounts for the first attestation of *indecipherable* in a letter of 1802 to the U.S. minister to France: "A favorable and a confidential opportunity offering by Mr. Dupont de Nemours, who is revisiting his native country gives me an opportunity of sending you a cipher to be used between us, which will give you some trouble to understand, but, once understood, is the easiest to use, the most **indecipherable**, and varied by a new key with the greatest facility of any one I have ever known." (The cipher involved using the names and residences of the two men as keys.)

Jefferson is also first in the *OED* with:

dutied (paid duty on, 1771)
circumambulator (1787)
reticulating (marked or networked, 1787)
revend (sell again, 1787)
bountied (paid bounty for, 1788)
monotonously (1778)
inheritability (1784)
inexactitude (1786)
authentication (1789)
countervailing (1793)
discountable (1813)
patricidal (1821)

The Deep-Drawn Sigh He has the first *OED deep-drawn*, in a letter of 1813 to John Adams on a loss in Adams's family: "I have ever found time and silence the only medicine, and these but assuage, they never can suppress, the **deep-drawn** sigh which recollection for ever brings up, until recollection and life are extinguished together."

Jefferson's Legalisms Apparently he was first to employ the Latin legal term *exequatur*, an official authorization of a government agent, in the formal language of a 1788 treaty with the French. Also:

commerciable (suitable for commerce, 1786)
uncommericable (1787)
unconciliatory (1789)
co-sovereign (1793)
amovability (capability of being dismissed, 1816)
enregistry (registering, 1825)

Whole phrases of Jefferson's still resonate in the American consciousness. Almost as familiar as the opening words of the Declaration of Independence is the phrase he invented for a letter to the Baptists of Danbury, Connecticut, in 1802: *wall of separation between church and state.* The context for that phrase is a lengthy sentence: "Believing with you that religion is a matter which lies solely between Man & his God, that he owes account to none other for his faith or his worship, that the legitimate powers of government reach actions only, & not opinions, I contemplate with sovereign reverence that act of the whole American people which declared that their legislature should 'make no law respecting an establishment of religion, or prohibiting the free exercise thereof,' thus building a **wall of separation between Church & State.**"

Failed Neologisms With the hindsight of two centuries, we know that not all of the new words Jefferson helped bring to the light of day were successes. He couldn't know, and probably wouldn't care, that more than two dozen creations attributed first to him in the *OED* are rarely to be seen or heard nowadays. They include:

unlocated (not surveyed, 1776)
dischargeable (payable, 1781)
intercolonnation (space between columns, 1782)
disrupture (disruption, 1785)
continuable (able to be continued, 1787)

inappreciable (immeasurably valuable, 1787)

spathic acid (hydrofluoric acid, 1788)

bonification (improvement, 1789)

debarrass (to un-embarrass, 1789)

on the creen (ready to turn or career either way, 1798)

graffage (a wooden frame to cross over water, 1798)

preordinate (superior, 1801)

misanthropism (misanthropy, 1813)

amphibologism (ambiguity, 1813)

palinoidal (recanting, 1813)

bibliograph (bibliographer, 1815)

cross-street (crossroads, 1825)

ralliance (rallying, 1826)

The Rough Writer

We have to advance a century to find another president in the forefront of neology. For all his expressiveness and prolificness, however—his collected works are more voluminous than those of any other president—Theodore Roosevelt doesn't make much of a splash in the *OED*. In comparison with Washington, John Adams, and Jefferson, Teddy didn't invent or help with the invention of that many individual words. But he gave an energetic spin to the words he used, and no other president can compare with him in creating colorful phrases.

Words of his that claim the earliest citations in the *OED* are mostly associated with the outdoor life: *to quirt* (to use the quirt, a short whip, 1888), with regard to Western horseback riding (*quirt* the noun is a word from 1845); and the abbreviation *bronc* (1893) for the earlier (1869) *bronco*: "I saddled up the bronc'," he wrote in *Wilderness Hunter* (1893), "and lit out for home."

A couple of animal entries in the *OED* carry first quotations from Roosevelt's writings: *bobcat* (1888), and *mussurana snake* (1914) from his book *Through the Brazilian Wilderness*.

From Africa, for his 1910 book *African Game Trails*, Teddy brought back *shenzi*, a Swahili term for someone who isn't civilized. It's the first example in the *OED* for that word.

There was the *whitecapper*, a kind of vigilante, for which Roosevelt provides the first *OED* evidence in an 1895 article on "The Issues of 1896."

The word is merely a variant of the already existing *whitecap* with the same meaning, but the article illustrates the ever-present vigorousness of his language: "The law-breaker, whether he be lyncher or **whitecapper**, or merely the liquor-seller who desires to drive an illegal business, must be made to feel that the Republican party is against him. Every ballot-box stuffer, every bribe-taking legislator, every corrupt official of any grade, must be made to feel that he is an outcast from the Republican party."

Roosevelt also provides the first *OED* example for *classified* (1889) in the sense of being arranged in classes, as in classes of jobs: "I expect from the President an extension of the classified service."

His Bully Pulpit Where Teddy really left his mark on our language was not with such *OED* firsts, but with his vivid use of words already established and his coining of memorable phrases. His colorful language makes the inventions of all other presidents pale in comparison. Because his distinctive words and phrases were so central to his message, they have already been discussed in the chapter on the Great Communicators: *muckraker, strong as a bull moose, hat in the ring, nail cranberry jelly to the wall, speak softly and carry a big stick*. And *bully*, of course. It's typical of T.R.'s way with language. *Bully*, with the meaning "splendid, first-rate," had been in use since before he was born, but it hit a high point of presidential usage with the first Roosevelt. For him, everything good was *bully*. And he invented the phrase *bully pulpit* for the presidency, a term that has been used ever since. As clergyman and social reformer Lyman Abbott said in his 1909 article telling of the origin of *bully pulpit* (quoted earlier in the chapter on the Great Communicators):

> *The episode is interpretative of the man. He has been ranchman, administrator, soldier, politician, statesman—but always and everywhere a moral reformer. I think there are two reasons for his enjoyment of his Presidential office: one, that it has enabled him to do things; the other, that it has given him a National platform from which to say things.*

Nowadays, with the fading of the feel-good adjective *bully*, we tend to misinterpret *bully pulpit* as the speaker bullying the audience from the lectern. There's a germ of truth to this.

We also have Theodore Roosevelt to thank for *lunatic fringe*. He tossed it into his review of the International Exhibit of Modern Art, the notorious "Armory Show" of 1913 in New York City. Some people liked the groundbreaking show that featured Marcel Duchamp's "Nude Descending a Staircase." For Teddy, it was just another progressive movement, but he couldn't make himself like it. His bully, infectious commentary is worth quoting:

> *It is vitally necessary to move forward and to shake off the dead hand, often the fossilized dead hand, of the reactionaries; and yet we have to face the fact that there is apt to be a* **lunatic fringe** *among the votaries of any forward movement. In this recent art exhibition the* **lunatic fringe** *was fully in evidence, especially in the rooms devoted to the Cubists and the Futurists, or Near-Impressionists.*
>
> *I am not entirely certain which of the two latter terms should be used in connection with some of the various pictures and representations of plastic art—and, frankly, it is not of the least consequence. The Cubists are entitled to the serious attention of all who find enjoyment in the colored puzzle-pictures of the Sunday newspapers. Of course there is no reason for choosing the cube as a symbol, except that it is probably less fitted than any other mathematical expression for any but the most formal decorative art. There is no reason why people should not call themselves Cubists, or Octagonists, or Parallelopipedonists, or Knights of the Isosceles Triangle, or Brothers of the Cosine, if they so desire; as expressing anything serious and permanent, one term is as fatuous as another.*

Once More the Bloviator

When it comes to extraordinary presidential language, time and again the focus comes to Warren G. Harding. He's back in this chapter as a noted resuscitator of obsolete words. One of them, of course, is his fancy term for fancy talk, *bloviate*. It's a word in the grand tradition of extravagant nineteenth-century American expressions: *absquatulate* (to sneak away), *callithumpian* (a noisy parade), *rambunctious, sockdolager* (something big), *splendiferous* . . . yes, *bloviate*, with its derivatives *bloviator* and *bloviation*, fits right in. Researcher Fred Shapiro has found it in a number of documents from that century, including the *Debates and Proceedings of the Convention for the Revision of the Constitution of the State of Ohio* in midcentury: "For doing my duty, I claim no credit—I seek no **bloviations**" and "The **bloviators** attempt to disturb the proceedings of this Convention." It may be no coincidence that Harding was from Ohio.

This word is conspicuously absent from the *OED*, perhaps because after its heyday with Harding it seemed to become obsolete. It was revived in the late twentieth century, however, and nowadays seems a fine word to describe fine words that mean nothing.

There's something likeable about *bloviate*, just as there was about Harding. He loved to bloviate and was unashamed to use that word for it. What's not to like? As Rabbi Robert J. Marx recently wrote, "It's more fun to say *bloviate* than to say 'orate verbosely.'"

In his *New Political Dictionary* William Safire notes that *bloviate* is defined in an 1889 slang dictionary as "verbosity, wandering from the subject, and idle or inflated oratory or blowing, by which word it was probably suggested, being partially influenced by 'deviate.'" And Safire also found a 1909 use of the word in the *Louisville Courier-Journal*. Louisville being just a hundred miles or so downriver from Cincinnati suggests that *bloviate* may indeed have been an Ohio specialty. Harding's biographer, Francis Russel, declared that *bloviate* was just an old Ohio word meaning "to loaf." But that diversion has fooled nobody.

An example of Harding's bloviation is seen in his use of *muniments* in an executive order. The word so bemused a *New York Times* reporter (who evidently had to look it up in a dictionary) that the *Times* devoted a short article to it in 1921:

Special to The New York Times.

WASHINGTON, Sept. 29—President Harding employed the seldom used word "muniments" today in writing the executive order transferring the Declaration of Independence and the Constitution of the United States from the State Department to the Library of Congress. The President wrote that the order was issued at the request of Secretary of State Hughes because the Secretary "has no suitable place for the exhibition of these muniments."

The Century dictionary states that a muniment is, in one sense, "a document by which claims and rights are defended or maintained. . . ."
[and so on, quoting the dictionary for the rest of a long paragraph]

Back to Normalcy Even more notorious than Harding's bloviating style was his use of the seemingly innocuous word *normalcy* in a 1920 campaign speech: "America's present need is not heroics but healing; not nostrums but **normalcy**; not revolution but restoration. . . ."

Inconspicuous as it may appear to the modern reader, the word shocked and perplexed reporters and editors when Harding argued for "normal times and a return to normalcy." They asked for an explanation. Harding obliged, as reported in the *New York Times* on July 21, 1920:

> *"I have noticed that word caused considerable newspaper editors to change it to 'normality,'" he said. "I have looked for 'normality' in my dictionary, and I do not find it there. 'Normalcy,' however, I did find, and it is a good word.*
>
> *"By 'normalcy' I do not mean the old order, but a regular, steady order of things. I mean normal procedure, the natural way, without excess. I don't believe the old order can or should come back, but we must have normal order, or, as I have said, 'normalcy.'"*

Labor leader Samuel Gompers took the opportunity to criticize Harding's word: "Senator Harding does not use the word 'normal.' He speaks of 'normalcy.' The word is obsolete, and so is the condition to which he would return."

And the British—well, they were still reeling from shock when Harding delivered his first presidential message to Congress the following April. The *Daily Chronicle* of London editorialized:

> *Mr. Harding is accustomed to take desperate ventures in the coinage of new words. In his election addresses he invented the hideous 'normalcy.' This message gives us 'hospitalization' which the English speaking world might surely have done very well without.*

Not just *normalcy* but *hospitalization*! What barbarities will that American think of next!

Despite such complaints, neither word was Harding's invention. *Normalcy* had been used, though primarily in mathematical contexts, long before Harding chose it over *normality*; *hospitalization* had been around for more than a decade. In the long run, of course, the opposition to such language crumbled. A letter in the *New York Times* of May 13, 1921, was prophetic:

> *Probably the word* [normalcy] *will remain in usage after its very spectacular resurrection. Indeed, its euphony recommends it. University "dry-as-dusts" of 2021 will amuse their classes in philology with its history, and will point to the heroic part played by a loyal partisan press in saving a situation and reanimating a dying word.*

The Neo-word-ist

Not since Jefferson has there been a coiner of words like George W. Bush. Nor has there been a president so enthusiastic about neology. Bush made the connection explicit in his remarks on Jefferson Day, April 12, 2001:

> *Most people don't realize this, but Thomas Jefferson and I share a hobby. We both like to make up words. According to the* Oxford English Dictionary, *Mr. Jefferson contributed more new words to the language than any other U.S. president. . . . The other day I tried a new word for our press corps:* misunderestimate. *It's not quite in Jefferson's league, but I am giving it my best shot.*

Despite his enthusiasm and his legendary lapses in language, George W. has not quite caught up with his mentor. His numerous novel expressions are for the most part mere malapropisms, failed attempts to use words he almost remembers, rather than coinages in their own right. Still, in just a few years, Bush has managed to come up with some stunning new words and phrases:

mential: This is still a dangerous world. It's a world of madmen and uncertainty and potential **mential** losses. (South Carolina, January 14, 2000)

subliminable: I don't think we need to be **subliminable** about the differences between our views on prescription drugs. (Orlando, Florida, September 12, 2000)

women of cover: I see an opportunity at home when I hear the stories of Christian and Jewish women alike, helping **women of cover**, Arab

American women, go shop because they're afraid to leave their home. (Speech to State Department employees, Washington, D.C., October 4, 2001)

punditry (pundits): Many of the **punditry**—of course, not you [laughter]—but other **punditry** were quick to say, no one is going to follow the United States of America. (Washington, D.C., January 21, 2003)

ooching: Let me tell you my thoughts about tax relief. When your economy is kind of **ooching** along, it's important to let people have more of their own money. (Boston, October 4, 2002) (In sailing, *ooching* is a sudden forward movement of the body, stopped abruptly.)

Perhaps his most ambitious and optimistic coinage is *embetterment*. Bush used it several times in 2002, first at the National Hispanic Prayer Breakfast on May 16: "I want to tell you it's an honor to be here amongst people who dedicate their lives to the embetterment of our fellow human beings." Later that year Bush was recorded as speaking of "the embetterment of mankind" and then "the embetterment of the lives of the Palestinian people." Chortler.com noted Bush's creation and offered this tongue-in-cheek definition:

embetterment (noun)—*The condition in which the lives of people is more good than before.* Synonyms: *disemworsenment, unimprovementlessness.*

As is typical of new words, *embetterment* comes naturally from old ones, a cross between *embitterment* and *betterment.* And also as is typical of new words, it is such a subtle innovation that it probably would have passed without notice if it hadn't been used by a president. You won't find *embetterment* in any dictionary, but that doesn't mean George W. was the first to use it; it just means that, as president, he was noticed when he did.

A search of the World Wide Web finds dozens of earlier examples. Back in 1998, Dave Leacraft was running for mayor of Washington, D.C. His "Declaration of Independence For the Residents Of the District of Columbia" begins, "We the People of the District of Columbia through Self-Embetterment, Cultural Development, and Community Empowerment can change the destiny of every resident of the District of Columbia." A poem by Heather Cole, copyright 1998, declares, "We are creatures of embetterment." Still further back, in February 1995, we find the *New World Reader* at Louisiana State University declaring, "Science is a group effort done for the good and embetterment of humanity."

Now it's not as if one person invented *embetterment* and all the others copied it; rather, it's such a natural invention that it has been created repeatedly. If it ever gains enough popularity to become a permanent resident in the English vocabulary, no one will be able to determine its exact origin. "If a word can be thought of, it can be thought of at different times by different people," notes Erin McKean, editor of the word magazine *Verbatim*, "and it's often the case that the thinker-upper with the best access to the media is anointed as the coiner even if your Great-Aunt Sadie said it every day of her life beginning in 1932."

The third edition of the *OED* is expected to be completed around 2010. We will find out then whether George W.'s *women of cover, misunderestimate*, and *embetterment* will have made their way into the permanent record alongside *belittle, muckraker*, and *normalcy*.

8 Presidential Accents

A ll presidents are not created equal in their speaking styles. Nor are they equal in their accents.

The differences in speaking styles, for the most part, are the result of individual choices and abilities: whether to be formal or down-to-earth, whether to use colorful language or plain, whether to speak at length or in brief, whether to embrace an opportunity to speak publicly or avoid it. Speaking styles reflect each president's character, personality, education, and individual preference. And skill.

But the differences in accent, for the most part, are accidental. They depend on the accidents of birth and nurture: where the president was born and raised, what family he came from. Skill doesn't play much of a role; luck is more like it. This is true for all of us. In most cases, unless we make a conscious effort to be different, we sound like the people we grew up with. We have the accent of the place we came from.

So while the presidents' speaking styles may be a surprise—who would have imagined that the great writer and conversationalist Thomas Jefferson would go to such lengths to avoid public speaking?— their accents are pretty much what one would expect.

We suspect this holds even for those who were president in the days before voice recording, because, in all the voluminous commentary on presidential ways of speaking, very little has been said about their accents. The accents were unremarked, and so we can tentatively conclude that they were unremarkable.

The early exceptions were presidents like Jackson and Lincoln, whose accents were noted because of their rusticity rather than their regionality. But as the profiles on those presidents in the final section of this book will explain, their rusticity has been exaggerated. Or rather, what rusticity they undeniably had in their youth was smoothed over and polished by the time they became president.

In the twentieth and twenty-first centuries, however, as recordings and broadcast media have carried the voices of presidents throughout the land, presidential accents have become more notable and noted. And as with speaking styles, so with accents: the notion that a president must follow a certain model has been shattered. But there once was a model for pronunciation. The demise of that model is the most notable event in the chronicle of presidential pronunciation.

The Atlantic Gentlemen

Since there are no voice recordings of the first 21 presidents, we can only guess how they sounded. But since speakers reflect region and class, we can at least make educated guesses. Of the first six presidents, in particular, the four gentlemen from Virginia most likely spoke with cultivated Virginia accents, and the well-educated John Adams and his even better educated son, John Quincy Adams, with cultivated Boston or New England accents. Otherwise their contemporaries and biographers would have noticed and let us know.

Though Washington, Jefferson, Madison, and Monroe came from the South and the Adamses from the North, in one particular their accents would have been different from those of the majority of Americans (and presidents) today. We can be pretty sure that they did not pronounce *r* after a vowel. That is, John and John Quincy Adams would have been the forebears of those who say "Pahk the cah in Hahvahd Yahd" today. Washington and his Virginia successors would have had slightly different vowels but the same lack of *r* after vowels that you will find today in much of the Old South, especially near the coast.

This is, of course, the British standard too, and was therefore, for many years of the early American republic, a mark of cultivation. Listen to a member of the British royal family, or the prime minister, or even Hugh Grant acting the part of the prime minister in the movie *Love, Actually*, and you'll "heah" the same *r*-less pronunciation.

The division between *r*-less and *r*-ful emerged in British English during the seventeenth and eighteenth centuries. It was a fashion adopted by the seaboard colonies, both north and south, in what was to become the United States; only Philadelphia of the major cities along the Atlantic coast kept its *r* after vowels. By the time the founders of the American republic were born, it was well established. It persists to this day, a distinction known to all Americans on both sides of the *r* divide. Some of us—in eastern New England, New York City, and the South along the Atlantic and Gulf coasts—leave out the *r* after vowels. The not-*r*'s will say *hahd* instead of *hard*, *fohd* instead of *ford*. Sometimes an "uh" sound will take the place of the omitted *r*, as in *fo-uh* for *four*, *ou-ah* for *our*, or *riv-uh* for *river*.

As the example of *riv-uh* shows, *r*'s at the start of words or syllables are always pronounced, even in the speech of the not-*r*'s. An *r* also is pronounced when a vowel immediately follows it, as in *miracle*. But it's not *hahd* to hear the difference, is it? *Fah* from it!

Meanwhile, Farther Inland

Inland pronunciation was another story. The English-speaking pioneers who pushed westward to populate the country in the late eighteenth and throughout the nineteenth centuries were for the most part *r*-speaking. So today's United States is, for the most part, *r*-ful.

It's an understatement to say that the Atlantic Coast remains politically and economically influential to this day. But a funny reversal has happened: Instead of the East serving as a model of cultivation for the rest of the country, influencing would-be cultivated speakers from other areas to drop their *r*'s, as used to be the case, the rest of the country now is influencing many Bostonians, New Yorkers, and Southerners to pronounce their *r*'s. This reflects a shift in prestige for *r*-lessness: Where once it seemed elegant to drop the *r*, now it seems pretentious, at least for those who grow up *r*-ful.

Thanks to the long history of recording the voices of the presidents, we can confirm that their accents illustrate and exemplify this shift. Like other Americans, presidents now are normally *r*-ful. Did the presidents instigate this change or merely reflect it? Probably the latter, be-

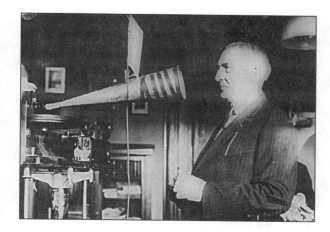

Warren G. Harding, as a presidential candidate in 1920, making a phonographic recording.

cause their accents were determined long before they were old enough to assume office. This chapter will focus on that major change in pronunciation and in the change in attitude that accompanied or caused it. We will also see how regional accents became both acceptable and even cherished at the end of the twentieth century. Other particulars of presidential pronunciation will be discussed in the profiles of individual presidents that conclude the book.

It should be emphasized that pronouncing *r* after vowels was never an impediment to getting elected, nor was dropping *r*'s. In the heyday of *r*-lessness, that is, in the nineteenth century, *r*-ful speakers like Andrew Jackson (who grew up with an Irish accent) were elected, and in the recent era of the dominance of *r*-fulness, *r*-less speakers like Jimmy Carter have won the popular vote. Nevertheless, in the nineteenth century an *r*-ful president aspiring to presidential dignity might well adopt an *r*-less pronunciation, although such a notion would be laughable today. For that matter, an *r*-less president would not stand to gain from changing to *r*-ful.

The Ohio Shift

So the most important change in American accents over the past two centuries is not a shift in pronunciation—that has remained fairly stable

Thomas A. Edison was photographed with his tin-foil phonograph in 1878 when he appeared before a meeting of the National Academy of Science at the Smithsonian Institution.

since the first settlements—but a shift in prestige. Even as the rest of the country was filling up with *r*-ful speakers, the *r*-less upperclass accents of New England, New York City, and the Old South remained the norm and even the goal, not just for those areas but for anyone who wanted to sound cultivated. But in the twentieth century the prestige of pronunciation in the two parts of the country reversed itself, and *r*-lessness was no longer necessarily an asset. Cultivated Ohioans once aspired to talk like New Englanders; now they, and even some New Englanders, are happier when they sound like they are from Ohio. Conveniently illustrating this shift, a series of cultivated Ohioans served as president in the late nineteenth and early twentieth centuries. They, and the other presidents of that previous turn of the century, exemplify the gradual turn from *r*-less to *r*-ful.

And we can hear their voices for ourselves, thanks to Thomas Edison's invention of the phonograph in 1878, and thanks to collections such as that of early Edison recordings at Michigan State University's G. Robert Vincent Voice Library. There are records of actual presidential voices, beginning with the twenty-second (and twenty-fourth) president, Grover Cleveland, and continuing in growing abundance for every subsequent president down to the ubiquitously recorded presidents of the present day.

Grover Cleveland, r-less Orator

Grover Cleveland, the first president whose voice has been preserved in a sound recording, was born in Caldwell, New Jersey, 15 miles west of r-less New York City, but his family soon moved to western New York State: Fayetteville, near Syracuse, and then Clinton, near Utica, both definitely in r-ful territory. At age 16, he moved to Buffalo, even farther to the west in New York state, and he lived there for the next quarter century. One would expect, then, that his speech would be r-ful.

But it's not. Instead, he is an exemplar of elegant not-r elocution. On the old Edison recordings you can hear Cleveland, president from 1885 to 1889 and again from 1893 to 1897, in an 1892 campaign speech, beginning with "Hail to the Chief" in the background. For this formal speech he adopts a highly formal style, not only dropping the r after vowels in *declaeh* (for *declare*) and *New Yohk* and *otheh* and *foehfathehs*, but also trilling the r in *every* and *over again, my friends*, and *carry*. As for *carry*, not only does he trill the r, but he also pronounces the *a* in the East Coast and British fashion, with the vowel sound of *hat* rather than that of *merry*.

In the person of President Cleveland's grandson George Cleveland, portraying his grandfather in a reenactment a century later, we can observe the change in American norms of pronunciation. George used his forebear's eloquent vocabulary, but not his treatment of *r*. The younger Cleveland had a fully developed *r* in all words, and no trills.

Benjamin Harrison, r-ful Ohioan

The fifth president from Ohio, and the first whose voice was recorded, was Benjamin Harrison. President from 1889 to 1893, in between Cleveland's presidencies, he was born in North Bend in the southwestern corner of Ohio and later made his home in Indianapolis, Indiana, both places in solid r-ful territory. We would expect his speech to be r-ful, and it is.

It could have been otherwise, however. He lived at the time of prestige for r-lessness. Furthermore, he was the grandson of William Henry Harrison, another of the Virginia gentleman presidents and almost certainly an r-less speaker. But Benjamin insisted on being his own man. Not only did he not use his ancestral connections to political advantage, he practically repudiated them, declaring, "I want it understood that I am the grandson of nobody." Being r-ful would be one way of showing his distance from a Virginian.

Only 28 seconds of Harrison's voice were preserved on an Edison recording in about 1889, but that's enough to establish him as *r*-ful. Harrison declares: "As president of the United States, I was present at the first Pan-American congress in Washington D.C. I believe that with God's help, our two countries shall continue to live side by side in peace and prosperity. Benjamin Harrison." In that statement he pronounces the *r* after the vowel in *first* and *our*. He also uses the vowel of *merry* in the first syllable of his last name. (Along the Atlantic coast, and in Cleveland's speech, that syllable would have the vowel sound of *hat*). His most unusual pronunciation in that short recorded segment is a long-drawn-out and rising vowel in *God's*.

William McKinley, r-less Ohioan

William McKinley was the first twentieth-century president, serving from 1897 until his assassination in 1901, but his speech has a pronounced nineteenth-century oratorical flavor. Like Harrison, McKinley hailed from Ohio. He was born in Niles in northern Ohio near the Pennsylvania border, solid *r*-ful territory, but he doesn't sound much like it. McKinley's

William McKinley delivering a speech from a review stand at the Pan American Expo in Buffalo, New York on September 5, 1901, the day before he was shot.

voice in an 1896 campaign speech is almost as formal and as Eastern as Cleveland's. He drops the *r* after vowels in *civil wah, ouh*, and *mahket*, though he also keeps it, as an Ohioan normally would, in *honor* and *preserve*. And in the same manner as Cleveland, his most notable affectation in speech is his trilling of *r*'s before vowels. As he nears the climax of his one-minute speech, we hear trills in *protection, reciprocity, foreign* (with a first syllable using the vowel sound of *far*), and *submit this declaration for the sober and considerate judgment of the American people.*

You can hear the same highly formal style in his 1901 speech at the Pan American Exposition in Buffalo, New York: not-*r* after vowels in *mahkets, hahmony, concohd,* and *wah*, and trilled *r*'s in *prosperity, interrupt, encourage, interest,* and *American*. On September 6, the day after he gave this speech, he was shot at close range by an anarchist. He died on the 14th.

Theodore Roosevelt, New York Rough Rider

When his young wife Alice died after childbirth, Theodore Roosevelt left his comfortable East Coast life behind to restore his health and spirits in the rugged American West. "I owe more than I can ever express to the West," he recalled later. But whatever he owed to the West, it wasn't his pronunciation. He never abandoned the highbrow New York accent that was his by birth and breeding.

Born and raised in a then-fashionable part of Lower Manhattan, and educated at Harvard, Roosevelt had the cultivated New Yorker's *r*-less accent: *ouah* for *our, pahties* for *parties, quatah* for *quarter,* and *watah* for *water,* for example. As he reached the climax of his speeches, he rolled the *r* a little: *sneering indifference, never ending.* His speech also betrays traces of what we nowadays would call Brooklynese: *foist* for *first, woid* for *word, woith* for *worth, toin* for *turn, soivice* for *service, consoins* for *concerns*—at least some of the time. And he pronounced *government* in two syllables: *govment.*

Clearly there was no disadvantage to *r*-lessness in Teddy's day. There were no complaints about his accent. He loved the whole country, and the whole country loved him.

William Howard Taft, Ohio r-ful

The next president, William Howard Taft, not only was from Ohio, but, in strong contrast to McKinley, also sounded like it. In the 1908 campaign speeches the Edison company recorded for him, his r's after vowels are pronounced, in both senses of that word. Taft had no Virginia ancestor to repudiate. He just spoke, without apology, in the r-ful manner he had grown up with in one of the leading families of Cincinnati.

To hear the r-dropping speeches of McKinley, who came from r-ful territory but affected an elegant not-r oratorical style, and then to compare them with the r-ful speeches of fellow Ohioan William Howard Taft less than a decade later, is to register firsthand the shift from East Coast to Midwestern norms.

Woodrow Wilson, r-ful Scholar

Woodrow Wilson, Ph.D., president during the teens of the twentieth century, grew up in Staunton, Virginia. Most of Virginia lacks the r pronunciation after vowels, but Staunton is in the western side of the state, in the Shenandoah Valley at the edge of the Appalachians. There, as well as in all points west as far as the Pacific Ocean, the r after vowels is pronounced. And so it was with Wilson. Evidently he too felt no need to adopt r-lessness to show his cultivation. True, his r is not as emphatic as Taft's, and in campaign speeches he recorded in 1912 it is possible to hear an occasional r-less pronunciation, like *farmah* instead of *farmer*. Wilson also used the more elegant British and eastern New England *ah* in words like *pass* and *demand*.

Warren G. Harding, Bloviator with an r

The next president from Ohio, and the last so far, was Warren G. Harding, the happy bloviator. He was born and raised near Marion, north of Columbus in the north central part of the state. Would he be a

A portion of the New York Times *article, dated April 13, 1921, in which Warren Harding's pronunciations were compared to the pronunciations of Woodrow Wilson.*

nineteenth-century orator, complete with *r*-lessness and rolling *r*, like his Ohio predecessor McKinley? Not a chance. This was well into the twentieth century, and like his other Ohio predecessor, Taft, he was an *r*-ful speaker, as in his famous phrase, "not nostrums but normalcy," with a clear audible *r* in *normalcy*. Harding did have a touch of elegance in pronouncing *rather* as *rahther*.

At Harding's inaugural address, a *New York Times* reporter made notes on the new president's pronunciation, contrasting it with Wilson's. Only in *advantage*, pronounced *advahntage*, and its opposite *disadvahntage*, did Harding use the genteel *ah* sound, the so-called long *a* or broad *a*. Furthermore, while Wilson had said *i-ther* and *ni-ther* for *either* and *neither*, Harding used the less genteel *ee-ther* and *nee-ther*.

Other contrasts noted by the reporter are more idiosyncratic. Wilson apparently used a French pronunciation for *personnel*, pronouncing it *pare-son-nel*, in the reporter's transcription, and strongly accenting the first syllable; Harding made it *purs-onel*. And Wilson, according to the reporter, said *maintained* with a weak *men* in the first syllable and then a strong *tained* in the second; Harding accented both syllables "with 'main' and 'tained' as spelled."

In the reporter's summary, Harding "was inclined to accent every syllable in some words while in many he exhibited a tendency to accent the first syllable strongly." To us today it is odd that such pronunciations should be heard as oddities; in fact it is hard to determine what the reporter found so odd about them.

Calvin Coolidge, r-less New Englander

Not-so-silent Calvin Coolidge, the vice president who succeeded to the presidency when Harding died and then earned a full term on his own, grew up in Plymouth Notch, Vermont, a tiny town just to the east of the historic east-west boundary between *r*-ful and *r*-less speech. Farther to the east of Plymouth Notch is the state of New Hampshire, fully *r*-less; farther to the west is upstate New York and the whole rest of the *r*-ful nation. By accident of location—just to the east of the dividing line—Coolidge's pronunciation was *r*-less. He regularly left out the *r* after vowels in words like *befoah* for *before, secuah* for *secure*, and *haht* for *heart*. In a 1920 Fourth of July campaign speech, you can hear *paht* for *part, dollahs* for *dollars, remaindah* for *remainder, yeah* for *year, woik* (yes, a kind of Brooklynese) for *work*, and *moah* for *more*, though once he also says *dollars* with an *r* after the vowel.

Coolidge was the first of the twentieth-century presidents with a noticeable regional as opposed to class accent. In his speech as well as his habits, he made a point of living up to the stereotype of rural New England frugality.

Herbert Hoover, Westerner

We get into modern times with Herbert Hoover, president from 1929 to 1932, who lived to age 90 in 1964. He was the first president born west of the Mississippi, in West Branch, Iowa. At the age of nine he was orphaned and went even farther west, to relatives in Oregon, and then to college at brand-new Stanford University in California, where he graduated with the first class in 1895. All these are *r*-pronouncing areas. Like all the presidents after McKinley who grew up in *r*-ful places, he gave no sign of any inclination to drop *r* after vowels.

Indeed, the West Coast has the ultimate blend of American English. As settlers moved westward from the different dialect areas of the Atlantic Coast, they intermingled, and the Rocky Mountains completely broke up the north-south differentiation characteristic of the East. The resulting West Coast blend is to most American ears bland and unremarkable. And getting back to Hoover, whatever praise he earned

From his private railroad car, Herbert Hoover delivers his final radio address of the 1932 presidential campaign against Franklin D. Roosevelt.

as a great engineer and humanitarian, whatever criticism he evoked for his inability to deal with the Depression, nobody bothered about his accent, one way or the other. That may be in part because he spoke in a monotone, but that's another story.

Another r-less Roosevelt

Franklin D. Roosevelt, like his fifth cousin Theodore, came from a patrician New York family. He grew up in sheltered opulence 50 miles up the Hudson River from New York City in his family's Hyde Park estate. There he learned an *r*-less accent not unlike Theodore's, and like Theodore he kept it all his life. Abundant recordings attest to Franklin D. Roosevelt's mastery of the media—radio, in his case—and to his accent, *r*-less after vowels in words like *ouah* for *our*. "We have nothing to *feah* but *feah* itself," FDR declared in his first inaugural address. Incidentally, his pronunciation of *again* rhymed with *train*, and his pronunciation of *Nazi* had the same vowel sounds as *nasty*.

Though Roosevelt had many vociferous enemies, they didn't attack his accent as unnatural or pretentious. He was what he was. By FDR's time, however, an Ohioan attempting to put on Rooseveltian airs in his speech would have been hooted off the platform.

Harry S. Truman, r-ful and Slightly Southern

After Franklin Roosevelt came Truman and Eisenhower, two more presidents born west of the Mississippi and both retaining the *r*-ful accents they were raised with. Truman was also the first of the twentieth-century presidents to sound a little Southern.

Truman was from Independence, pronounced by him *Indy-pendence,* on the outskirts of Kansas City at the western edge of Missouri. Like any Missourian, it should be emphasized, he pronounced all his *r*'s. But like other Missourians from that part of the state, he had a hint of Southern pronunciation in his speech. Occasionally he would use the Southern *ah* vowel, as in *sahlence* for *silence, vahlated* for *violated, Ah* for *I,* and *mah* for *my,* though more often he pronounced such words with the Northern long *i* sound. Furthermore, in a fashion more typical of the South than of the North, he pronounced *the* as *thuh* not just before words with consonants, as everyone does, but even before words beginning with vowels, as in *thuh allies* and *thuh evil.* He also had a bit of the Southern manner of raising the short *e* before *n* almost to the level of short *i,* so that *defense,* for example, would sound something like *definse.*

Dwight D. Eisenhower: Unremarkably r-ful

After Truman came Dwight D. Eisenhower, who grew up in Abilene, Kansas, about 160 miles west of Independence. Kansas, like Missouri, is *r*-ful, far from any *r*-less territory, and Eisenhower, like Truman, pronounced all his *r*'s. If Eisenhower ever had a hint of a Southern accent like Truman's, it must have been weeded out during his long experience as an officer in the military. Critics have fussed about the grammaticality of Eisenhower's sentences and his military-style pronunciation of *nuclear* as "nucular," but not about any particulars of his accent.

En route to Baltimore on September 26, 1952, Dwight D. Eisenhower speaks to an audience gathered around his train at Silver Spring, Maryland.

The Kennedy r-lessness: A Different Perception

Like his predecessors Franklin Roosevelt, Calvin Coolidge, Theodore Roosevelt, William McKinley, and Grover Cleveland—not to mention earlier presidents like the Adamses—John F. Kennedy grew up *r*-less. He too came by his *r*-dropping naturally, being from Boston. But the shift in prestige from *r*-less to *r*-ful was now so complete that, instead of admiring Kennedy for his accent or accepting it as to be expected of a person of his origins, the rest of the country was bemused and even amused by Kennedy's pronunciations.

Granted, Kennedy's pronunciation was less patrician than FDR's, but such a distinction between two *r*-less styles was lost on most Americans. It was American attitudes that had changed. What they heard from FDR and his *r*-dropping predecessors was a pronunciation that seemed to express the highest degree of cultivation; by Kennedy's time that same kind of pronunciation seemed merely atypical, an aberration. A best-selling record by humorist Vaughn Meader, *The First Family*, took advantage of the changed attitude, satirizing the Kennedys' accents as well as their style.

To an America by now fully attuned to *r*-ful presidents, Kennedy's *r*-less Boston accent attracted immediate notice. Like previous *r*-less presidents, Kennedy said *outah* for *outer, ovah* for *over, othah* for *other, hahd* for *hard, noath* for *north, caeh* for *care, Novembah* for *November, theuhfoah* for *therefore, feah* for *fear*. Like a good Bostonian, he said *lahst* for *last*.

The shift away from *r*-lessness is apparent in the younger generation of Kennedys. For that matter, it's even apparent in John Kennedy's own generation. His younger brother, Senator Ted Kennedy, nowadays is much more *r*-ful than he was when he first was elected to the Senate.

Kennedy's Extra r One more thing Kennedy did in accord with Boston practice: He kept the *r* at the end of a word when the next word began with a vowel. So he would be *r*-ful in saying *there is* or *air of progress* or *whatever action*. Furthermore, when one word ends with a vowel and the next one begins with a vowel, speakers of his Boston dialect insert an *r* that isn't there to begin with. This is where Kennedy's famous pronunciation of *Cuba* with an *r* at the end comes from. If you listen to his speech of October 18, 1962, on the Cuban Missile Crisis, you will hear plain *Cuba* without an *r* again and again—until he says *launched from Cubar against any nation of the Western Hemispheah*. Or later says *conspiracy which has turned Cubar against your friends*. (In that phrase Kennedy does pronounce the *r* in *turned*. Not all of his *r*-less opportunities become *r*-less.) Only when *Cuba* is immediately followed by a vowel does it sprout an *r* in Kennedy's speech.

At this press conference in the State Department Auditorium on November 20, 1962, John F. Kennedy announced that the Soviet Union had agreed to withdraw all IL-28 bombers from Cuba within one month's time.

Lyndon Johnson: r-ful and Southern

The abrupt transition from Kennedy to Lyndon B. Johnson was a shock in language as well as in events. Johnson had grown up in rural West Texas. The eastern edge of Texas is *r*-less territory, but Johnson was from the west, and he was properly *r*-ful. He said *I* with a Northern pronunciation too, most of the time, instead of the Southern *ah* predominant in most of Texas. The Texas flavor of his speech came more from lengthening the vowels in many of his words, so that *sound*, for example, and *love* in his pronunciation became two-syllable words.

The election of Boston-accented Kennedy over neutral-accented Richard Nixon in 1960 and Texas-accented Johnson over neutral-accented Barry Goldwater in 1964 marked a major change in American attitudes toward regional pronunciations. Just as *r*-ful had developed into the norm for American pronunciation during the early and mid twentieth century, so the acceptance of diversity in American pronunciation developed during the latter part of that century. It had happened before it was noticed by commentators. Satirist Lenny Bruce, for example, confidently asserted that a Southerner couldn't be elected president because of his accent. Before Lyndon Johnson proved him wrong in the 1964 election, Bruce had a routine that managed to satirize three different accents:

> *Now, Lyndon Johnson. Good guy. Good American. Brilliant craftsman,* brilliant *politician. But because there's a lot of bigots in this country, Lyndon Johnson never had a chance. Why? Bigotry, man, out-and-out. His whole culture is into the shithouse. No matter how profound Lyndon Johnson could ever be, as soon as he opens up his mouth—*
> "Folks, ah *think new-cleer fishing—*"
> "You think your putz, *you dummy! Get that* schlub *outta here!*"
> "But ah th—"
> "You don't think *anything,* schmuck!"
> 'Cause *bigots say that*
> "Anybody tawks that way's a shitkickuh, Daddy, He cain't know a damn thing."

In one short sentence fragment, Johnson is characterized by coupling a Southern *ah* with ignorance about the proper pronunciation of *nuclear fission.* It should be noted, however, that *new-cleer* is approximately the standard *r*-ful pronunciation of that word, and the "proper" one at that, rather than *nucular,* though the spelling implies ignorance. Of course, there's *r*-lessness, as well as *tawks* and *cain't,* in the language of the "bigots," and the first unnamed respondent to Johnson liberally uses Yiddish slang.

Bruce turned out to be wrong about Southern accents getting in the way. After his pronouncement came Lyndon Johnson, and then Jimmy Carter, Bill Clinton, and now George W. Bush.

Two r-ful Neutrals

After Johnson came Nixon, a Californian with the neutral (and *r*-ful) accent characteristic of that state. His speech mannerisms, including an effort at folksiness that clashed with his stiff formality, are fascinating, but his accent has little to comment on.

Just as unremarkable for his accent was Nixon's successor, Gerald Ford. Ford's unremarkable and *r*-ful accent is from Michigan. If you listen for nonstandard pronunciations, you can hear Ford talking about "our *childern*" and "our *childern's childern,*" but that's about it.

Jimmy Carter, True r-less Southerner

But then a true Southerner came along—Jimmy *Cahtah* of *Geogia.* His is a cultivated not-*r* pronunciation: *moah* for *more, wah* for *war, evuh* for *ever, ah* for *are.* He speaks of the *govement* without using an *r.* And he has the Southern *ah* for *I, hah* for *high, ahdealism* for *idealism, sasahtih* for *society.*

Reagan and Bush the Elder: More r-ful Neutrals

After Carter came a remarkable speaker with an unremarkable *r*-ful accent: Ronald Reagan. He spent his early years in *r*-ful Dixon, Illinois.

Any hint of a local accent was whittled away by Reagan's years as a radio broadcaster and then his many years in Hollywood as an actor. This wasn't inevitable. He began his radio and acting career in the 1930s, when an *r*-less accent still was widely affected by actors and broadcasters, and of course Reagan's hero as president was *r*-less Franklin D. Roosevelt. But Reagan wasn't the type. True to his upbringing, he remained unaffectedly *r*-ful.

The Bush family that provided two of the next three presidents has a variety of accents. George H. W. Bush, Reagan's vice president, who succeeded him to the presidency, grew up in *r*-ful western Connecticut, and his *r* is pronounced, in both senses of that word. That was where he acquired his neutral pronunciation, little affected by his move as an adult to Texas, where his children were raised.

Bill Clinton, Arkansawyer

Before the second Bush, the Southern flavor returned yet again with the election of Bill Clinton. But Arkansas is outside the *r*-less limits of the deep South. What it has for Southern flavor instead is the *ah* pronunciation for *I*. So you can hear Clinton say *tahm* for *time* and *rahsing* for *rising*, but he won't miss an *r*. His education outside the South at Georgetown University, Oxford, and Yale Law School didn't have an appreciable effect on his down-home accent. If it had, he would have run the risk of being accused of snobbery. He had other accusations to face, but snobbery wasn't one of them.

The Texas Bush

It's not heredity but environment that determines how a person speaks. The only aspect of language hardwired in the human brain is the ability to learn whatever language(s) a child hears as he or she is growing up. And when parents speaking one way move to a place that speaks in another way, the children have a choice: talk like mom and dad, or talk like your friends. Sooner or later the friends usually win out.

So it is that George W. Bush, born in New Haven, Connecticut, but raised in Texas, should talk with a Texas twang, even though his parents do not. When he was 2, his family moved to Odessa in west Texas; two years later they moved to nearby Midland, where he spent his boyhood and language-formative years. The Midland Chamber of Commerce declares: "George W. Bush benefited from his father's decision to break free of the 'noble' life of the Eastern establishment. Instead of limousine rides, young George pedaled a bike around the streets of Midland. . . ."

Not-so-young George holds to that attitude today. "The values Midland holds near to its heart are the same ones I hold near to my heart," Bush has said. He was referring to optimism and the notion that "the sky's the limit," but he could be referring to language too. And despite the best of Eastern educations, Dubya has held on to those Midland values, in accent as well as worldview. It may have helped that he returned to Midland after his education elsewhere, living there from 1975 to 1987.

Dubya's speech is *r*-ful. His part of Texas, like Lyndon Johnson's, and like Clinton's Arkansas, is well beyond the limits of *r*-less Southern territory. But more than Johnson's, though less than Clinton's, Bush's speech has the Southern and Texan *ah* for *i*. It's not pure *ah* in words like *lives* and *child* and *mind*, but it's not a strong Northern long *i* either. He also has a folksy style that sometimes changes *–ing* to *–in'* in words like *talkin'* and *gettin',* and that leaves out some syllables and consonants. He will say *lemme* and *gotta* and *gonna*—not in prepared remarks, but freely in press conferences and interviews. His nickname *Dubya* comes from his pronunciation of his middle initial. More peculiarities of Dubya's speech will be discussed in the profile on his presidency at the end of this book. He has quite a few—giving future presidential aspirants a clear indication that anything goes when it comes to presidential pronunciations.

Accentuating the Presidents

We have available the recorded voices of 21 presidents, going back as far as the late nineteenth century. From that evidence can we draw any conclusions about what kind of accent best becomes a president, or best becomes someone who wants to become president? Only this: an *r*-less, Atlantic Coast, semi-British accent is no longer something that anyone from the rest of the country should aspire to. But nowadays it's hardly necessary to warn against that; indeed, there are few who remember the days when an r-less accent intimated sophistication and good breeding.

What may not be quite so obvious is that the r-ful neutral accent isn't required either. Really, almost anything goes. You can have a noticeable r-less accent, like Kennedy and Carter; you can have a noticeable r-ful accent, like Johnson, Clinton, and the younger Bush; or you can have an unremarkable neutral r-ful way of speaking, like Nixon, Ford, and Reagan. Nowadays, at least, your regional accent won't earn you the presidency or keep you from it, or determine your success, failure, or popularity while in office. The only difference is that if you have a noticeable accent, your political friends will like it and your political enemies will be annoyed with it, while if your accent is neutral, friends and foes will find other things about you to praise or blame.

9 Acting Presidents: Movies and Television

As the previous chapters have made clear, American presidents have had vastly different speaking styles and abilities. There have been orators and communicators as gifted as John Adams and Franklin Roosevelt; there have been reluctant public speakers like Thomas Jefferson and Gerald Ford, and all kinds in between. Even their admirers have to admit that some of our presidents have been mediocre speakers at best. But that doesn't keep us from hoping that a president will have great power of utterance to match great leadership and statesmanship. We can find that perfect combination in our dreams—or in the movies and on television.

What kind of speaker would we like our presidents to be? Maybe we should look to the left coast instead of the right for an answer. The make-believe presidents of Hollywood movies and television have their speaking abilities made to order, while, for many reasons, the real-life presidents in Washington may not conform to our wishes or ideals. We don't elect presidents primarily for their manner of speaking—in fact, the nine who were elevated from the vice presidency hadn't been elected president at all—but when we go to the movies, we elect to hear those who speak uncommonly well.

If we want to discover what Americans really hope for in a president, then, perhaps we should look to the dream factories of Hollywood. There, presidents can take on any character their creators wish, unencumbered by the constraints of history. In the movies and on television, you won't come across a president who gives a two-hour lecture on the Constitution, as William Henry Harrison did in his inaugural address, or who reads a speech in a monotone like Herbert Hoover, or who stumbles over words like George W. Bush. Perhaps not coincidentally, you won't find many movies or television shows about those particular presidents either.

Hollywood presidents make great speeches with feeling, and even in private conversation they never mangle a sentence. Without exception, every president portrayed in a movie, whether the usual good guy or the occasional villain, is well spoken. This holds true both for movies that portray actual presidents and for those whose presidents are figments of the filmmakers' imagination.

Historical Presidents

When reel presidents depict real presidents, they tend to be all that we hope a president would be. It's hard to think of a single movie that portrays a historical president in less than a flattering light unless the president is poor Richard Nixon.

Not surprisingly, the most fabled president of all, Abraham Lincoln, has been a favorite for movies. His is a fabulous rags-to-riches—or at least log-cabin-to-presidency—story, climaxed by four years of the nation's most desperate struggle since the presidency began and finished by a martyrdom. The Lincoln story is also blessed with a real-life protagonist of down-home modesty, good humor, sharp wit, and soaring oratory. Just find an actor who does him justice, and you're in business.

As soon as talking movies were invented, Lincoln was in them, portrayed by Walter Huston in D. W. Griffith's *Abraham Lincoln* in 1930. More than forty movies since then have featured Lincoln, and Hollywood has found its most admirable and sympathetic character actors to embody him. There was Henry Fonda in John Ford's *Young Mr. Lincoln* (1939), portraying Lincoln as a country boy with a rustic twang who chooses law as a profession and wins difficult court cases through his down-to-earth humor and brilliant arguments. There was Raymond Massey winning the Lincoln-Douglas debates in John Cromwell's *Abe Lincoln in Illinois* in 1940.

Lincoln the great presidential orator, delivering the Gettysburg Address, was the subject of *The Perfect Tribute*, a 1935 movie with Charles "Chic" Sale as Lincoln and then a 1991 remake with Jason Robards as the president. In this dramatization, failing to get much applause from his Gettysburg audience, Lincoln learns the next day how much of an impression the text of his speech has made on a dying Southern soldier in a Washington hospital.

The list of distinguished Lincolns goes on. For example, Sam Waterston played Lincoln in *Gore Vidal's Lincoln*, a 1988 portrayal of the embattled Civil War president, and Hal Holbrook took the part of Lincoln in the miniseries *North and South* (1995–96).

No other actual president comes close to Lincoln for number of movie portrayals. George Washington, of course, has been depicted in the movies, but it's telling that none stands out in movie history. Almost all recent movies featuring Washington are made-for-television semidocumentaries. Among the actors who have portrayed Washington in these TV movies are Richard Basehart (*Valley Forge*, 1974), Barry Bostwick (*George Washington*, miniseries 1984 and 1986), Cliff Robertson (*The American Revolution*, 1994), Brian Dennehy (*Founding Fathers*, miniseries 2000), Jeff Daniels (*The Crossing*, 2000), and Kelsey Grammer (*Benedict Arnold: A Question of Honor*, 2003).

Among twentieth-century presidents, Franklin Roosevelt, Harry Truman, and John F. Kennedy have been notable as subjects of movies. Ralph Bellamy portrayed FDR in *Sunrise at Campobello* (1960) as well as in the television miniseries based on Herman Wouk's *Winds of War* (1983) and *War and Remembrance* (1988). Gary Sinise was the title character in the 1995 made-for-TV biopic *Truman*. Cliff Robertson played John F. Kennedy in *PT 109* (1963), the story of the boat Kennedy commanded in World War II, and Henry Fonda was Kennedy in a 1966 NBC documentary. Martin Sheen, later to be transmogrified into President Josiah Bartlet on *The West Wing*, portrayed Kennedy in the eponymous 1983 TV miniseries. Bruce Greenwood played him in the 2000 movie *Thirteen Days*.

And then there is the exception, Richard Nixon. The only president who has had to resign in disgrace is the only president predominately portrayed in disgrace. Nixon's fall could be tragedy or comedy, and it has been portrayed as both, in neither case to his advantage.

Oliver Stone was drawn to the dark vision of Nixon as one whose downfall was brought about by his tragic flaws—Nixon's paranoid fear and hatred of enemies in particular. In Stone's motion picture *Nixon* (1995), Anthony Hopkins is a scheming, brooding Nixon who also happens to be a good family man. Stone provides lots of opportunity for Nixon's brooding as the president listens to tapes and thinks back on episodes in his life; the film is more than three hours long.

There's the comic version of Nixon too, manifested in director Andrew Fleming's flick *Dick* (1999), a snappy 94-minute riff on the great Watergate movie *All the President's Men* (1976). That movie made Nixon such a remote, sinister figure that he never appears onscreen except in short television clips. *Dick*, in contrast, brings him front and center as a bumbling chief conspirator, played by Dan Hedaya. For that matter, it presents Bob Woodward and Carl Bernstein, the *Washington Post* reporters who covered and uncovered the Watergate scandal, as bumblers too. In *Dick*, the Watergate secrets are revealed not by those journalists but inadvertently by two lively and clueless teenage girls (Kirsten Dunst and Michelle Williams).

It would take too long to relate the movie's ingenious explanations of how the girls bring the scandal to light without realizing it, but it all begins when they take a White House tour and find a piece of paper listing "Creeps" to be paid off. Those would be members of Nixon's famous Committee to Re-Elect the President, a fund-raising organization that surreptitiously paid half a million dollars to the Watergate burglars to keep them from talking about their break-in at Democratic national headquarters.

Aside from Nixon, however, Hollywood knows to treat presidents respectfully—or else. This was demonstrated in 2003 in the controversy over a TV miniseries on the Reagans. In the eyes of many Reagan supporters, it was grossly negative in its portrayal of Reagan. The Drudge Report on the World Wide Web, and then the *New York Times*, reported the shocking news that the TV version would have James Brolin as Reagan telling his wife, in refusing to aid AIDS victims, "They that live in sin shall die in sin"—something Reagan never actually said, in public or in private, to the best of anyone's knowledge. In response to the criticism, the movie was re-edited to remove that scene, and it was downgraded to the CBS cable affiliate Showtime rather than being broadcast on the CBS network.

In Your Dreams

When the president is purely hypothetical, not a re-creation of an actual historical figure, Hollywood is tempted to extremes. Unlike most of the people who have actually held the office, generic movie presidents are mostly pure heroes or pure villains. Imaginary movie presidents usually make the American dream come true—or the American nightmare. Our dream president is all-wise, all-talented, and trustworthy, loyal, helpful, friendly, courteous, kind, brave, clean, and reverent—in short, a grownup Boy Scout or an Indiana Jones. Our nightmare is the opposite, either a hapless fool or a corrupt schemer.

The dream and the nightmare follow a variety of patterns, but one pattern is pervasive: the president is almost always at least a glib speaker, if not a glittering one.

One dream pattern is the rags-to-riches story, where the president is plucked as if by magic from obscurity. It's not too much of a stretch, actually, considering that nine real presidents have been plucked from the obscurity of the vice presidency to take over the top office. The wishful difference is that, in the course of stepping from ordinary citizen to leader of the country, the movie citizen always rises to the occasion.

Take the case of Mays Gilliam in Chris Rock's 2003 movie *Head of State*. He's an obscure alderman in a tough district of Washington, D.C., who is made his party's nominee when the original presidential and vice-presidential candidates die in a midair collision. At first Gilliam goes along with his cynical handlers, who expect him to lose but to draw black voters to the party so they can win with a white candidate four years later. Finally, though, in a Chicago meeting hall he breaks away from his scripted platitudes to address the true concerns of his black and white audience:

> *How many of you workin' two jobs just to be broke? Let me hear you say That ain't right!*
> (Audience: *That ain't right!*)
> *How many of you workin' in cities you can't afford to live in? Cleaning up hotels you can't afford to stay in? We got nurses working in hospitals they can't afford to be sick in? That ain't right!*
> (Audience: *That ain't right!*)
> *How many schools have old books but they have brand new metal detectors? Now, that ain't right!*
> (Audience: *That ain't right!*)

That speech turns the campaign around, bringing him believability and a big upsurge in the polls. It's quite an act.

A similar fairy-tale triumph belongs to the 1993 movie *Dave*. Kevin Kline as Dave Kovic is busy running a temporary employment agency in Washington, D.C., when the Secret Service recruits him to impersonate immoral president Bill Mitchell at a luncheon. While Dave is doing his impersonation, the philandering real president becomes unconscious from a stroke. So Dave takes over full time, winning the affections of everyone from the real president's wife to the whole country as he outmaneuvers the evil White House chief of staff. He dazzles reporters and the country in a press conference where, like Mays Gilliam, he confronts the nation's problems:

> . . . *things aren't fine. And you know that and I know that. And we can keep lying to ourselves, but it's a little late for that. We've got water we can't drink and air we can't breathe. We've got bars on our windows and graffiti on our doors.*
>
> *If you get sick, you can't afford to go to the doctor, and if you get laid off, you can't find a new job. We're trillions of dollar in debt. Our roads are cracking, our bridges are crumbling, and everything we used to build is made in Japan. We've got people sleeping in cardboard boxes, and ten-year-old kids who are doing drugs. We've been living together for four hundred years, and we're still trying to kill each other. But that isn't even the worst part. The worst part is we feel like we can't do anything about it.*
>
> *So I've decided that while I'm President, I should actually try to do things, even if they seem impossible.*
>
> *First off I'm initiating a program to try to find a decent job for every American who wants one.*
>
> *Why start here? Because if you've ever seen the look on someone's face the day they get a job—I've had some personal experience with this—they look like they could fly. And unless we start tapping into that kind of spirit again, there's no way we're gonna fix anything in this country.*
>
> *So let's get to work.*

Not since the Great Depression has a presidential speech about employment been such a hit. The press corps sit in stunned silence, then jump to their feet to report the electrifying news. Nina Totenberg on the *NBC Nightly News* (yes, real journalists make cameo appearances) gushes that it is "the boldest initiative yet of the 'new Bill Mitchell' presidency, a full employment program unparalleled since the days of FDR." Robert Novak of *Evans and Novak* calls it "dangerous," Chris Mathews of *Good Morning America* calls it "courageous, challenging, visionary," and four others chime in with similarly extreme reactions.

Is the speech all that brilliant? Well, Dave delivers it forcefully, but it's hardly the first time a president has said something like this, with somewhat less of a response. The difference is in the script. In a script you can make the audience go wild over anything. A real politician could only wish.

To bring the movie to a satisfying romantic conclusion, Dave makes another supposedly breathtakingly candid speech to a joint session of Congress in response to an accusation of corruption. He ends the speech with a dramatic presidential moment unparalleled since Teddy Roosevelt was shot in Milwaukee, collapsing as if suffering a heart attack and being carried off so that the now-dead real president can be substituted as his corpse. With the true president truly dead, the good-guy vice president takes over and Dave returns to civilian life—and a romance with the ex-president's widow.

Then there's Michael Douglas as President Andrew Shepherd in *The American President* (1995), where the rags-to-riches story is lonely-heart-widower-to-romance. The screenplay was by Aaron Sorkin, later the creator and writer for *The West Wing*. Like Dave, President Shepherd stuns the press corps and wins the applause of the citizenry, in this case with an impromptu declaration of love for his country and his environ-mentalist-lobbyist-girlfriend.

> *This is a country made up of people with hard jobs that they're terrified of losing. The roots of freedom are of little or no interest to them at the moment. We are a nation afraid to go out at night. We're a society that has assigned low priority to education and has looked the other way while our public schools have been decimated. We have serious problems to solve, and we need serious men to solve them. . . .*
>
> *. . . I've loved two women in my life. I lost one to cancer, and I lost the other 'cause I was so busy keeping my job, I forgot to do my job. Well, that ends right now.*
>
> *Tomorrow morning the White House is sending a bill to Congress for its consideration. It's White House Resolution 455, an energy bill*

requiring a 20 percent reduction of the emission of fossil fuels over the next ten years. It is by far the most aggressive stride ever taken in the fight to reverse the effects of global warming. . . . If you want to talk about character and American values, fine. Just tell me where and when, and I'll show up. This is a time for serious men, Bob [his opponent], and your fifteen minutes are up. My name's Andrew Shepherd, and I am the President.

The audience response is enthusiastic, in contrast with the reception such a speech might get in real life. For example, in 1979 President Carter gave a major speech calling for reduction in the use of fossil fuels—with a decidedly unfavorable response from the public. But that was real life; this is the movies.

The American President concludes with an even more dramatic occasion for speechmaking, the president's State of the Union address. What could he possibly say to top the bold declaration he made at his press conference? Sorkin makes the brilliant choice of leaving it entirely to our imagination. The doorkeeper announces, "Mr. Speaker, the president of the United States!" and, in the words of the screenplay, "The chamber leaps to its feet in a thunderous ovation, shouts of 'Bravo!' from the gallery" . . . and the movie comes to an end.

The Presidential Action Hero

Another Hollywood scenario portrays the president as action hero. No matter; he's still a great communicator. In *Air Force One* (1997), for example, President James Marshall appears to be a reincarnation of Indiana Jones—which isn't so surprising, considering that the president is played by Harrison Ford. In Russia, President Marshall addresses an audience at a dinner celebrating a victory over terrorists. Then he folds up his written speech, takes off his glasses, and addresses unscripted remarks to the audience:

What we did here was important. We finally pulled our heads out of the sand. We finally stood up to the brutality and said we've had enough. Every time we ignore these atrocities—the rapes, the death

squads, the genocides—every time we negotiate with these—these
thugs to keep them out of our country and away from our families,
every time we do this, we legitimize terror.

Terror is not a legitimate system of government. And to those who
commit the atrocities, I say: we will no longer tolerate, we will no
longer negotiate, and we will no longer be afraid. It's your turn to be
afraid.

Not to worry about audience response, of course. Applause is in the script. This is just the beginning of the story, though, and Indiana Jones—oops, James Marshall—has a lot of commando fighting to do, and some piloting, when terrorists hijack Air Force One and take him and his family hostage. For the rest of the movie, he's just too busy to make speeches. At the end he wordlessly salutes when the pilot of a fighter plane says, "Welcome aboard, sir."

And then there's *Independence Day* (1996). Funny, in this movie too the president happens to be a war hero and pilot. President Thomas J. Whitmore, played by Bill Pullman, addresses U.S. fighter pilots ready to take off for the greatest military challenge humanity has ever faced: attacking the spaceship of an alien civilization that is about to conquer and destroy the earth. He uses these words:

Good morning. In less than one hour planes from here and all
around the world will launch the largest aerial battle in the history of
mankind.

Mankind. The word has new meaning for all of us now. We are re-
minded not of our petty differences but of our common interests.

Perhaps it's fate that today, July the Fourth, we will once again
fight for our freedom. Not from tyranny, persecution, or oppression.
But from annihilation. We're fighting for our right to live, to exist.
From this day on, the fourth day of July will no longer be remembered
as an American holiday but as the day that all of mankind declared
we will not go quietly into the night. We will not vanish without a
fight. We will live on. We will survive.

Once again, applause and cheers are in the script. So, for that matter, is the convenient coincidence of July 4. Whitmore has spoken perfectly well, but in this movie actions speak louder than words. It turns out that the president is himself a pilot, and he suits up and goes after the alien spacecraft hovering overhead, succeeding in causing the initial damage to the bad spaceship. When it's all over, he merely says, "We're getting reports from all over. Their ships are going down!"

Life imitates art. Whitmore's bold piloting might have been a foreshadowing of President George W. Bush's landing in a fighter jet on the U.S.S. *Abraham Lincoln* on May 1, 2003, to announce "Mission accomplished" in Gulf War II. For that matter, the speeches of Presidents Marshall and Whitmore aren't that different from the bold antiterrorist declarations Bush has made from time to time.

Bombs Away

Before the present era of presidential action heroes, there were some notable presidential action failures in the movies, especially in the nervous early Cold War era. Two 1964 movies took up the theme of accidental nuclear war raised by Eugene Burdick and Harvey Wheeler's 1962 book *Fail Safe*. The movie of that name took the peril seriously. Henry Fonda was the noble president unable to prevent an American bomber from destroying Moscow. In return, to prevent the Soviet Union from retaliating, he has another American plane destroy New York City. He is repeatedly on the hot line to the Soviet premier in Moscow: "Mr. Chairman, my wife is in New York today on a shopping trip and I have her on the phone right now. . . . Mr. Chairman, the phone has gone dead."

The same story is told as grim farce in *Dr. Strangelove: Or How I Learned to Stop Worrying and Love the Bomb*, with Peter Sellers in three roles, one as President Merkin Muffley, who is as muffled as his name implies. He too spends his time on the hot line with the Soviet premier, to little avail:

> Hello? Hello, Dimitri? Listen, I can't hear too well. Do you suppose you could turn the music down just a little? Oh, that's much better. Yes. Fine, I can hear you now, Dimitri. Clear and plain and coming through fine. I'm coming through fine too, eh? Good, then. Well then, as you say, we're both coming through fine. Good. Well it's good

that you're fine and I'm fine. I agree with you. It's great to be fine.
[Laughs.] Now then, Dimitri. You know how we've always talked
about the possibility of something going wrong with the bomb. . . .

Dimitri, look, if this report is true and the plane manages to bomb
the target, is it . . . is this going to full . . . is this going to set off the
Doomsday Machine? Are you sure? Well, I . . . I guess you're just go-
ing to have to get that plane, Dimitri! . . . (And Dmitri doesn't, of
course, thereby setting off the Doomsday Machine nuclear explosion
that renders the earth uninhabitable.)

If Muffley's words to a drunken and befuddled Dmitri are a little
shaky, that's understandable, considering that it's the end of the world
as we know it. Neither the president in *Fail Safe* nor the president in
Dr. Strangelove makes any communication to Congress, the press corps,
or the public, as the more heroic presidents of the nineties movies are
pleased to do.

In addition to bumblers like Muffley, there have been outright villains
in recent presidential movies too. The president in *Wag the Dog* (1997),
for example, is caught in a Lewinskyesque escapade just before the election. His media consultant arranges a phony war in Albania to divert attention from the president's misbehavior. And in Tom Clancy's *Clear and
Present Danger* (1994), the president (played by Donald Moffat) schemes
to get the virtuous CIA operative Jack Ryan (played by Harrison Ford)
killed by Colombian drug lords. In these cases, though, it should be
noted that the criticism of the presidency is not as bold as it could be:
the president's advisers are the really bad guys, and the president himself has little screen time and little to say. Similarly, in *Love Actually*
(2003), Billy Bob Thornton plays an American president with a roving if
not roguish eye for the British Prime Minister's pulchritudinous assistant—but he doesn't get involved with her, and instead emboldens the
Prime Minister to make his own approach, so it all ends happily.

On Television: President Palmer

Two of the most successful recent television series have featured imaginary presidents with great speaking ability, one more admirable than

Publicity still of Dennis Haysbert as President David Palmer on the television series 24.

the next. On *24*, there is David Palmer, played by Dennis Haysbert. Each season the show goes through 24 consecutive hours of a terrorist-threatened day, and each time Palmer is caught up in the terror: first as a presidential candidate and then as a president so virtuous that the villains can't stand to leave him alone. Palmer, we learn, earned a law degree from the University of Maryland, was a basketball All-American for Georgetown, and served as a congressman and senator before attaining the presidency. Oh, and he is the first African-American president. Haysbert's Palmer speaks with a deep, resonant voice and has a dignified, well-spoken manner reminiscent of James Earl Jones.

He faces and survives scenarios just as bad as Marshall's, Whitmore's, or Muffley's. By odd coincidence, convenient for the producers of the show, all of Palmer's troubles occur in Los Angeles. In the first 24-hour sequence, while he is a presidential candidate, he is the target of assassins. In the second, terrorists are attempting to detonate an atomic bomb in Los Angeles. In the third, the villains' weapon of choice is bioterrorism. Unlike Marshall and Whitmore, however, while Palmer is in peril, he isn't on the front line. Action hero Jack Bauer (Kiefer Sutherland) takes care of that. Palmer merely remains in close touch with Bauer by phone or in person.

Action is paramount in *24*, but speeches by Palmer are important too. All are impressive. In the first season of *24*, while he is on the verge of winning the California primary, Palmer makes a crucial speech at an evening press conference. Like so many movie and television presidents, he differentiates himself from the usual politicians by speaking the truth and admitting his errors. "Doing the right thing is the only thing to do," he declares in his rich baritone, as he presents evidence that his financial backers had been involved in a murder and apologizes that he hadn't known about it.

In the second season of *24*, Palmer has been president for a year. Members of his staff and cabinet scheme to use the Twenty-fifth Amendment to the Constitution to declare him unfit for office and replace him with his vice president. Palmer makes a dignified plea to his cabinet not to oust him as president and another dignified speech when he is restored to the presidency after having been ousted. There was every expectation of another dignified, significant, and successful speech or two for every subsequent season of *24* during Palmer's presidency.

The third season has Palmer in his fourth year as president, back in Los Angeles at the University of Southern California for a debate with his opponent, Senator John Keeler—but it's cut short by a threat of a bioterror attack.

The President Who Argued with God

The acme of presidential speechmaking comes in the person of Josiah "Jed" Bartlet, played by Martin Sheen on *The West Wing*. Unabashedly, *The West Wing* shows how much of a president's remarks should be credited to the speechwriters. The debate among speechwriters and aides is often the focus of an episode. But Bartlet is above them all. We are told that he comes from a distinguished New Hampshire family of American patriots; the fictitious president is given a distant ancestor by the name of Josiah Bartlet, who really did sign the Declaration of Independence. In Aaron Sorkin's scripts, Jed is presidential not only by virtue of holding the office, but by his demeanor, intelligence, wisdom, and speech. (Although said to be from New Hampshire, he has no trace of a New England accent.)

Actor Martin Sheen, as President Josiah Bartlet, in a publicity still on the set of The West Wing.

President Bartlet speaks eloquently not only to his aides, to visitors, to reporters, to Congress, and to the American people. In private, and less formally, he even dares to speak defiantly to God—in God's home, Washington's National Cathedral. Bartlet asks that the doors be closed and then declares:

> *You're a son-of-a-bitch, you know that? She [his secretary] bought her first new car and you hit her with a drunk driver. What, was that supposed to be funny?* "You can't conceive, nor can I, the appalling strangeness of the mercy of God," says Graham Greene. I don't know whose ass he was kissing there 'cause I think you're just vindictive. . . .
>
> There's a tropical storm that's gaining speed and power. They say we haven't had a storm this bad since you took out the tender ship of mine last year in the North Atlantic last year—68 crew. Do you know what a tender ship does? Fixes the other ships. Doesn't even carry guns. Floats around and fixes the other ships and delivers that mail. That's all it can do.
>
> [angry] Gratias tibi ago, domine. [I give thanks to you, Lord.] Yes, I lied. It was a sin. I've committed many sins. Have I displeased you, you feckless thug?
>
> 3.8 million new jobs, that wasn't good? Bailed out Mexico, increased foreign trade, 30 million new acres for conservation, put Mendoza on the bench, we're not fighting a war, I've raised three children—That's not enough to buy me out of the doghouse? Haec credam a deo pio? A deo iusto? A deo scito? Cruciatus in crucem! Tuus in terra servus, nuntius fui; officium perfeci. [angry] Cruciatus in crucem. [waves dismissively] Eas in crucem!
>
> [Bartlet turns away in anger. He descends to the lower sanctuary and lights a cigarette. He takes a single puff, drops the butt to the floor, and grinds it defiantly with his shoe. He looks back at the altar.] You get [Vice President] Hoynes!

God doesn't need a translation of his Latin, so the broadcast didn't provide one. The official translation of the Latin passage goes like this:

> *Am I really to believe that these are the acts of a loving God? A just God? A wise God? To hell with your punishments! I was your servant*

here on Earth. And I spread your word and I did your work. To hell
with your punishments. To hell with you!

The show depicts Bartlet's speechwriters helping him with his remarks on other occasions, but this clearly is Bartlet himself speaking from the heart, in the presence only of God and the television audience.

There's never been a real president, or even a fictitious one, quite like this. You'd have to go back to James Garfield, former college professor of classics, who was said to be able to write Latin with one hand and Greek with the other simultaneously, and who, by the way, campaigned in German as well as in English. But it's quite unlikely that Garfield would have addressed God so boldly.

The Ultimate Hollywood President

If a movie president became a real president, what would the real president be like? There's an answer to this question already: Ronald Reagan.

Reagan never played a president in the movies, but he knew the script. He wasn't the action hero type, but he did play the role of ordinary citizen become president while keeping to his deeply felt beliefs and speaking the plain truth. He polished and rehearsed his lines carefully when giving a major address, and when there wasn't time for rehearsal he was quick with a quip. He always had a story to tell about an ordinary citizen caught in the snares of government—or maybe a story to get a laugh as well as to make a point. Here's one he told the National Association of Evangelicals on March 8, 1983, when he also made his famous remark about the "evil empire":

An evangelical minister and a politician arrived at Heaven's gate one day together. And St. Peter, after doing all the necessary formalities, took them in hand to show them where their quarters would be. And he took them to a small, single room with a bed, a chair, and a table, and said this was for the clergyman. And the politician was a little worried about what might be in store for him. And he couldn't believe it then when St. Peter stopped in front of a beautiful mansion with lovely grounds, many servants, and told him that these would be his quarters.

And he couldn't help but ask. He said, "But wait, how—there's something wrong—how do I get this mansion while that good and holy man only gets a single room?" And St. Peter said, "You have to understand how things are up here. We've got thousands and thousands of clergy. You're the first politician who ever made it." [Laughter]

It's ironic, then, that with an actor playing the president so well, television still felt the creative urge to find an actor to play an actor playing the president for the CBS miniseries *The Reagans*. It's not surprising that those who admired Reagan and agreed with his views were outraged at anything less than a hagiographic portrayal. But it is, after all, a Hollywood temptation frequently indulged to remake a successful movie.

There is one major difference, though, between the Reagan presidency and an actor's imaginary portrayal of him as president: In reality, the audience reaction isn't scripted. Today, as it was during his presidency, there are those who admire Reagan for his principles and actions, and those who dislike him for the same reasons. Those who admire him and his principles include his speeches in their admiration; those who dislike him and his principles dismiss the speeches. For all his skill at communication, like most other real-life politicians, he didn't change many hearts and minds through his speeches, though he did attract enough undecided voters and "Reagan Democrats" to make an electoral difference.

10 How to Talk Like a President

So you'd like to be president! Well, after all this discussion of presidential voices, you should be able to draw some useful conclusions about how you should talk if you're president or if you aspire to be one.

To be frank, though, if you haven't been elected president yet, the odds are against you no matter how you talk. The U.S. population is nearly 300 million. Minus nearly 35 million foreign-born who are excluded by the Constitution from the presidency, that leaves odds of about 265 million to one. Subtract the nearly 100 million who won't yet be the constitutionally mandated age of 35 by the time the election of 2008 comes around, and you still have odds of 165 million to one against being chosen president that year.

But don't be discouraged. Aside from nativity and age, there are no other minimum requirements for president. In the twenty-first century, certainly, you don't have to be white or male. And best of all, as history has shown, you don't have to be particularly talented. It's clear, furthermore, that if you don't happen to be a good speaker, that lack won't keep you from being president either. A disinclination for public speaking didn't keep Thomas Jefferson from the presidency, and scrambling his words didn't diminish George W. Bush's popularity.

Still, as president, you might want to present yourself in the best light possible. How should you go about it? A key to the answer comes in the following recent conversation on WNYC radio:

Daniel Max, WNYC: *I think there is a division in the administration, and has been since the* [September 11, 2001] *attacks, over whether the president should sound like he just rode into Dodge* [City] *or like he's speaking to the U.N. So that on the one hand he'll say, we're going to smoke bin Laden out of his cave, or we want him dead or alive, and then he'll speak about the rights of man in the next moment. It's an oddity.*

Bob Garfield, *New York Times: So do you believe the American public wants our president to speak presidentially, or do you think they want to see the real guy, the genuine article?*

—(Radio interview, October 20, 2001)

In a nutshell, the answer to Garfield's question is: Yes—we want both. We want our president to speak presidentially. But we also want him to be a real guy—or gal, when it comes to that in the twenty-first century.

It's easy to learn how to assume the more formal of the two roles, that is, to speak presidentially. Look no further than George Washington for a model. Or go ahead and look further: you'll find a similar dignified style associated with all presidents, whether or not they used it well. For the essence of that style, read through the inaugural addresses. Then, for your own inaugural address, pick up some of those stirring phrases. If you use them in your own inaugural, you will have saved some effort and will have the added advantage of reporters and historians catching the allusions to your predecessors' remarks. They will admire your erudition and your respect for tradition.

If you don't have time to write your inaugural address yourself, and if your budget has been so exhausted by the election campaign that you can't afford a speechwriter, here's a ready-made version (with credits to the original sources) that can do in a pinch:

All-Purpose Presidential Inaugural Address

"Fellow citizens" (Washington and successors), *conscious of "the magnitude and difficulty of the trust to which the voice of my country called me"* (Washington), *but knowing that "the will of the people is the source, and the happiness of the people the end, of all legitimate government upon earth"* (John Quincy Adams), *I pledge my "attachment to the Constitution of the United States, and a conscientious determination to support it"* (John Adams).

"The business of our nation goes forward" (Reagan). *"The only thing we have to fear is fear itself"* (Franklin Roosevelt). *"Much time has passed since Jefferson arrived for his inauguration. . . . But the themes of this day he would know: our nation's grand story of courage and its simple dream of dignity"* (G.W. Bush).

"So let us begin anew . . . a struggle against the common enemies of man: tyranny, poverty, disease and war itself" (Kennedy). *"We must be willing, individually and as a nation, to accept whatever sacrifices may be required of us"* (Eisenhower). *"Beyond that, my fellow citizens, the future is up to us"* (Clinton).

"With malice toward none; with charity for all; with firmness in the right, as God gives us to see the right, let us strive on" (Lincoln). *"God bless you and may God bless America"* (Reagan and successors).

This weighs in at just under 200 words, short enough to be the next shortest inaugural after Washington's second. So it will earn applause for its brevity as well as its sentiments.

Well, that takes care of the inaugural address. After that, you'll have a White House budget to pay for speechwriters. They'll keep your speeches on a dignified diet of this sort, making sure you sound presidential. It's their necks if they don't. Be sure they finish with "God bless America"—nowadays it seems to be as necessary as playing the national anthem at a sporting event.

But for down-to-earth occasions, for photo opportunities and broadcast interviews and meetings with voters, speechwriters won't be the answer. Those speechwriters will be inclined to make you sound presidential, no matter what, either out of respect for the office or out of dreams for their own immortality. But when you're down-to-earth, you're you, not some generic president. Worse yet, you will be called on to speak impromptu, without a script, on unforeseen occasions. You can't choose to remain silent, as long-ago presidents could in the days before voice amplification and broadcast, so you'll have to put some thought into this yourself.

It's a dilemma. Throughout history, peoples everywhere have expected high language from their leaders on high occasions, solemn words to match solemn situations, and that basic principle of rhetoric has hardly been abolished, even in America. On the other hand, as the founders declared, as we the people have enthusiastically discovered for ourselves (hence the slow but inexorable extension of rights to all), as observers from the time of Alexis de Tocqueville have discovered—we Americans are profoundly democratic, and we definitely want our leaders to be down-to-earth.

So it is not just looking over their shoulders at their most eminent predecessors—What would Washington do? What would Theodore Roosevelt do?—that produces anxiety for presidents and their advisers, but the dilemma of expectations that require the president to be both dignified and down-to-earth. Some presidents can manage this; some can't. Some, like Washington, and perhaps Franklin D. Roosevelt, were especially good at dignity; Truman was especially good at being down-to-earth. Who has been good at both? Lincoln, above all; and in the twentieth century, perhaps Teddy Roosevelt or Ronald Reagan, the Great Communicator.

Be careful about your models, though. When it comes to being down-to-earth, don't bother trying to imitate Harry S. Truman. He was one of a kind. If in imitating him you try to cuss 'em and give 'em hell, chances are you'll just end up sounding mean and nasty.

Furthermore, though we're inured to foul language in the movies, in the lyrics of popular music, and in every kind of publication except daily newspapers and the *Reader's Digest*, don't let loose with obscenities. They are too unpresidential, even when you're trying to be down-to-earth. No matter how good you are at invective, that type of language won't be appreciated from a president. Look at the harm it did Nixon when the tapes of his private conversations were made public.

A better model might be Ronald Reagan. His famous off-the-cuff remarks in debate with Jimmy Carter in 1980, and Walter Mondale in 1984, were plain, down-to-earth, and unforgettable. During the October 28, 1980, debate, Carter elaborated on his view of Reagan's view of Medicare,

> . . . *Governor Reagan, as a matter of fact, began his political career campaigning around this nation against Medicare. . . . These are the kinds of elements of a national health insurance, important to the American people. Governor Reagan, again, typically is against such a proposal.*

How to Talk Like a President 179

The truth of this charge didn't matter, because Reagan upset Carter's applecart with a simple "There you go again" prefacing his rebuttal. The details didn't matter; "There you go again" was enough to dismiss Carter's whole argument.

His final statement in that debate sticks in mind, too, because of its simple nonrhetorical question:

> *Next Tuesday all of you will go to the polls, will stand there in the polling place and make a decision. I think when you make that decision, it might be well if you would ask yourself, are you better off than you were four years ago?*

That led to the simple conclusion:

> *If you don't agree, if you don't think that this course that we've been on for the last four years is what you would like to see us follow for the next four, then I could suggest another choice that you have.*

Four years later, on October 28, 1984, in presidential debate with Fritz Mondale, reporter Henry Trewhitt of the *Baltimore Sun* threw this hardball at him:

> Trewhitt: *You already are the oldest President in history, and some of your staff say you were tired after your most recent encounter with Mr. Mondale. I recall, yes, that President Kennedy had to go for days on end with very little sleep during the Cuba missile crisis. Is there any doubt in your mind that you would be able to function in such circumstances?*

Reagan, off-the-cuff, hit that ball out of the park:

> Reagan: *Not at all, Mr. Trewhitt, and I want you to know that also I will not make age an issue of this campaign. I am not going to exploit for political purposes my opponent's youth and inexperience.*

Poor Mr. Mondale, Mr. Trewhitt hadn't done him any favor.

From Reagan you can also learn the value of distilling the nation's problems and anxieties into a single down-to-earth sound bite, one simple message you can repeat again and again. In Reagan's case, as he declared in his 1981 first inaugural, it was "Government is not the solution."

So when you're not at an occasion that requires elevated language, do your best to sound down-to-earth. Speak simply and without a hint of evasion. Even if you're lying through your teeth, make it seem as if you tell the unvarnished truth.

And use words of one syllable. Words like this: "I have just been shot. But it takes more than that to kill a Bull Moose."

Pay attention to your audience. And do have something to say. That will make all the difference.

Here's a fine down-to-earth example of how to sound like a president. It's the official White House transcription of George W. Bush's remarks at Ground Zero in New York City on Friday, September 14, 2001:

On September 14, 2001, George W. Bush stood among the rubble of the World Trade Center and thanked the police, firefighters, and rescue workers for their efforts.

> 4:40 p.m. EDT
> Crowd: *U.S.A.! U.S.A.!*
> The president: *Thank you all. I want you all to know—*
> Q: *Can't hear you.*
> The president: *I can't talk any louder.* [Laughter] *I want you all to know that America today—that America today is on bended knee in prayer for the people whose lives were lost here, for the workers who work here, for the families who mourn. This nation stands with the good people of New York City, and New Jersey and Connecticut, as we mourn the loss of thousands of our citizens.*
> Q: *I can't hear you.*

The president: *I can hear you.* [Applause] *I can hear you. The rest of the world hears you.* [Applause] *And the people who knocked these buildings down will hear all of us soon.* [Applause]

Crowd: *U.S.A.! U.S.A.!*

The president: *The nation sends its love and compassion to everybody who is here. Thank you for your hard work. Thank you for making the nation proud. And may God bless America.* [Applause]

Crowd: *U.S.A.! U.S.A.!*

[The President waves a small American flag. Applause.]

Profiles of the Presidents

George Washington

[1732–99]
President 1789–97

Though he had fine manners and was skilled in everything from playing the flute to riding a horse, Washington was not a trained orator and didn't care to be. But as chapter 1 explains, he did have an awareness of setting the proper precedents for presidents in speechmaking, as in every other aspect of the office. As he wrote to James Madison on May 5, 1789, five days after his first inaugural address:

My dear Sir:

Notwithstanding the conviction I am under of the labor which is imposed upon you by Public Individuals as well as public bodies; yet, as you have begun, so I could wish you to finish, the good work in a short reply to the Address of the House of Representatives (which I now enclose) that there may be an accordance in this business.

Thursday 12 Oclock, I have appointed to receive the Address. The proper plan is with the House to determine. As the first of everything, in our situation, will serve to establish a Precedent, it is devoutly wished on my part, that these precedents may be fixed on true principles. With Affectionate regard etc.

He was asking Madison, who had been the principal author of the inaugural address, to write a suitable reply to the House of Representatives' suitable reply to that address. Washington was definitely not a monarch, but in these formalities as in so many other ways, he invested the presidency with the dignity of a monarch.

His contemporaries remarked that Washington had a quiet, low voice. It was his bearing that was imposing, not his speech. Aside from any other factors, his false teeth made sure of that. His voice was said to be shaky and soft as he delivered that first inaugural address to the members of Congress and distinguished guests on April 30, 1789.

Washington's first inaugural was also his first speech before the first session of the First Congress. Every year thereafter, following the Constitutional mandate that the president "shall from time to time give to the Congress Information of the State of the Union," Washington gave a similarly dignified speech to his fellow-citizens of the Senate and House of Representatives, inaugurating the custom of delivering a State of the Union address in person. Congress, in turn, would send a delegation to the president's house to give a courteous formal reply.

Washington could easily have interpreted the Constitution to require merely a written report on the State of the Union, but he wanted to give it a proper presidential presence. It was one precedent that was interrupted after a short while. Washington's successor, John Adams, happily gave his State of the Union address in person, but it was too monarchical for Thomas Jefferson when he became president. Jefferson sent written State of the Union messages to Congress, a more modest practice followed by his successors for more than a century, until Woodrow Wilson once again delivered the State of the Union in person.

During his presidency, Washington made several ceremonial tours covering the entire country, much as a monarch might have "made a progress" through the countryside. He traveled in the North in 1789, on Long Island in 1790, in the South in 1791. After he was given a jubilant reception by the populace, the leading citizens of a town would greet him with elegant speeches using as many rhetorical ruffles and flourishes as they could muster, and the next day he would reply in kind.

Like a monarch in formality, but unlike a monarch in sentiment, Washington encouraged allegiance to the new form of government rather than to his person. The people praised him for his leadership; he praised them for their patriotism and their adherence to the brand-new Constitution.

Speechwriters helped him throughout his career. As noted above, Madison was the primary author of Washington's first inaugural address, as well as of his reply to the House's reply to this address. (At least the authorship remained presidential, as events later turned out.) The Farewell Address was the work of several advisers. But there is no doubt that the sentiments and the words are as Washington wanted them.

What was Washington's style of speaking before he had help from the likes of Madison, Hamilton, and Jay? Much the same. In 1775, for example, Washington achieved fame for a brief speech to the Continental Congress when he accepted command of the army. This one was apparently unscripted and composed by himself. Here it is in full, as transcribed in the journal of the Congress:

> *Mr. President, Tho' I am truly sensible of the high Honour done me, in this Appointment, yet I feel great distress, from a consciousness that my abilities and military experience may not be equal to the extensive and important Trust: However, as the Congress desire it, I will enter upon the momentous duty, and exert every power I possess in their service, and for support of the glorious cause. I beg they will accept my most cordial thanks for this distinguished testimony of their approbation.*
>
> *But, lest some unlucky event should happen, unfavourable to my reputation, I beg it may be remembered, by every Gentleman in the room, that I, this day, declare with the utmost sincerity, I do not think myself equal to the Command I am honored with.*
>
> *As to pay, Sir, I beg leave to assure the Congress, that, as no pecuniary consideration could have tempted me to have accepted this arduous employment, at the expence of my domestic ease and happiness, I do not wish to make any proffit from it. I will keep an exact Account of my expences. Those, I doubt not, they will discharge, and that is all I desire.*

By the way, the general was not merely gentlemanly in refusing a salary and taking only expenses, he was shrewd. He used his expense account as generously as might a modern CEO. After studying Washington's accounts, humorist Marvin Kitman wrote, "There are 43 basic principles of expense account writing. Washington used 42 of them. . . . The rules include: be specific about smaller expenses and vague on the larger ones. Describe, in some depth, the purchase of a ball of twine (Brown, 2-3/4" circumference, $1.98) and casually throw in 'Dinner for one army, $1,010.'" In all, during the eight years of the Revolutionary War, Washington managed to run up expenses of $449,261.51—and that's in 1780 dollars, the equivalent of many millions today.

Washington was not only the father of his country, but the father, or godfather, of a goodly number of everyday words in the English language, as the chapter on vocabulary explains. Because of his fame, he may be credited with more innovations in vocabulary than were actually his, but the prestige of his using them would have helped them get established.

John Adams

[1735–1826]
President 1797–1801

B orn and raised on a farm in what is now Quincy, Massachusetts, on the coast south of Boston, Adams most likely spoke with an edu-cated Boston accent. And as Boston educations go, Adams had the best, graduating from Harvard.

But George Washington was still a hard act to follow. Compared with Washington, Adams was a little giant. Like Washington, he inclined toward the regal, but his posturing didn't have the same effect as Washington's noble manner. Colleagues ridiculed his desire for for-mal titles of respect by calling him "His Rotundity."

And Adams didn't come near to greatness as president, despite his great abilities. In one respect, however, Adams surpassed the first presi-dent. Adams was a great orator, probably the greatest ever in the office of president.

"I had some faculty for public speaking," Adams modestly yet boast-fully observed in his later years. Indeed he did. As a Boston lawyer in the 1770s, Adams heard himself praised as "the equal to the greatest orator that ever spoke in Greece or Rome"—and he conscientiously recorded the praise. Biographer David McCullough gives the example of a time when Adams spoke in court for five hours while a client was getting a document. "At the end he was roundly applauded because, as he related the story, he had spoken 'in favor of justice.'"

As chapter 2 has explained, Adams's speeches were almost all extemporaneous. Even he didn't know exactly what he would say until he said it. Perhaps the most important, as well as the best, such speech of Adams's life was to the Continental Congress on July 1, 1776. John Dickinson of Pennsylvania had argued long and forcefully against American independence; after a moment of silence, Adams was the one who rose to reply. We know little about his speech except that he won the day. As his grandson Charles Francis Adams wrote in his 1856 biography:

> Of his speech, not a word has been transmitted to posterity. But all the accounts given by persons present agree in representing it as having been in the highest class of oratory.

About this speech Jefferson commented that Adams was "not graceful nor elegant, nor remarkably fluent," but his "deep conceptions and nervous style . . . gave him a power of thought and expression that moved us from our seats."

Adams's speech went on for a good hour. When he was nearly finished, several delegates arrived late and asked him to give it again, which he obligingly did in a slightly shorter version.

Adams himself, according to his grandson, thought that the speech had been a waste of time, because everything possible had already been said during the previous six months of debate. Still, he was full of enthusiasm, writing to his wife the next day: "Yesterday, the greatest question was decided which ever was debated in America, and a greater, perhaps, never was, nor will be decided among men." And in the aftermath of Adams's speech, the representatives of the united colonies indeed declared for independence.

Thomas Jefferson

[1743–1826]
President 1801–09

Born, raised, and making his home for his entire life near Charlottesville in central Virginia, Jefferson most likely had the cultivated *r*-less accent of a Virginia gentleman. Too bad he was born long before the time of Edison; he would have been among the first to use the newfangled phonograph to record his voice for posterity. Fortunately, however, we have a considerable number of firsthand accounts of his speaking ability and manner, as well as considerable writings by Jefferson himself on language.

When it comes to vocabulary, as it did in chapter 7, Jefferson deservedly stands head and shoulders above all other presidents. But when it comes to oratory, as it did in chapter 2, he isn't even a candidate. The man who penned the most famous document in American history, declaring, "We hold these Truths to be self-evident, that all Men are created equal, that they are endowed by their Creator with certain unalienable rights, that among these are Life, Liberty, and the Pursuit of Happiness," was not a great orator. Indeed, he was not much of an orator at all. He was known for having a voice unsuited to public speaking.

A contemporary of Jefferson, William Wirt, a prominent lawyer and U.S. attorney general from 1817 to 1829, explains:

> *He had all the attributes of the mind and the heart and the soul which are essential to eloquence of the highest order. The only defect was a physical one: he wanted volume and compass of voice for a large deliberative assembly; and his voice, from the excess of his sensibility, instead of rising with his feelings and conceptions, sunk under their pressure and became guttural and inarticulate. The consciousness of this infirmity repressed any attempt in a large body, in which he knew he must fail. But his voice was all sufficient for the purposes of judicial debate; and there is no reason to doubt that if the services of his country had not called him away so soon from his profession, his fame as a lawyer would now have stood upon the same distinguished ground which he confessedly occupies as a statesman, an author, and a scholar.*

When it came to writing, Jefferson had no peer. Wirt again, for example:

> *It has been thought that Mr. Jefferson made no figure at the bar: but the case was far otherwise. There are still extant, in his own fair and neat hand, in the manner of his master, a number of arguments which were delivered by him at the bar upon some of the most intricate questions of the law, which, if they shall ever see the light, will vindicate his claims to the first honors of the profession.*

Jefferson preferred writing to speaking, and he wrote copiously all his life—legal and political documents, articles, books, and above all, letters. He didn't lack convictions or the courage to express them. Indeed, he was among the most outspoken of presidents. He just lacked the taste for the public arena. In that way, as a Virginia gentleman, he had something in common with Washington; he preferred not to stoop to debate. As a later biographer, John T. Morse, said, Jefferson "instinctively preferred to remain silent when confronted with wrangling and conflict."

Jefferson was such a poor public speaker that he changed the whole state of the union for the next century. Well, make that State of the Union. Where Washington and Adams had presented their

Constitutionally mandated reports ("He shall from time to time give to the Congress Information of the State of the Union") in person, Jefferson began the practice of sending his in writing, a custom observed until Woodrow Wilson's presidency more than a hundred years later.

In private conversation, Jefferson was quite different. He dazzled his guests. John Bernard, an Englishman who visited Jefferson in 1801, later recalled:

> *His information was equally polite and profound, and his conversational powers capable of discussing moral questions of deepest seriousness, or the lighter themes of humor and fancy. Nothing could be more simpler than his reasonings, nothing more picturesque and pointed than his descriptions. On all abstract subjects he was plainness—a veritable Quaker; but when conveying his views of human nature through most attractive medium—anecdote—he displayed the grace and brilliance of a courtier.*

Margaret Bayard Smith, wife of a Washington, D.C., newspaper publisher and the author of *The First Forty Years of Washington Society*, left vivid descriptions of Jefferson's manner in private. When she first met him it was a while before she discovered "the stranger whose deportment was so dignified and gentlemanly, whose language was so refined, whose voice was so gentle, whose countenance was so benignant, to be no other than Thomas Jefferson." Much later, in 1823, she wrote for the *Richmond Enquirer:*

> *Every one who has known, has acknowledged the colloquial powers of this excellent man. He is frank and communicative in his manner, various and delightful in his conversation. With a mind stored by much reading, long experience, accurate observation, deep research, an intimate acquaintance with the great and good men of Europe and America; with the events, and scenes and customs of both countries; he possesses a store of intellectual wealth, which falls to the lot of few; and of those, how many possess the treasure, have not the faculty of imparting it to others. But, Mr. J, has not only the sterling gold, but has the baser coins, which afford an easy currency of thought, and are so important in social intercourse. No subject could*

be started, which he did not illustrate by luminous observations, or enliven by sprightly anecdotes.

One quality he has, which I never knew equalled in any other man: a quick and intuitive perception of the character, taste and feelings of his guests, and with a benevolence, equalling in warmth, the greatness of his perception; he always turned the conversation, so as to draw forth the powers and talents of each guest, bestowing on all, the same gracious attention: he, above all men, has the art of pleasing, by making each pleased with himself. Why can I not recollect every word which fell from his lips, during these charming conversations, for every word deserved to be remembered!

Regarding manner of writing and speaking, Jefferson left no doubt that he preferred the plain and direct variety. In his 1821 autobiography he fondly recalled discussions by a group of French "patriots" under the leadership of the Marquis de Lafayette in his Paris residence at the time of the French Revolution:

The discussions began at the hour of four, and were continued till ten o'clock in the evening; during which time I was a silent witness to a coolness and candor of argument unusual in the conflicts of political opinion; to a logical reasoning, and chaste eloquence, disfigured by no gaudy tinsel of rhetoric or declamation, and truly worthy of being placed in parallel with the finest dialogues of antiquity, as handed to us by Xenophon, by Plato and Cicero.

And he was a confirmed "permissive linguist" when it came to language use. In chapter 7 we saw how he argued for the necessity of neology—not just allowing, but requiring new words for new circumstances. He was equally permissive about grammar, as in this August 16, 1813, letter to John Waldo, author of a book on English grammar:

Mine has been a life of business, of that kind which appeals to a man's conscience, as well as his industry, not to let it suffer, and the few moments allowed me from labor have been devoted to more attractive studies, that of grammar having never been a favorite with me. The scanty foundation, laid in at school, has carried me through a life of much hasty writing, more indebted for style to reading and memory, than to rules of grammar. I have been pleased to see that in all cases you appeal to usage, as the arbiter of language; and justly consider that as giving law to grammar, and not grammar to usage. I concur entirely with you in opposition to Purists, who would destroy all strength and beauty of style, by subjecting it to a rigorous compliance with their rules. . . .

I am no friend, therefore, to what is called Purism, but a zealous one to the Neology which has introduced these two words without the authority of any dictionary. I consider the one as destroying the nerve and beauty of language, while the other improves both, and adds to its copiousness. . . .

Certainly so great growing a population, spread over such an extent of country, with such a variety of climates, of productions, of arts, must enlarge their language, to make it answer its purpose of expressing all ideas, the new as well as the old. The new circumstances under which we are placed, call for new words, new phrases, and for the transfer of old words to new objects.

Thomas Jefferson would have enjoyed a book like this. In fact, alone among American presidents, he could have written a book like this. In addition to his talents in such fields as paleontology, botany, and anthropology, Jefferson was a serious scholar of language.

The book Jefferson could have written about language would include his letter advocating neology excerpted in chapter 7. It would include his admonitions for simplicity in language and his diatribes against purism like the one given above. It would include his praise of the modern French language for adding so many words since their Revolution, and of the ancient Greek language for allowing so many words to be created from one basic form. Scribble, scribble, scribble, Mr. Jefferson!

It would include his "Essay towards Facilitating Instruction in the Anglo-Saxon and Modern Dialects of the English Language," prefaced by a letter explaining why educated people, and especially students of law, should study the Anglo-Saxon or Old English language of a thousand years ago (for better understanding of "a multitude of law-terms"). He would facilitate instruction in Anglo-Saxon by simplifying the grammar, spelling, and typography of Anglo-Saxon texts to keep them from being "muffled" by the "learned apparatus" of scholars.

And it would include his study of the comparative vocabularies of Indian languages with the aim of reconstructing the history and connections of the various tribes, something that comparative linguists continue to do today. Not content to make do with just a few specimens, Jefferson had a list of common English terms printed and issued to military officers in the West, including Lewis and Clark, so they could obtain equivalents in the languages of the Indians with whom they came in contact.

James Madison

[1751–1836]
President 1809–17

The Virginia presidencies continued with Jefferson's protégé, the "Father of the Constitution" in his own right, James Madison. He was born and raised in King George County in the Tidewater area of Virginia, not far from where Washington spent his early years. He too would have had a gentlemanly *r*-less Virginia accent.

And like Jefferson, Madison had too quiet a voice for public speaking. He was diminutive in every respect: five feet four, 100 pounds, voice too soft to permit the career in the ministry he originally wanted, or in the law. Furthermore, he would rock back and forth when speaking.

His first inaugural address, like Jefferson's, was "spoken in a tone of voice so low that scarcely any part of it was heard by three-fourths of the audience," according to John Quincy Adams, who was there. During Madison's first term, that inaugural address was the only speech he actually delivered in person; all others he sent to Congress to be read.

Nevertheless, he was not at a loss for words. And his most important words, spoken as well as written, came at the time of the Constitutional Convention of 1787, when delegates from the thirteen states met to determine a new form of government. Madison was a central and indispensable figure in these deliberations. He had spent the better part of the previous year in research, reading everything he could find about governments and federations (and helped by Jefferson, who sent him books from France). Approaching the issue with an open mind, Madison wanted to discover what kind of federal government would succeed. He concluded that a strong central government would be needed to hold the federation together. After more than two centuries, we now know how right he was.

A Georgia delegate to the Constitutional Convention, William Pierce, described him:

> In the management of every great question he evidently took the lead in the Convention, and tho' he cannot be called an Orator, he is a most agreeable, eloquent and convincing Speaker. From a spirit of industry and application which he possesses in a most eminent degree, he always comes forward the best informed Man of any point in debate, . . . a Gentleman of great modesty, with a remarkable sweet temper.

And there is no doubt that Madison could be eloquent in advocating his ideas for the new government. Consider, for example, the 15 or so essays he contributed to the *Federalist Papers* arguing for the adoption of the Constitution. He sometimes wraps his careful and logical reasoning in flights of elegance, as in this passage from *Number 10:*

> Liberty is to faction what air is to fire, an aliment without which it instantly expires. But it could not be less folly to abolish liberty, which is essential to political life, because it nourishes faction, than it would be to wish the annihilation of air, which is essential to animal life, because it imparts to fire its destructive agency.

Above all, the impression one gets from Madison's writing is that of thoughtfulness and fairness, a goal he explicitly aims for, as he says in *Federalist Paper Number 37:*

> It is a misfortune, inseparable from human affairs, that public measures are rarely investigated with that spirit of moderation which is essential to a just estimate of their real tendency to advance or obstruct

the public good; and that this spirit is more apt to be diminished than promoted, by those occasions which require an unusual exercise of it.

From his copious writings, and from the abundant testimony of his contemporaries, we can get a good idea of Madison the writer and speaker. Here is Jefferson in his autobiography, admiringly summing up Madison's early career and abilities:

> *Mr. Madison came into the House in 1776, a new member and young; which circumstances, concurring with his extreme modesty, prevented his venturing himself in debate before his removal to the Council of State in November 1777. From thence he went to Congress, then consisting of few members. Trained in these successive schools, he acquired a habit of self-possession which placed at ready command the rich resources of his luminous and discriminating mind, & of his extensive information, and rendered him the first of every assembly afterwards of which he became a member.*
>
> *Never wandering from his subject into vain declamation, but pursuing it closely in language pure, classical, and copious, soothing always the feelings of his adversaries by civilities and softness of expression, he rose to the eminent station which he held in the great National convention of 1787 and in that of Virginia which followed, he sustained the new constitution in all its parts, bearing off the palm against the logic of George Mason, and the fervid declamation of Mr. Henry. With these consummate powers were united a pure and spotless virtue which no calumny has ever attempted to sully. Of the powers and polish of his pen, and of the wisdom of his administration in the highest office of the nation, I need say nothing. They have spoken, and will forever speak for themselves.*

Twenty years later, presiding over the government he fathered, Madison was neither the best nor the worst of presidents, neither the best nor the worst of speakers. But he wasn't always easy to follow. His second inaugural address in 1813 focused on the war with the British and included sentences as challenging as these:

> *And now we find them, in further contempt of the modes of honorable warfare, supplying the place of a conquering force by attempts*

to disorganize our political society, to dismember our confederated Republic. Happily, like others, these will recoil on the authors; but they mark the degenerate counsels from which they emanate, and if they did not belong to a sense of unexampled inconsistencies might excite the greater wonder as proceeding from a Government which founded the very war in which it has been so long engaged on a charge against the disorganizing and insurrectional policy of its adversary.

Get it? He seems to be saying that the British are doing to us what they complained about us doing to them. But it's not an easy read, let alone an easy listen.

Madisonianisms

Compared to his three prolific predecessors, Madison is far behind in helping new words enter the English language. There are just a handful of words for which Madison provides the first citations in the *Oxford English Dictionary*. One of them, however, represents a major contribution to the American system of government.

The word is *Federalist* itself, designating those who support the Federalist Party and political philosophy in favor of a strong central government for the United States. *Federalist* Number 10, of November 22, 1787, written by Madison, concludes: "In the extent and proper structure of the Union, therefore, we behold a republican remedy for the diseases most incident to republican government. And according to the degree of pleasure and pride we feel in being republicans, ought to be our zeal in cherishing the spirit and supporting the character of **Federalists**."

Surprisingly, in all of the 85 installments of *The Federalist*, that is the only instance of *Federalist* in the text. So though the very title is *The Federalist*, Madison may fairly be called the author of the first use of that word—in a sentence. The case for this truly being the first use is strong, because *Federalist* is a word that arose in connection with the campaign to ratify the newly written Constitution, and the authors of *The Federalist* were the leaders of that campaign. Of course, the invention of the word, as opposed to its first use in a published sentence, may have been the doing of any of the three authors of *The Federalist*: Madison or Alexander Hamilton or John Jay.

Madison also provides the first *OED* evidence for another term that becomes important in American history: *squatter,* designating someone who settles unauthorized on land belonging to another or to the government. It was a growing problem in the new country. A 1788 letter of his constitutes the first quotation for *squatter* in the *OED*: "Many of them and their constituents are only **squatters** upon other people's land, and they are afraid of being brought to account."

Madison is quoted first in the *OED* for *caption* in the modern meaning of the heading or label of a document. In a May 1789 letter to Jefferson regarding the new Constitution, he employs the word in a democratic rejection of fancy titles: "Inclosed is the Speech of the President with the Address of the House of Reps. & his reply. You will see in the **caption** of the address that we have pruned the ordinary stile of the degrading appendages of Excellency, Esqr. &tc. and restored it to its naked dignity. *Titles* to both the President & vice President were formally & unanimously condemned by a vote of the H. of Reps. This I hope will shew to the friends of Republicanism that our new Government was not meant to substitute either Monarchy or Aristocracy, and that the genius of the people is as yet adverse to both."

Madison also provides the earliest *OED* evidence for *amenability* (1789) meaning answerable to an authority: "A unity in each has been resolved on, and an **amenability** to the President alone, as well as to the Senate by way of impeachment."

Madison is credited with the first example of *misthinking,* an obsolete term that he may have playfully coined on the spur of the moment to contrast with *unthinking* in a sentence in the *Federalist* (1788): ". . . it may inflame the passions of the unthinking, and may confirm the prejudices of the **misthinking**."

And finally, Madison is quoted as the *OED*'s first example for *rising sun,* in his famous description of the final moment of the Constitutional Convention of 1787: "Whilst the last members were signing it Doctor Franklin looking towards the President's Chair, at the back of which a rising sun happened to be painted, observed to a few members near him, that Painters had found it difficult to distinguish in their art a rising from a setting sun. I have, said he, often and often in the course of the Session, and the vicissitudes of my hopes and fears as to its issue, looked at that behind the President without being able to tell whether it was rising or setting: But now at length I have the happiness to know that it is a **rising** and not a setting **sun**."

Madison's writings are scarce in the current *OED*, even for quotations that are not first examples. But in the new third edition, at present including little more than the letter *M*, the editors have made generous use of Madison's writings to provide citations, though not first ones, for *magical, maxim* (premise), *mean* (average), *merit, mingled, misjudged, more so*, and *the most*.

James Monroe

[1758–1831]
President 1817–25

Yet another Virginian from the neighborhood of Washington and Madison was James Monroe. He was born and raised in Tidewater area Westmoreland County, not far from where Washington was born. He too presumably would have had the *r*-less accent of a Virginia gentleman.

The early presidents seem to have alternated between tall and short. Washington was a tall six feet two inches; John Adams a short five feet seven; Jefferson a tall six feet two-and-a-half; Madison the shortest of all presidents at five feet four; and Monroe another tall one at about six feet.

Monroe had been an officer under Washington in the Revolutionary War. He was George Washington's ambassador to France for a time, and later negotiated the Louisiana Purchase from the French for his mentor, Thomas Jefferson. He was governor of Virginia and U.S. secretary of state, and then secretary of war during the War of 1812. But his speaking ability, evidently, was at best unremarkable—neither especially good nor especially bad.

One lasting consequence of his residence in France as a young man was an appreciation for French fashion. And he and his wife found it useful to speak to each other in French about personal matters when they were in the White House.

Monroe was the last of the Revolutionary War presidents, and he dressed the part. By the time he became president, knee britches and stockings were going out of fashion in favor of long pants, but he kept to the old style. He had Washingtonian height, Washingtonian style in clothing, Washingtonian dignity, and Washingtonian formality, but nobody said he spoke like Washington.

Nevertheless, Monroe is remembered for one of the most famous statements in American history. His 1823 State of the Union message, delivered in writing of course, and written primarily by his successor John Quincy Adams, nevertheless expressed Monroe's own view of the responsibility of the United States to preside over the independence of the New World, and the need for European powers to keep out:

> *We owe it, therefore, to candor and to the amicable relations existing between the United States and those* [European] *powers to declare that we should consider any attempt on their part to extend their system to any portion of this hemisphere as dangerous to our peace and safety. With the existing colonies or dependencies of any European power we have not interfered and shall not interfere, but with the* [Latin American] *Governments who have declared their independence and maintained it, and whose independence we have, on great consideration and on just principles, acknowledged, we could not view any interposition for the purpose of oppressing them, or controlling in any other manner their destiny, by any European power in any other light than as the manifestation of an unfriendly disposition toward the United States. . . .*
>
> *. . . It is impossible that the allied powers should extend their political system to any portion of either continent without endangering our peace and happiness; nor can anyone believe that our southern brethren, if left to themselves, would adopt it of their own accord. It is equally impossible, therefore, that we should behold such interposition in any form with indifference.*

A firm statement, but couched in the most diplomatic terms: European interference in the Americas would be "manifestation of an unfriendly disposition." How polite is that? Very appropriate, coming most likely from a secretary of state, John Quincy Adams, who had been involved in diplomatic missions since his teen years.

The use of *manifestation* in this message was distinctive enough to be quoted in the *Oxford English Dictionary*, the only quotation attributed to Monroe in that entire work. It is the first example the *OED* gives for what it calls a rare meaning of the common word *manifestation*: "A public act on the part of a government intended as a display of its power and determination to enforce some demand."

A much better-known term associated with Monroe is *Monroe Doctrine*, the name given to the policy announced in that 1823 State of the Union message. But neither Monroe nor John Quincy Adams came up with that term; the earliest example of *Monroe Doctrine* found so far by the *OED* is in 1850, a quarter century later.

John Quincy Adams

[1767–1848]
President 1825–29

John Adams's son, the sixth president John Quincy Adams, was born and raised in exactly the same place as his father, in Braintree, now Quincy, south of Boston. Also like his father, he was relatively short—five feet seven inches—and rotund in his maturity.

It can reasonably be assumed that he too acquired an *r*-less cultivated Boston accent, perhaps refined further by his frequent sojourns in Europe as a youth and young man, first on his father's diplomatic missions for the U.S. government and then on his own.

Through travel, education, and experience, Quincy was as well prepared to be president as anyone before or since. Diplomatic missions to France, Holland, Russia, England, and Portugal; a term in the U.S. Senate while he was also Boylston Professor of Rhetoric, lecturing occasionally at Harvard; and serving as secretary of state to James Monroe were just some of his qualifications. After his presidency, he was "Old Man Eloquent" in the House of Representatives, taking every opportunity to speak out against slavery.

Like his father, Quincy was one of the great presidential orators. There is no question that he knew how to speak, and spoke often and well. As evidence of the esteem in which he was held as a speaker, he

206

was called on to make the major addresses at the fiftieth anniversary of the Constitution before the New York Historical Society in 1839, and for the fiftieth anniversary of Washington's inauguration in that same year. His oratorical prowess and career are treated in chapter 2.

He was a poet too, or at least aspired to be. In one of his poems, a lighthearted disquisition on "The Wants of Man," he expresses these wishes:

> *I want a keen, observing eye,*
> *An ever-listening ear,*
> *The truth through all disguise to spy,*
> *And wisdom's voice to hear;*
> *A tongue, to speak at virtue's need,*
> *In Heaven's sublimest strain;*
> *And lips, the cause of man to plead,*
> *And never plead in vain.*

Nevertheless, according to historian Simon Schama,

> *The tragedy of his life was that although he was nicknamed "Old Man Eloquent" and although he looked as though you could set his bust alongside Demosthenes and Cato the Elder, and although his speaking style was with "kindled eyes and tremulous frame," the organ itself was apparently shrill and piercing so that in an age of the honey-smooth oratory of the young Daniel Webster and John Calhoun, Adams's Presidential speeches, which sounded fine when he rehearsed them before the Cabinet—his Farewell to Lafayette or the panegyric to the Erie Canal—seemed barked at, rather than voiced to, the public.*

A French Word or Two

One talent for which he was not particularly noted was innovations in vocabulary. Aside from his possible authorship of the special use of *manifestation*, credited publicly to Monroe, Adams registers in the *Oxford English Dictionary* only twice. Both occasions are for French words of marginal interest. The *OED* lists his as the first and only example of the obscure French term *are*, a measure ten meters square.

The *OED* says Adams's 1819 use of *are* is quoted in an 1871 book on *The Metric System*, but there is no quoted sentence.

Quincy uses the name of the French faction *Fronde* in reference to French history. The *OED* finds a 1798 use of that term by J.Q. Adams published in the collected *Works* of his father, John: "The history of France during the periods of the League and the **Fronde**."

Andrew Jackson

[1767–1848]
President 1829–37

What a difference Andrew Jackson made! His election erased the established model for a president. If one were to draw conclusions from the examples of the first six presidents, an American president would have to come from a privileged background, a family with both property and culture. The president (well, every president after Washington) would be a college graduate, in a day when only a small fraction of the population went to college. He would be a born gentleman. And he would follow the coastal and British fashion of dropping *r* after vowels.

But then along came Old Hickory, hero of the Battle of New Orleans, farmer of Tennessee, Sage of the Hermitage. His predecessor (and loser to Jackson in the election of 1828), John Quincy Adams, in a letter to a relative, disgustedly characterized Jackson as "a barbarian who cannot write a sentence of grammar and can hardly spell his own name." The long knives were out—and Jackson himself was sometimes labeled Sharp Knife.

We can thank Jackson for making Abraham Lincoln possible—or rather, for making possible serious consideration of Lincoln's candidacy. Jackson was the first president born in a log cabin, as opposed to a town house or mansion. Seven other presidents in the nineteenth century followed Jackson in claiming the advantage of log-cabin birth.

Jackson was born and raised in the rural Waxhaw settlement at the boundary between North and South Carolina, so far west in both states that the line separating them had not yet been surveyed in 1767. His parents were Scotch-Irish immigrants from Carrickfergus, County Antrim (now in Northern Ireland), and so were many of his neighbors. And so his speech, like that of Ireland, would have been *r*-ful.

As an adult he became one of the first citizens (in both senses) of Tennessee, another *r*-pronouncing state. It is possible that, as a well-spoken president, he might have affected an *r*-less pronunciation, but most likely he kept all *r*'s. Either way, he would have reinforced the notion that *r*-less was the cultured pronunciation: *r*-ful would have been in accord with his humble background; *r*-less would have shown him overcoming it.

He was always a forceful speaker, and he gradually became a polished one too. In *U.S. Presidents as Orators*, Thomas M. Lessl summarizes:

> *The younger Jackson appears to have been carried away by his own emotions, shaking a long forefinger as he spoke and, in moments of great excitement, spraying his startled listeners with saliva as he declaimed in a North Irish accent inherited from the immigrant settlement where he grew up. But observers of the elder Jackson describe a speaker whose self-control only increased as his anger mounted, enabling him to articulate cool political reprisals.*

There is no question that Jackson, like all other presidents, learned to read quite well. He did go to school in Waxhaw, but in the 1828 presidential campaign, as chapter 6 notes, he was accused of being unable to spell. That charge didn't hurt him as much as a similar one did Vice President Dan Quayle more than a century and a half later. As for his ability to spell, you be the judge of whether the charge was excessive. Here is a transcription of a letter he wrote in 1816 to his wife while negotiating an Indian treaty in Mississippi:

Chikesaw council house Sept. 18th. 1816
My Love,
   I have this moment recd. your affectionate letter of the 8th. Instant,
I rejoice that you are well & our little son. Tell him his sweet papa

hears with pleasure that he has been a good boy & learns his Book, Tell him his sweet papa labours hard to get money to educate him, but when he learns & becomes a great man, his sweet papa will be amply rewarded for all his care, expence, & pains—how thankfull I am to you for taking poor little Lyncoya home & cloathing him—I have been much hurt to see him there with the negroes, like a lost sheep without a sheperd.

we have had a long and disagreable time of it here, our servants have been all sick, Doctor Bronaugh very low, Jame had like to have went, but is on the mend—I hope we will get through our business tomorrow & leave here day after for Turkey town in the cherokee nation, I hope to reach home about the 5th. or 6th. of october we have made a conditional Treaty with the cherokee delegation and are to meet a full council at Turkey Town on the 28th. Instant to have it fully ratified—I have a sanguine hope we will be fully successfull with the chikesaw and once more, regain by tribute, what I fairly, & hardly purchased with the sword, so much trouble & cost has been occassioned by the rashness, folly, & Ignorance of a great little man. But as successfull as I have reason to believe we will be at present, I shall be contented—I have truly noted the conduct of the overseer, & negros, as soon as I return will take a satisfactory order on all—and you will charge him to sell nothing without your express orders—I will make him more than answerable for the Vallue—with my sincere prayers for your health and happiness, and my little son & all the family believe me to be affectionately yours.

Andrew Jackson

P.S. I Thank you for your admonition I hope in all my acts & conduct through life they will measure with propriety and dignity, or at least with what I believe true dignity consists, that is to say honesty, propriety of conduct, & honest independence – A.j.

Mr James Jackson on your application will take order on Sampson if necessary, that family will sell any where, better below than in Nashville, but I suppose in Nashville for $14. or 1500-

His spelling is not perfect, but considering that this is a personal letter not intended for publication, it is quite *satisfactory* and shows *propriety of conduct*, at least in orthography. He goes for double *l* in *thankfull, successfull,* and *vallue,* uses the British spelling for *labours,* uses old-fashioned spellings for *expence*, *cloathing*, and *sheperd*, and is somewhat indifferent about capital letters for proper nouns—not too surprising, in all, for any writer of the early nineteenth century. Even words like *sanguine* and *affectionately* follow standard orthography.

Dead Ducks, Sky High

Despite his humble background, Jackson provides two first quotations in the *OED*, though neither of them is likely to have been a term of his own creation. One is *land scrip*, a document awarding possession of government land to a private holder. Jackson wrote in 1834, "Mr. St. Clair . . . had permitted the clerk in his office to be the agent of speculations in **land scrip**."

Jackson also provides first *OED* evidence of the variant *Missourian* (1833) for the Missouri Indians: "Treaty with the united bands of Ottoes and **Missourians**, made 21st September, 1833."

As befits the first presidential "man of the people," Jackson is the first president to be quoted in the *OED* for slang expressions. These are not, however, the first quotations for the terms, but merely illustrative ones; the *OED* shows only that Jackson had them in his vocabulary. One is *dead duck*, in an 1844 letter saying that his enemy Henry Clay "is a **dead** political **duck**." There is an *OED* example of this term from fifteen years earlier.

Jackson is also quoted as one of the users, not the first, of the term *sky high* in an 1845 letter: "Put your veto upon them both, or you and your Secretary will be blown **sky high**." The *OED* has two examples of *sky high* before Jackson's, going back to 1818.

In his first administration, early in the 1830s, Jackson was criticized for having a *Kitchen Cabinet*, so called because it consisted of unofficial advisers instead of the quarrelsome official cabinet. For several years he met mostly only with the Kitchen Cabinet. The term was invented not by Jackson but by his opponents, and it wasn't meant as a compliment.

Martin Van Buren

[1782–1862]
President 1837–1841

After Jackson, there's not much to remark about the language of the next few presidents. It was much too early for voice recordings, so we can't hear what they sounded like. They neither rose to the level of great orators nor descended to that of great blunderers.

So the most notable linguistic observation about Martin Van Buren is that, through the accident of where he was born, he helped *OK* become the most famous and successful invention of all time in the American language.

No, he didn't invent *OK*. That honor goes to a Boston newspaper editor. In March 1839, amid a craze for supposedly humorous abbreviations like *O.F.M.* for "our first men," *N.G.* for "no go," and *O.W.* for "all right," the editor of the Boston *Morning Post* came up with "*o.k.*—all correct." He had to include the explanation, because as with *O.W.*, the humor of *o.k.* (soon to use capital letters like the other abbreviations) came from blatant misspellings of the words of the initial letters.

O.F.M., *O.W.*, and most of the other abbreviations faded from sight within the year, but *O.K.* was saved from oblivion by the timing of

Martin Van Buren's campaign for a second term. His supporters formed "O.K. Clubs" in New York City and elsewhere—because it happened that Van Buren was known as "Old Kinderhook," on account of his birthplace, Kinderhook, New York. That made it possible to say "O.K. is OK." The rest is history—a rather long and complicated history that leads to the proliferation of *OK* in everyday conversation today, here and around the world.

Incidentally, Van Buren lost that election.

Except for his years in Washington, D.C., Van Buren lived in Kinderhook all his life. Kinderhook was a long-established Dutch settlement on the Hudson River in upstate New York near Albany, the sort of place celebrated and caricatured by Washington Irving. In fact, Irving wrote "The Legend of Sleepy Hollow" at Van Buren's home in Kinderhook.

So what would a man from Kinderhook sound like? At the time, it would have been possible to hear something of a Dutch accent in the relatively isolated community, and Van Buren himself is said to have had spoken with a slight Dutch accent when excited. In any case, like Jackson, and unlike the first six presidents, his speech would have been *r*-ful. Van Buren's accent otherwise would have been quite different from Jackson's—more like the general speech of the northern and western United States nowadays.

The *Oxford English Dictionary* passes over him in silence.

William Henry Harrison

[1773–1841]
President 1841

The next two presidents, William Henry Harrison and John Tyler, were from the same *r*-less Tidewater region of Virginia. Harrison, to be sure, was presented to the public as a Western man "content to sit in his log cabin and drink hard cider," but he was actually from a distinguished Virginia family and college-educated as well.

The "log cabin and hard cider" slogan of his Whig supporters in the 1840 presidential election came from their portraying him as a farmer living in a log cabin on the banks of the Ohio River. That stretched the truth a little, as did the claim that he won a great battle when he actually suffered a defeat against Tecumseh and the Shawnee Indians in 1810 at the Tippecanoe River in Indiana. That was the source of the other slogan of the 1840 campaign, "Tippecanoe and Tyler, too" (John Tyler being his vice presidential running mate).

Harrison was born and raised at Berkeley Plantation in Charles City County, Virginia. True, he did head west in his twenties, fighting Indians and then serving as governor of Indiana Territory for a dozen years. He didn't live in a log cabin in Indiana, however, but in a handsome brick Federal-style mansion known as Grouseland, in Vincennes on the

Wabash River in the southwestern corner of the present-day state. There he entertained Indian delegations and negotiated treaties that ceded their lands to the United States. There is no reason to suppose that he would have abandoned his cultivated Virginia accent during those years. He was bringing civilization to the West, after all.

Harrison had the shortest presidency on record, dying of pneumonia a mere month after his inauguration. That inauguration appears to have been the instigator of his illness, since he insisted on speaking outdoors without hat or coat in a cold rain, and since his inaugural address is today still unsurpassed for length—nearly 8500 words and almost two hours long.

He too is not quoted at all in the *Oxford English Dictionary*.

John Tyler

[1790–1862]
President 1841–45

L ike Harrison, the man he unexpectedly succeeded, John Tyler was born and raised on a plantation in Charles City County in the Tidewater region of Virginia. After he became president, he bought a house there in which his descendants still live today—the longest frame house in America, over 300 feet long. Like Harrison, Tyler too went to college. He would surely have had a cultivated *r*-less accent like Harrison's. He is said to have been an impassioned orator; his voice has been described as lilting and silvery.

President Tyler is the one who nicknamed his Virginia home "Sherwood Forest," in good-humored recognition of his position as a political "outlaw." A Democrat, he had been put on the 1840 Whig ticket as vice president to balance the Whig presidential candidate, Harrison, as reflected in the campaign slogan "Tippecanoe and Tyler, too." No president had ever before died in office, so the Whigs were happy to have relegated him to the harmless obscurity of the vice presidency.

Much to their shock, then, he became president only a month after Harrison had taken office. As president, Tyler maintained a strong Democratic states' rights position against the wishes of the Whigs.

He still holds the record for greatest number of Supreme Court nominations rejected, a total of five.

And what orotund eloquence he displayed! Here is a sample sentence from his December 1841 (written) Message to Congress:

> *In pursuance of a pledge given to you in my last message to Congress, which pledge I urge as an apology for adventuring to present you the details of any plan, the Secretary of the Treasury will be ready to submit to you, should you require it, a plan of finance which, while it throws around the public treasure reasonable guards for its protection and rests on powers acknowledged in practice to exist from the origin of the Government, will at the same time furnish to the country a* **sound paper** *medium and afford all reasonable facilities for regulating the exchanges.*

That's one of the most grammatically complex sentences found in any presidential statement. Relative clauses and subordinate clauses intertwine to render it almost incomprehensible, though it is in fact impeccably grammatical.

The phrase *sound paper* appears in bold type in that sentence because it is Tyler's one contribution to the *Oxford English Dictionary*. He provides the first example for the phrase *sound paper*, derived from the older term *sound money*. Tyler used it not just once but several times in 1841 and 1842.

James K. Polk

[1795–1849]
President 1845–49

After the two Virginians Harrison and Tyler, both from Tidewater territory near the Atlantic coast, came a Westerner who followed almost literally in Jackson's footsteps. He followed his mentor "Old Hickory" so closely, in fact, that he was called "Young Hickory."

James K. Polk was born in Mecklenburg County in western North Carolina near the border between North and South Carolina, just a little to the west of where Jackson was born. He lived there till age 11 and then, like Jackson at 21, moved to Tennessee. Both places would be *r*-ful territory.

After a few years of school in Tennessee, he returned to North Carolina to attend the University of North Carolina at Chapel Hill, in the middle of the state, where he joined a debating society and graduated cum laude with honors in mathematics and the classics. It was at that university, Polk later said, "that I spent near three years of my life. It was here that I received lessons of instructions to which I mainly attribute whatever of success or advancement has attended me in subsequent life."

For all his education, Polk was known to be plainspoken. John Quincy Adams, who had been so disdainful of Jackson, didn't even try to fault Polk for grammar or spelling, but he went after him for his plainness: "He has no wit, no literature, no point of argument, no gracefulness of delivery, no elegance of language, no philosophy, no pathos, no felicitous impromptus; nothing that constitutes an orator, but confidence, fluency, and labor." He said that Polk was hardly even qualified "for an eminent County Court lawyer."

From 1825 to 1839 he was a representative from Tennessee in the U.S. Congress, the last four years as Speaker of the House. Despite Quincy's quibbling, Polk was said to be a powerful debater as well as a master of parliamentary procedure. For his down-to-earth eloquence and persuasiveness he was labeled "Napoleon of the Stump."

The modern musical group They Might Be Giants has a song celebrating, or at least commemorating, President Polk. It includes these lines:

Austere, severe, he held few people dear.
His oratory filled his foes with fear.

Shackling Remarks

Despite his plainness, Polk does get modest attention from the *Oxford English Dictionary*. He provides the first, and only, *OED* example (1846) for the term *President's Mansion*: "He had not been in my office or at the **President's mansion** for many weeks." Pretty clearly, though, Polk was not the first to use *President's Mansion* for what we now call the *White House*. It had been known as the *President's House* or *President's Mansion* from its earliest days half a century earlier.

The *OED* also cites Polk in nonprimary examples of *specific* in a specific use, *Secretary of State*, and *Missouri Compromise*; the first and only example of *reception evening*; and the curious word *shackling*, though his is not the first evidence for that either. It's a somewhat old-fashioned and folksy word meaning ramshackle or rundown. *Shackling* goes back as far as the 1780s, according to the *Dictionary of American Regional English*, which has an earlier first quotation than the *OED*. Polk used the word in his meticulous diary for June 9, 1846, during his presidency: "Mr. Bancroft reminded Mr. Buchanan of a remark which he had made in the Cabinet some months ago, that the title of the United States north of 49° was a **shackling** one."

Zachary Taylor

[1784–1850]
President 1849–1850

The last of the nineteenth-century Virginia-born presidents was Zachary Taylor. His exact birthplace isn't known, but it was on the Montebello estate just north of Charlottesville in western Virginia, not far from the Appalachians. That's on the boundary between *r*-ful and *r*-less speech. But for the purpose of determining his manner of speech, or indeed any other aspect of his upbringing, his birthplace doesn't matter, because while he was still an infant his family moved west to a farm near Louisville, Kentucky, in *r*-ful territory. Later in life he owned a plantation in Mississippi.

Taylor was a career military man and a military hero, leading major victories against the Seminole Indians in Florida in the 1830s and against the Mexicans in the 1840s. The former earned him the nickname "Old Rough and Ready"; the latter brought about the vast expansion of U.S. territory through the Mexican War of 1846–48. He had never even voted before, but in 1848 the Whig party took advantage of his popularity to nominate him for a successful run for the presidency. A year and a half later, he died in office, supposedly of acute indigestion.

Taylor was not very eloquent. He is said to have been "a poor speaker, often stammering, and unable to put together a string of ideas."

The *Oxford English Dictionary* has a single citation from Taylor, of *looped*, referring to loopholes in buildings. His 1846 letter, written during the Mexican War, is the only *OED* example for this obscure word: "The houses are of stone . . . all **looped** up for musketry."

Millard Fillmore

[1800–1874]
President 1850–53

When Taylor died, he was succeeded by "His Accidency," Millard Fillmore. Fillmore was a man of the North and the West, born and raised in central New York State, in solidly *r*-ful territory, on a farm that was then on the frontier. He was mostly homeschooled at a time when that was the only option in the pioneer territory of Cayuga County.

At age 20, pursuing his ambition to become a lawyer, he moved further west to Buffalo. By the time he was 30, he was one of the most prominent lawyers in the state. By then he was also involved in politics. He served four terms in the U.S. House of Representatives and ran unsuccessfully for governor of New York before he was named vice president on the successful Whig ticket in 1848. He then became the second vice president to assume the presidency through the president's death.

Robert Raybeck's biography of Fillmore cites contemporary accounts to give this description of his way of speaking:

> *As Fillmore began to appear before the public* [in 1830, age 30],
> *the kind of performer he would be for the rest of his life became clear.*

He spoke slowly, almost deliberately. The low pitch and masculine timbre of his voice seemed to be in keeping with his hulking frame and jovial eye. Usually he chose common household words to express himself, and these he arranged in short, direct sentences. Except for careful inflections, little that was precious clung to his speech and his audiences gained the impression of good-natured, simple sincerity. . . .

In his own day, however, no one ever credited him with great oratorical ability. He was at his best in private conversations and small groups. He lacked the elegant language and the turgid figures of speech which the nineteenth century usually associated with masterful orators. In situations where accepted elocution required impassioned utterances that fused thought and feeling, he resorted to logic, simple exposition, and called for reasonableness. He neither timed his quips, measured his cadence, nor felt out the whims of his audience. He was not a showman, but rather a citizen-in-office, and about him was always an aura of dignity.

In keeping with this character, it should be noted that he refused to accept an honorary degree from Oxford on the grounds that he had "neither literary nor scientific attainment." His real reasons, according to biographer Glyndon G. Van Deusen, were "partly because he was reluctant to accept a degree in Latin, which he could not read, and partly because he feared that the Oxford students would make jokes at his expense."

For whatever reasons, Fillmore's words entirely escaped the notice of the *Oxford English Dictionary.*

Franklin Pierce

[1804–69]
President 1853–57

After Fillmore came Franklin Pierce of New Hampshire, in solidly *r*-less eastern New England. His inauguration had two firsts. He was the first, and so far the only president to *affirm* rather than *swear* to uphold the Constitution, choosing *affirm* for religious reasons. It wasn't because he was an Episcopalian; ten other presidents have been Episcopalians, and they have had no hesitation in swearing. But Pierce took personally Jesus' statements in Matthew 5:33–37, as he would have read them in the King James Bible:

> *Again, ye have heard that it hath been said by them of old time, Thou shalt not forswear thyself, but shalt perform unto the Lord thine oaths: But I say unto you, Swear not at all; neither by heaven; for it is God's throne: nor by the earth; for it is his footstool: neither by Jerusalem; for it is the city of the great King. Neither shalt thou swear by thy head, because thou canst not make one hair white or black. But let your communication be, Yea, yea; Nay, nay: for whatsoever is more than these cometh of evil.*

No politician could restrict himself merely to *Yea, yea* and *Nay, nay*, but he did avoid the *swear* word. He proceeded then with his other inaugural first, the first and only inaugural address to be delivered without notes, all 3333 words of it.

The unrehearsed words of his inaugural have been preserved for posterity, however. His only son had been killed in a train wreck two months earlier, so he began the address on a sad personal note:

> *It is a relief to feel that no heart but my own can know the personal regret and bitter sorrow over which I have been borne to a position so suitable for others rather than desirable for myself.*
>
> *The circumstances under which I have been called for a limited period to preside over the destinies of the Republic fill me with a profound sense of responsibility, but with nothing like shrinking apprehension. I repair to the post assigned me not as to one sought, but in obedience to the unsolicited expression of your will, answerable only for a fearless, faithful, and diligent exercise of my best powers. I ought to be, and am, truly grateful for the rare manifestation of the nation's confidence. But this, so far from lightening my obligations, only adds to their weight. You have summoned me in my weakness; you must sustain me by your strength.*

No less a writer than his old friend Nathaniel Hawthorne, a former classmate at Bowdoin College, wrote Pierce's campaign biography. Here's what Hawthorne had to say about Pierce's manner of speaking:

> *When he spoke, it was not only because he was fully master of the subject, but because the exigency demanded him, and because no other and older man could perform the same duty as well as himself. Of the copious eloquence—and some of it, no doubt, of a high order— which Buncombe* [that is, what we now dismiss as *bunk*] *has called forth, not a paragraph, nor a period, is attributable to Franklin Pierce. He had no need of these devices to fortify his constituents in their high opinion of him; nor did he fail to perceive that such was not the method to acquire real weight in the body of which he was a member.*
>
> *In truth, he has no fluency of words, except when an earnest meaning and purpose supply their own expression. Every one of his*

speeches in Congress, and, we may say, in every other hall of oratory,
or on any stump that he may have mounted, was drawn forth by the
perception that it was needed, was directed to a full exposition of the
subject, and (rarest of all) was limited by what he really had to say.
Even the graces of the orator were never elaborated, never assumed
for their own sake, but were legitimately derived from the force of his
conceptions, and from the impulsive warmth which accompanies the
glow of thought.

Owing to these peculiarities—for such, unfortunately, they may be
termed, in reference to what are usually the characteristics of a legisla-
tive career—his position before the country was less conspicuous than
that of many men, who could claim nothing like Pierce's actual influ-
ence in the national councils. His speeches, in their muscular texture
and close grasp of their subject, resembled the brief but pregnant argu-
ments and expositions of the sages of the Continental Congress, rather
than the immeasurable harangues which are now the order of the day.

. . . As we have already remarked, he seems, as a debater, to revive
the old type of the Revolutionary Congress, or to bring back the noble
days of the Long Parliament of England, before eloquence had become
what it is now, a knack, and a thing valued for itself.

After all that definite information, however, Hawthorne issues a dis-
claimer:

It has never been the writer's good fortune to listen to one of
Franklin Pierce's public speeches, whether at the bar or elsewhere;
nor, by diligent inquiry, has he been able to gain a very definite idea
of the mode in which he produces his effects.

So that's where we are left in regard to a president of the days before
voice recordings.

Pierce is quoted twice in the *Oxford English Dictionary*, both times
providing earliest examples. One quotation is for *violative*, a less-than-
brilliant turn of phrase expressed in a convoluted sentence of Pierce's
1856 Message to Congress:

I confidently trust that now, when the peaceful condition of
Kansas affords opportunity for calm reflection and wise legislation,

either the legislative assembly of the Territory or Congress will see
that no act shall remain on its statute book **violative** *of the provi-*
sions of the Constitution or subversive of the great objects for which
that was ordained and established, and will take all other necessary
steps to assure to its inhabitants the enjoyment, without obstruction
or abridgment, of all the constitutional rights, privileges, and immu-
nities of citizens of the United States, as contemplated by the organic
law of the Territory.

Pierce also provides the first *OED* example of *enabling act*, also in an
1856 message to Congress. But this term had been long in use by that
time, beginning with the *Enabling Act* of Congress in 1791 authorizing
the formation of a state government in Kentucky. It's a reminder that
being a first instance in the *OED* does not always reflect the actual origin of a term.

James Buchanan

[1791–1868]
President 1857–61

Yet another frontier-born president was James Buchanan, still the only president to have come from Pennsylvania. He was born in Cove Gap, near Mercersburg, among the mountains in south central Pennsylvania, where his father, an Irish immigrant, operated a trading post. Buchanan went east to college, Dickinson College in southeastern Pennsylvania, and then established himself still farther east in Lancaster, 80 miles west of Philadelphia. All are well within *r*-ful territory, and the Irish accent of his father would have been *r*-ful too.

In Lancaster he became a successful lawyer and politician. He served 10 years in the U.S. House of Representatives, 12 years as a U.S. senator, and as U.S. secretary of state under James K. Polk. Despite his success, he disliked making speeches, in part because he didn't project well in the days before amplification. In small groups, however, he enjoyed himself and was said to be a great conversationalist.

Buchanan is quoted twice in the *Oxford English Dictionary*, providing earliest examples for two terms that must have been new or odd to him, too, since he puts them in quotation marks when he writes them. The *OED* credits him as the instigator of *Africanize*, in an 1853 letter:

"A violent . . . article in the Washington *Union* charging them with an intrigue with Spain to '**Africanize**' Cuba."

And then there is the rare term *frock-dress*, for which Buchanan provides the only example in an 1854 letter. It was no light matter. At the time he was in London as the American ambassador to Great Britain, and the invitation to appear "in frock dress" had been the result of lengthy diplomatic negotiations. It seems that in the previous year the American secretary of state had instructed all American representatives to appear at foreign courts "in the simple dress of an American citizen." What exactly that meant the secretary didn't specify, but it was enough to ruffle royalty by the implied snub of elegant European fashion.

Buchanan described the problem in a letter to his niece dated February 21, 1854: "I dined on Wednesday last with the Queen at Buckingham Palace. Both she and Prince Albert were remarkably civil, and I had quite a conversation with each of them separately. But the question of costume still remains, and from this I anticipate nothing but trouble in several directions. I was invited 'in **frock dress**' to the dinner." Three days later he was happier: "The dress question, after much difficulty, has been finally and satisfactorily settled. I appeared at the levee on Wednesday last in just such a dress as I have worn at the President's a hundred times—a black coat, white waistcoat and cravat, and black pantaloons and dress boots, with the addition of a very plain black-handled and black-hilted sword—this to gratify those who have yielded so much, and to distinguish me from the upper court servants."

Abraham Lincoln

[1809–65]
President 1861–65

Abraham Lincoln was born in Kentucky—the first president born west of the Appalachians—and raised in southern Indiana. Then as now, there was more than a hint of a Southern accent in the speech of southern Indiana, but it's not *r*-less, just Ah-ful (that is, inclined to say *ah* for *I*). As a young man, Lincoln struck out north and west, and lived the rest of his life in central Illinois, except for certain intervals in Washington, D.C. With that exception, he spent his entire life far from any *r*-less territory.

Coming from so deep in the back woods, he attracted notice for his pronunciation, and there are some tantalizing tidbits in the notes of contemporaries. Horace White, reporting for the *Chicago Press and Tribune* on a Lincoln speech in September 1854, wrote that Lincoln "had the accent and pronunciation peculiar to his native state, Kentucky." In early 1860, when Lincoln delivered his famous Cooper Union speech in New York City, a long way from home, another reporter noted, "He said 'Mr. Cheerman,' instead of 'Mr. Chairman,' and employed many other words with an old-fashioned pronunciation."

Lincoln was also reported to say *git* for *get, thar* for *there,* and *heared* for *heard,* and to speak with a "backwoods twang." But early during Lincoln's presidency, when young Robert Gould Shaw of Massachusetts visited him at the White House, Shaw heard a very different voice: "His voice is very pleasant; and though, to be sure, we were there only a few minutes, I didn't hear anything like Western slang or twang in him. He gives you the impression, too, of being a gentleman." Evidently Lincoln polished his language for use in the White House.

He didn't have much in the way of formal education. Lincoln himself explained in a short 1859 autobiographical article:

> There were some schools, so called; but no qualification was ever required of a teacher beyond "readin, writin, and cipherin" to the Rule of Three. If a straggler supposed to understand Latin happened to sojourn in the neighborhood, he was looked upon as a wizard. There was absolutely nothing to excite ambition for education. Of course when I came of age I did not know much. Still somehow, I could read, write, and cipher to the Rule of Three; but that was all. I have not been to school since. The little advance I now have upon this store of education, I have picked up from time to time under the pressure of necessity.

In a longer 1860 article Lincoln wrote about himself in the third person:

> Abraham now thinks that the aggregate of all his schooling did not amount to one year. He was never in a college or academy as a student, and never inside of a college or academy building till since he had a law license. What he has in the way of education he has picked up. After he was twenty-three and had separated from his father, he studied English grammar—imperfectly, of course, but so as to speak and write as well as he now does.

The Stump Speaker

If any president could be called a stump speaker, it would be Lincoln. That's a judgment of his contemporaries, not just of historians. Learning that Lincoln would be debating him in the 1858 Senate race, Stephen Douglas said, "I shall have my hands full. He is the strong man of his party—full of wit, facts, dates—and the best stump speaker, with his droll ways and dry jokes, in the West. He is as honest as he is shrewd, and if I beat him my victory will be hardly won."

Stump speaker? Yes, the picture of him as a youth standing on a tree stump and preaching in imitation of a sermon he had just heard is not entirely apocryphal. And as for his later political career, you can go to downtown Decatur, Illinois, and see a statue of Lincoln with this legend: "Lincoln mounted a stump by Harrell's Tavern facing this square and defended the Illinois Whig Party candidates near this spot at age 21 in the summer of 1830."

As a stump speaker, he was something to see. He used extravagant gestures. His law partner, William Herndon, recalled, "When the sentiment was one of detestation, denunciation of slavery for example, both arms, thrown upward and fists clenched, swept through the air. This was one of his most effective gestures." Adding to the extravagance was his towering height, six feet four inches.

But what about his speech? Those who heard him were unanimous on this: He had a high-pitched voice. One even described it as a falsetto: "He had a thin tenor, or rather falsetto voice, almost as high pitched as a boatswain's whistle." Those who heard him are unanimous, too, in their testimony that his voice carried clearly to the far reaches of any crowd. But hearers disagree about whether that high-pitched, far-carrying voice was an agreeable one.

Waldo W. Braden, in his book *Abraham Lincoln, Public Speaker*, collected examples of the contradictory opinions. In Lincoln's favor, Colonel Clark Carr, who sat near Lincoln when he delivered the Gettysburg Address, praised "those high clarion tones which the people of Illinois had so often heard," and added, "His was a voice that, when he made an effort, could reach a great multitude, and he always tried to make everyone hear."

On the other hand, a reporter for the *New York Herald* said Lincoln's voice had "a frequent tendency to dwindle into a shrill and unpleasant sound." Carl Schurz, an influential supporter of Lincoln in the 1860 campaign, described Lincoln's manner of speaking in some detail in an 1891 article in *Harper's Magazine*:

> *His rich natural gifts, trained by long and varied practice, had made him an orator of rare persuasiveness. In his immature days, he*

*had pleased himself for a short period with that inflated, high-flown
style which, among the uncultivated, passes for "beautiful speaking."
His inborn truthfulness and his artistic instinct soon overcame that
aberration, and revealed to him the noble beauty and strength of simplicity. He possessed an uncommon power of clear and compact
statement, which might have reminded those who knew the story of
his early youth of the efforts of the poor boy, when he copied his com-
positions from the scraped wooden shovel, carefully to trim his expressions in order to save paper.*

*Although he had never studied the rules of logic, he was a mas-
ter of logical lucidity. His reasoning he loved to point and enliven
by humorous illustrations, usually anecdotes of Western life, of
which he had an inexhaustible store at his command. These anecdotes had not seldom a flavor of rustic robustness about them, but
he used them with great effect, while amusing the audience, to give
life to an abstraction, to explode an absurdity, to clinch an argument, to drive home an admonition. The natural kindliness of his
tone, softening prejudice and disarming partisan rancor, would
often open to his reasoning a way into minds most unwilling to
receive it.*

*Yet his greatest power consisted in the charm of his individuality.
That charm did not, in the ordinary way, appeal to the ear or to the
eye. His voice was not melodious; rather shrill and piercing, especially when it rose to its high treble in moments of great animation.
His figure was unhandsome, and the action of his unwieldy limbs
awkward. He commanded none of the graces of oratory as they are
commonly understood.*

Noah Brooks, a reporter, tried to make the best case for Lincoln:
"Lincoln's voice was not sonorous, and at times it rose to a high somewhat shrill key. In ordinary conversation his tones were agreeable, and
his enunciation clear."

In a letter in 1887, nearly a quarter century after Lincoln's death,
Herndon ventured a description: "Lincoln's voice was, when he first began speaking, shrill, squeaking, piping, unpleasant. . . . As Mr. Lincoln
proceeded further along with his oration . . . he gently and gradually
warmed up—his shrill-squeaking-piping voice became harmonious,
melodious—musical, if you please."

The Reticent President

Lincoln had made his reputation both as lawyer and as politician by speaking. As politician, or candidate for lesser office than the presidency, he spoke at every opportunity. But that stopped abruptly when he became a candidate for president. From then on, and throughout his presidency, Lincoln was cautious in the extreme about speaking in public. He made fewer than a hundred speeches, many very brief, during his presidential years. Here are two of them, in their entirety, delivered at Frederick, Maryland, on October 4, 1862. In them he gives his reason for his reticence:

> In my present position it is hardly proper for me to make speeches. Every word is so closely noted that it will not do to make trivial ones, and I cannot be expected to be prepared to make a matured one just now. If I were as I have been most of my life, I might perhaps, talk amusing to you for half an hour, and it wouldn't hurt anybody; but as it is, I can only return my sincere thanks for the compliment paid our cause and our common country.

Five minutes later he gave another little speech, almost as short:

> Fellow citizens: I see myself surrounded by soldiers, and a little further off I note the citizens of this good city of Frederick, anxious to hear something from me. I can only say, as I did five minutes ago, it is not proper for me to make speeches in my present position. I return thanks to our soldiers for the good service they have rendered, for the energies they have shown, the hardships they have endured, and the blood they have so nobly shed for this dear Union of ours; and I also return thanks not only to the soldiers, but to the good citizens of Maryland, and to all the good men and women in this land, for their devotion to our glorious cause. I say this without any malice in my heart to those who have done otherwise. May our children and our children's children to a thousand generations, continue to enjoy the benefits conferred upon us by a united country, and have cause yet to rejoice under those glorious institutions bequeathed us by Washington and his compeers.

This does not mean that Lincoln refused to speak in public as president—far from it. The few speeches he gave include some of the most memorable in American history, in particular his second inaugural address and the Gettysburg Address. Those he worked over meticulously, advised by his aides. Their pithy incisiveness raises them to a different sphere than almost any other presidential remarks, before or since. And of course that raises the bar for presidents and their speechwriters, who must prepare their remarks to be judged against the Lincoln standard.

Lincoln's Wooling

The *Oxford English Dictionary* takes considerable note of Abraham Lincoln, quoting him nearly two dozen times. Most of these, however, are far from being the first examples of the words in question. They are words and phrases like *shut mouth* (keep quiet) and *pegging away* and *peter out*, and the maxim *Actions speak louder than words*, as well as *liquor law, re-express, that few* (instead of *those few*), *Washingtonian* (referring to George W.), and as basic a word as *struggle*. For the last example of *half . . . half*, the *OED* has the famous Lincoln statement of 1858: "I believe this Government cannot endure permanently half slave and half free."

But there are also a handful of first instances. The young Lincoln provides the first *OED* example of *wooling*, that is, pulling someone's hair. A 1927 *Life of Lincoln* quotes him in his early twenties (around 1831) as saying, "I never use tussle and scuffle. I don't like this **wooling** and pulling."

Still in his twenties, in 1834 Lincoln the surveyor used what became the first *OED* example for the well-known word *relocate* and its companion *relocation* in its modern sense: "To view and **relocate** a part of the road . . . we have made the said **relocation** on good ground." For *relocation*, the *OED* gives as first instance this 1837 quotation, even though the quotation for *relocate* provides an earlier example: "I also tacked a provision on to a fellow's bill, to authorize the **relocation** of a road."

And the *OED* attests to his role while a congressman in giving residents of Michigan the curious designation *Michigander*.

LINCOLN GOOSES MICHIGAN

L argely because of Lincoln's wit while he was a member of Congress, the inhabitants of Michigan have the curious designation *Michiganders*. This is how it came about. On July 27, 1848, Lincoln addressed the House of Representatives in sarcastic reference to General Lewis Cass, the Democratic nominee for president. Cass was a veteran of the War of 1812 and had governed the territory of Michigan from 1813 to 1831. In the 1848 speech, Lincoln, a member of the opposition Whig party, joined in the chorus of those who had mocked Cass as a "goose." In Lincoln's speech the goose became a gander.

"But in my hurry I was very near closing this subject of military tails [*sic*] before I was done with it," said Lincoln. "There is one entire article of the sort I have not discussed yet—I mean the military tail you Democrats are now engaged in dovetailing into the great Michigander. Yes, sir; all his biographies (and they are legion) have him in hand, tying him to a military tail, like so many mischievous boys tying a dog to a bladder of beans."

He wasn't the first to sarcastically call Cass the "great Michigander"; the epithet had appeared in a Xenia, Ohio, newspaper published that same day, July 27, 1848, without reference to Lincoln, a clear indication that it was already in circulation among the Whigs. But Lincoln's speech, often reprinted, made *Michigander* famous. At first it was used just in reference to General Cass, always in the phrase "great Michigander." But by the time of the Civil War, a decade later, *Michigander* instead of a more neutral word like *Michiganite* or *Michiganian* was being used to designate any person from Michigan. Thus, thanks in large part to Lincoln, Michigan was permanently goosed.

This has been something of an embarrassment. Since that time, respectable citizens have tried to substitute *Michiganian* for *Michigander*. Michigan historical societies and publications prefer *Michiganian*, and so does the *Detroit News*. But its rival, the *Detroit Free Press*, holds for *Michigander*, and that term remains a favorite among the people. A "Michigania" website explains the distinction: "You may be a Michiganian if—you're a Michiganian for official occasions, but a Michigander in your heart." A Michigan resident wrote in 2002 to the editor of the *National Review*, "Thanks for using ▶

'Michigander' instead of 'Michiganian'! The latter term was something imposed on us, like the metric system and soccer."

Or it could be said, as Bob Linsenman does in *Midwest Fly Fishing* magazine, that "A Fudgie is a Michigan Yuppie. . . . The Fudgie drives a foreign car, says 'Michiganian' instead of 'Michigander,' and comes north only to visit the shops in Petoskey or on Mackinac Island." And on the Beliefnet website, "Budlong Brown" proclaimed, "Born in Bay City. . . . Proud alumnus of the great University of Michigan. Never going to accept the term 'Michiganian'. Until the day I die, I shall be a very proud *Michigander!!!*" Clearly, the Lincoln effect remains strong.

Point Well Taken and Common-Looking

Lincoln is credited in the *OED* with the first example of *point well taken* (1863): "The point made in your paper is well taken." He also has the first attestation for the phrase *common-looking*, in a story told by his secretaries and later biographers John G. Nicolay and John Hay:

> One night he had a dream, which he repeated the next morning to the writer of these lines, which quaintly illustrates his unpretending and kindly democracy. He was in some great assembly; the people made a lane to let him pass. "He is a **common-looking** *fellow*," someone said. Lincoln in his dream turned to his critic and replied, in his Quaker phrase, "Friend, the Lord prefers **common-looking** people: that is why he made so many of them."

The *OED* gives the dates 1860–65 for this story, since Nicolay and Hay don't specify when Lincoln told it.

Lincoln provides the earliest *OED* evidence for the phrase *come to stay* in an 1863 letter: "I hope it [peace] will come soon, and **come to stay.**"

There is a Lincoln version of the maxim *change horses in midstream*, the earliest example of that maxim in the *OED*, quoted twice from 1864:

> I do not allow myself to suppose that either the Convention or the League have concluded to decide that I am either the greatest or best man in America, but rather they have concluded that it is not best to

swap horses while crossing the river, *and have further concluded that I am not so poor a horse that they might not make a botch of it in trying to swap.*

I am reminded . . . of a story of an old Dutch farmer, who remarked . . . that it was not best to swap horses when crossing a stream.

The *OED* also credits Lincoln with the first example of *long-felt* in a prosaic context in his December 1862 Annual Message to Congress:

The suspension of specie payments by the banks soon after the commencement of your last session made large issues of United States notes unavoidable. In no other way could the payment of the troops and the satisfaction of other just demands be so economically or so well provided for. The judicious legislation of Congress, securing the receivability of these notes for loans and internal duties and making them a legal tender for other debts, has made them an universal currency, and has satisfied, partially at least, and for the time, the **long-felt** *want of an uniform circulating medium, saving thereby to the people immense sums in discounts and exchanges.*

Bass-Ackwards Abe

Honest Abe should also be credited with the first known use of *bass-ackwards* as a supposedly humorous twist on the supposedly humorous term *ass-backwards*. The *OED* and the *Historical Dictionary of American Slang* have it only as early as the twentieth century, but researcher Fred Shapiro found, in *The Collected Works of Abraham Lincoln*, an undated "piece" by Lincoln that begins like this: "He said he was riding **bass-ackwards** on a *jass-ack*, through a *patton-cotch*, on a pair of *baddle-sags*. . . ."

Andrew Johnson

[1808–75]
President 1865–69

Following more or less in the footsteps of both Jackson and Polk, Andrew Johnson grew up in poverty in Raleigh, North Carolina, near the western edge of *r*-less territory, and made his later life and his political career in *r*-ful Tennessee.

John S. Wise, a gentlemanly author who personally met many of the nineteenth-century presidents, said of Johnson in his 1906 book *Recollections of Thirteen Presidents*:

> He grew up an obscure and ignorant boy of the very humblest, and possibly even doubtful, antecedents, of that class of people known in the South as "poor whites"; he drifted from North Carolina into Tennessee, where his youth was spent in the little village of Greenville. . . .
>
> Mr. Johnson's very remarkable career in Tennessee was, from its beginning, based upon the strong, fierce, aggressive appeal to what he was pleased to call the "masses" against the other elements of the community denominated by him as the "classes."

Harper's Weekly in 1866 told its readers the story of Johnson's education:

> *During the seven years of his apprenticeship [to a tailor] he learned to read, an acquisition due, in part, to accident but still more to his own ingenuity and untiring perseverance. His first reading-book—and that was a borrowed one—was a volume of speeches, chiefly those of British statesmen. In 1826, at the age of 18, he removed to Greenville, in East Tennessee, where he was so fortunate as to marry a young lady who was competent to teach him writing and the first rudiments of arithmetic. This was the completion of Andy's schooling.*

Nevertheless, he studied to improve his knowledge and his speaking ability, spending much of his free time at the Library of Congress after he had been elected to the House of Representatives in 1843. He served ten years in Congress, then four years as governor of Tennessee, and then a term in the U.S. Senate before being named military governor of Tennessee during the Civil War and then Lincoln's running mate in the 1864 election.

In September 1866, with Johnson increasingly at odds with the Radical Republican Congress that opposed his discriminatory attitude toward blacks and conciliatory attitude toward Southern whites, *Harper's Weekly* declared,

> *His exhibition of temper, his intemperate, and often indecent, denunciation of his political opponents remind us rather of the demagogue than of the unimpassioned and well-balanced statesman. . . .*
>
> *The strongest speeches he has ever made—and those most free of the characteristic weakness to which we have alluded—were those made by him in the Senate in the winter of 1860 and the following summer. Indeed when speaking before the Senate he appeared as a very different style of orator than when addressing the people. Before the latter his speeches are disconnected, full of repetitions, and not even his official position as Chief Magistrate of the United States is sufficient to keep him within the limits of good sense and decorum.*

In 1867, Johnson removed Secretary of War Edwin Stanton from office despite the newly passed Tenure of Office Act that prohibited such an action without the Senate's consent. Told that if he did so, he would be impeached, he uttered his most famous statement, "Impeach and be damned!" He came within one vote in the Senate of being removed from office in 1868.

So what did his speeches sound like? There were no recording machines during his presidency, but there is a stenographic transcript of a speech he made in Cleveland in September 1866 while touring the nation to rally support against the Congress. Here are some excerpts:

And let me say tonight that my head has been threatened. It has been said that my blood was to be shed. Let me say to those who are still willing to sacrifice my life [derisive laughter and cheers], if you want a victim and my country requires it, erect your altar, and the individual who addresses you tonight, while here a visitor ["No," "No," and laughter], erect your altar if you still thirst for blood, and if you want it, take out the individual who now addresses you and lay him upon your altar, and the blood that now courses his veins and warms his existence shall be poured out as a last libation to Freedom. I love my country, and I defy any man to put his finger upon anything to the contrary. . . .

And because I stand now as I did when the rebellion commenced, I have been denounced as a traitor. My countrymen here tonight, who has suffered more than I? Who has run greater risk? Who has borne more than I? But Congress, factious, domineering, tyrannical Congress has undertaken to poison the minds of the American people, and create a feeling against me in consequence of the manner in which I have distributed the public patronage.

While this gang—this common gang of cormorants and bloodsuckers, have been fattening upon the country for the past four or five years—men never going into the field, who growl at being removed from their fat offices, they are great patriots! Look at them all over your district! Everybody is a traitor that is against them. I think the time has come when those who stayed at home and enjoyed fat offices for the last four or five years—I think it would be more than right for them to give way and let others participate in the benefits of office. Hence you can see why it is that I am traduced and assaulted. I stood by these men who were in the field, and I stand by them now. . . .

Then in parting with you tonight, I hang over you this flag, not of 25 but of 36 stars; I hand over to you the Constitution of my country,

*though imprisoned, though breaches have been made upon it, with
confidence hoping that you will repair the breaches; I hand it over
to you, in whom I have always trusted and relied, and, so far, I have
never deserted—and I feel confident, while speaking here tonight, for
heart responds to heart of man, that you agree to the same great
doctrine.*

Discrimination

Johnson is cited only three times in the *Oxford English Dictionary*, but,
in his statement of March 27, 1866, vetoing a civil rights bill, he provides the first examples for *discriminating* and *discrimination* as they
refer to civil rights. He scolds Congress for attempting to abolish discrimination:

> *If it be granted that Congress can repeal all State laws* **discrimi-
> nating** *between whites and blacks in the subjects covered by this bill,
> why, it may be asked, may not Congress repeal in the same way all
> State laws* **discriminating** *between the two races on the subjects of
> suffrage and office? . . . Thus a perfect equality of the white and col-
> ored races is attempted to be fixed by Federal law in every State of the
> Union over the vast field of State jurisdiction covered by these enu-
> merated rights. In no one of these can any State ever exercise any
> power of* **discrimination** *between the different races.*

He also provides an *OED* example, though not the first, for *civil
rights*, the subject of much discussion throughout his presidency, as
well as of that veto.

Ulysses S. Grant

[1822–1885]
President 1869–1877

The great general and not-so-great president U. S. Grant was born at the southwestern edge of Ohio, in Point Pleasant on the Ohio River, upriver from Cincinnati. When he was a year old, his family moved to Georgetown, twenty miles to the east. All parts of Ohio are *r*-ful, so Grant would have grown up in an *r*-ful environment.

He attended a one-room school for seven years, starting at age 6, and two local academies for a year each before going to the U.S. Military Academy. Grant was the first of two West Point graduates who became president; the second would be Eisenhower in the next century.

Of all the presidents, Grant was perhaps the most flatly opposed to public speaking, and not just for himself. He had this to say about it:

> *You all know how unaccustomed I am to public speaking, how undesirable a talent I think it is to possess, how little good it generally does, and how desirous I am to see more of our public men follow the good example . . . I have set them.*

His dislike of public speaking began at an early age. A classmate from his one-room school later recalled that Grant hated declaiming: "He spoke a selection from Washington's Farewell Address, but he made fearful work of it." Well, as we have seen, even Washington didn't speak that address.

The remarks Grant had to make in public—as a general, secretary of war, and president—were unremarkable. But he was notable as a soldier who hated war, and as perhaps the first president who was a one-worlder. He talked about both these stances in his second inaugural address of 1873:

> Under our Republic we support an army less than that of any European power of any standing and a navy less than that of either of at least five of them. There could be no extension of territory on the continent which would call for an increase of this force, but rather might such extension enable us to diminish it. . . .
>
> I do not share in the apprehension held by many as to the danger of governments becoming weakened and destroyed by reason of their extension of territory. Commerce, education, and rapid transit of thought and matter by telegraph and steam have changed all this. Rather do I believe that our Great Maker is preparing the world, in His own good time, to become one nation, speaking one language, and when armies and navies will be no longer required.

Though a military man, he didn't use off-color language, even in private. "I am not aware of ever having used a profane expletive in my life," he once stated, "but I would have the charity to excuse those who may have done so, if they were in charge of a train of Mexican pack mules."

Grant was known, if anything, for keeping silent. But he was an impressive writer, even long before he became president. His plain, direct character is reflected in his writing. According to historian Bruce Catton:

> Anyone who has been required, in the line of duty, to spend many hours examining the letters, dispatches, orders and reports in those bulky and usually dusty volumes, The Official Records of the War of the Rebellion, is likely sooner or later to notice an unexpected phenomenon: he gets so that he can generally identify the material that was written by General Ulysses S. Grant without waiting to see the signature. . . .

. . . Grant's stands out. Quite simply, it had its own style. It was, to begin with, always very clear. The man knew exactly what he wanted to say and knew exactly how to say it so that the man at the other end of the line would get it without any chance of misunderstanding. It was not a polished style at all, and now and then it contained locutions which would pain a teacher of rhetoric. The man was just plain careless about spelling, and at times he would spell the same word two or three different ways in one letter. But the style was there, and it was a style many a professional writing man might like to have.

There was never anything flabby about it. What Grant wrote never rambled, made the same point twice, or stabbed around in a blind hunt for an obscure target. He had an extremely clear mind, and his prose style reflected it. He had a knack for coining an occasional phrase or sentence that stands alone and lives on; he had, as well, a quiet sense of humor that will be remembered by anyone who has read his Memoirs.

And a recent biographer remarks that Grant "wrote the only memoir by an American general or president that belongs among the classics of American literature."

Contemporary Grant

Grant's memoirs were published to great acclaim in 1885, when editing and publishing of the *Oxford English Dictionary* had just begun. The *OED* editors mined those memoirs for quotations to illustrate current usage. So the *OED* contains contemporary examples from Grant, rather than first instances, for *report* (for duty), *gunning, man* (the guns), *fortify, major-generalcy,* (military) *operations, involve, leading, lying* (idle), *get through, growth, grown up* meaning "crowded," *follow* (a way of life), *pick up* meaning "to capture," *into hospital* (boats for repair), *cordelle* meaning "to tow a boat with a cordelle, that is, a rope," and *run* (a pair of millstones).

Among the nearly twenty *OED* quotations from Grant's memoirs are two that are first instances. One is *bring up* in a military sense: "The troops from Corinth were **brought up** in time to repel the threatened movement without a battle." The other is *points* to mean destinations:

"Vicksburg was important to the enemy because it occupied the first high ground coming close to the river below Memphis. From there a railroad runs east, connecting with other roads leading to all **points** of the Southern States."

No Lobbyist

It's widely claimed that Grant coined the word *lobbyist*. As one source tells it,

> *After a long day in the Oval Office, he used to escape the pressures of the presidency with a brandy and cigar in the Willard [Hotel] lobby. As many leaders and business people approached him on individual causes, President Grant began referring to these folks as "lobbyists."*

There are only two problems with this. First, the Oval Office was not built until 1909. Second, the *OED* has a quotation for *lobbyist* dated 1863, while Grant was busy in Vicksburg and Chattanooga and long before he became president. For that matter, the verb *lobby* with the meaning of pestering legislators for favors had been used for two centuries, deriving from the lobby of the House of Commons in England.

Rutherford B. Hayes

[1822–93]
President 1877–81

Rutherford B. Hayes came from Delaware, Ohio, north of Columbus in the middle of that *r*-ful state. He went to private schools in Norwalk in northern Ohio and in Middletown in Connecticut, then back to Ohio to Kenyon College, not far from his home, where he graduated as valedictorian. He then went east again to Harvard Law School, where he was head of his class. His education resulted in what biographer Harry Barnard called "an interesting mixture of New England 'gentleman' and Ohio 'Buckeye.'" It's possible that the New England part of the mixture included *r*-less pronunciation.

Though his managers seemingly stole the presidential election from Samuel J. Tilden so blatantly that he became known as "Rutherfraud," Hayes himself was honest, incorruptible, and hardworking. He pledged not to seek a second term so that he would give no appearance of appealing for votes. And he thought a single-term limit was a good idea for all presidents.

Hayes was a capable speaker but not a brilliant one. He was a proponent of education and, in contrast to some other presidents, most notably Johnson, of racial equality. His inaugural address shows his matter-of-fact manner of advocating these policies:

248

At the basis of all prosperity . . . lies the improvement of the intellectual and moral condition of the people. Universal suffrage should rest upon universal education. To this end, liberal and permanent provision should be made for the support of free schools by the State governments, and, if need be, supplemented by legitimate aid from national authority. . . .

Let me assure my countrymen of the Southern States that it is my earnest desire to regard and promote their truest interest—the interests of the white and of the colored people both and equally—and to put forth my best efforts in behalf of a civil policy which will forever wipe out in our political affairs the color line and the distinction between North and South, to the end that we may have not merely a united North or a united South, but a united country. . . .

In furtherance of the reform we seek, and in other important respects a change of great importance, I recommend an amendment to the Constitution prescribing a term of six years for the Presidential office and forbidding a reelection.

For whatever reason, Hayes is missing from the pages of the *Oxford English Dictionary*.

James A. Garfield

[1831–1881]
President 1881

A nother of the Ohio presidents was James A. Garfield, the "preacher president," who holds a deserved place among the great presidential orators discussed in chapter 2.

He was born and raised on a farm near Orange, a suburb of Cleveland in the far north of the state, deep in *r*-ful territory. At age 21 he went to Western Reserve Eclectic Institute (now Hiram College), 20 miles southeast of his birthplace. After two years there he transferred to Williams College in Massachusetts. He took to education so well that after graduating from Williams in 1856, he returned to Hiram, teaching classics for a year and then becoming the college's president in 1857.

There is an account of the first sermon Garfield ever preached. It was while he was still a student (but also an instructor) at the Eclectic Institute in the winter of 1853–54. His topic was "The First and Second Comings of Christ." According to the eyewitness,

> *In beginning, Mr. Garfield drew a most startling historic parallel—
> so it seemed to those who heard the sermon—between the first and
> second coming of Napoleon Bonaparte and Jesus Christ. With great
> vividness he sketched the life of the great Napoleon, from the time he*

entered the military school in Paris, in 1784, an unknown youth, to the time when all France gathered to receive the remains of the dead conqueror, who under the flag of the empire, whose glory he sought on so many battle fields, was entering the gates of the city once more.

He then turned and traced the history of Jesus Christ, from the manger, in the village of Bethlehem, until he took his departure from the mountain in Galilee to heaven, where he should reign until every enemy was subdued and then he would come again, not as the babe, in helplessness, nor as the man of sorrows, but as Him whom the armies of heaven followed, and whose name written on vesture and thigh is "King of kings and Lord of lords." At the conclusion of his sermon the attention was intense and the stillness most profound, and from that time onward until he ceased to preach, no one heard him without great pleasure.

Garfield was so erudite—or so much of a showman—that it was said he could simultaneously write Greek with one hand and Latin with the other. And in 1876 he developed a new proof for the Pythagorean theorem, which holds that the sum of the squares of the sides of a right triangle is equal to the square of the hypotenuse.

In 1860 he left the college for a career in law, politics, and the military (he became the youngest major general for the Union in the Civil War). In 1863, in the midst of the Civil War, he was elected to Congress, where he served until 1878, making a name for himself as an orator and writer.

Beyond his inaugural address, he didn't have much time to develop his presidential rhetorical style. On July 16, 1881, barely four months after he was sworn in, he was shot by Charles J. Guiteau, a would-be lawyer frustrated in his demand for an ambassadorship in the new administration. During the 1880 election campaign, Guiteau had given unsolicited speeches for Garfield and imagined he alone was responsible for Garfield's victory.

Misadjustment

Garfield is credited with the first instance in the *Oxford English Dictionary* of the word *misadjustment* with the meaning "lack of agreement." The third edition of the *OED* labels this meaning of the word both obsolete and rare, and indeed gives no other examples. The word occurs in a long 1878 article by Garfield on "The Army of the United States" in the *North American Review*. Here's the word in context: "In fact, most of the **misadjustments** between the Secretary of War and the army, so much complained of in recent years, originated with a Secretary of War who had been a soldier and could hardly refrain from usurping the functions of command." A very diplomatic way of saying they disagreed.

From Garfield's journal of a visit to London in 1867 while he was a member of Congress, the *OED* picked up his use of *hobbling* (meaning something like *wobbling* in movement or in speech), not as a first instance, but as a contemporary example. Garfield wrote that a certain member of Parliament "has a full, rotund voice, and, like Gladstone, is un-English in his style—that is, he speaks right on, with but little of that distressful **hobbling** which marks the mass of Parliamentary speakers."

Chester A. Arthur

[1830–86]
President 1881–85

Chester A. Arthur was born and raised in Fairfield in northwestern Vermont, where his father, an Irish immigrant, was a Baptist preacher. Fairfield is in the r-ful western half of Vermont, not far from Lake Champlain and the Canadian border. He went south and a little farther west to Union College in Schenectady, New York, also in r-ful territory, where he graduated with the class of 1848.

A career in law and politics brought him to New York City, and in 1871 he was appointed chief customs collector of the Port of New York. That operation was notorious for corruption. Arthur himself was honest, but during President Hayes's cleanup of the civil service in 1878, Arthur was removed from office for standing by his corrupt subordinates. As "Gentleman Boss" of the Republican Party in New York, Arthur achieved the vice presidential nomination on the 1880 ticket with Garfield. He came into the presidency after Garfield died from an assassin's bullet.

He was apparently a capable, though not remarkable speaker. His most memorable speech was the brief one he gave on being sworn in as president by the chief justice of the Supreme Court on September 22, 1881:

> *The wisdom of our fathers, foreseeing even the most dire possibilities, made sure that the government should never be imperiled because of the uncertainty of human life. Men may die, but the fabrics of our free institutions remain unshaken. No higher or more assuring proof could exist of the strength and permanence of popular government than the fact that, though the chosen of the people be struck down, his constitutional successor is peacefully installed without shock or strain, except the sorrow which mourns the bereavement.*
>
> *All the noble aspirations of my lamented predecessor which found expression in his life, the measures devised and suggested during his brief administration to correct abuses and enforce economy, to advance prosperity and promote the general welfare, to insure domestic security and maintain friendly and honorable relations with the nations of the earth, will be garnered in the hearts of the people, and it will be my earnest endeavor to profit and to see that the nation shall profit by his example and experience.*
>
> *Prosperity blesses our country, our fiscal policy is fixed by law, is well grounded and generally approved. No threatening issue mars our foreign intercourse, and the wisdom, integrity, and thrift of our people may be trusted to continue undisturbed the present assured career of peace, tranquility, and welfare. The gloom and anxiety which have enshrouded the country must make repose especially welcome now. No demand for speedy legislation has been heard; no adequate occasion is apparent for an unusual session of Congress. . . .*
>
> *Summoned to these high duties and responsibilities, and profoundly conscious of their magnitude and gravity, I assume the trust imposed by the Constitution, relying for aid on Divine guidance and the virtue, patriotism, and intelligence of the American people.*

And despite his tolerance and even defense of corruption in the civil service while he was in New York, he made civil service reform the most important accomplishment of his administration. Arthur makes one of the best examples of the sometimes ennobling effect of the presidency.

John S. Wise, the Virginia gentleman who published *Recollections of Thirteen Presidents* in 1906, said of Arthur,

Now and then one hears people discussing which of the Presidents have been gentlemen. . . . In America whether a particular person is or is not a gentleman is largely dependent upon the notions of each person concerning what constitutes a gentleman. But I have yet to hear anybody familiar with the personal attributes of our Presidents, and trying to classify them socially, who did not declare that Chester A. Arthur was a "gentleman," whatever that term may mean in America.

There is no mention of Arthur's words in the *Oxford English Dictionary*.

Grover Cleveland

[1837–1908]
President 1885–89, 1893–97

With Grover Cleveland, we arrive at the presidents whose voices have been recorded. No longer is it necessary to guess what they sounded like. In Cleveland's case, though he was born in New Jersey, his preacher-father moved the family to Fayetteville, near Syracuse, in western New York when he was 4. He lived there until age 18, when he went further west to Buffalo, where he eventually became a lawyer. Since he grew up in western New York State, we might expect his speech to be *r*-ful, but as chapter 8 explains, he used the elegant *r*-less style of the East Coast.

We're told that Cleveland "cussed openly," and that he delighted in hearing Negro dialect stories. A friend later remembered: "He was not a great talker. Once in a while something would start him going, and he would run on for half an evening, but for the most part he let others do the talking; he listened."

During his second term, he developed a cancer of the mouth. On June 13, 1893, in an operation hidden from public notice on a friend's yacht, his entire upper left jaw was removed, along with a bit of the soft palate. A second operation, on July 17, removed some additional suspicious tissue. For a few months that summer, Cleveland kept to his retreat on Cape Cod. This gave him time to practice talking in a natural way with a prosthesis replacing his jaw and teeth. Evidently it worked better than Washington's false teeth. Dr. W. W. Keen, one of the surgeons involved, told the story many years later:

After the first operation, while the President was at Gray Gables, Dr. Kasson C. Gibson, of New York, fitted Mr. Cleveland with an artificial jaw of vulcanized rubber. This supported the cheek in its natural position and prevented it from falling in. When it was in place the President's speech was excellent, even its quality not being altered. On October fourteenth Mr. Cleveland, in a letter to Doctor Gibson, expressed his lively satisfaction after trying a new and even better and more comfortable plate also made by Doctor Gibson. . . .

On September fifth he opened the First Pan-American Medical Congress, in Washington, when his voice was "even clearer and more resonant" than on March fourth at his inauguration. Two weeks later he spoke at the Centenary of the Founding of the City of Washington. He met many persons officially and socially. No scar or other evidence of an operation existed, neither eyeball was displaced, his cheek was not fallen in, his voice did not betray him, and his general health was evidently as good as could be expected by one who for four months had endured a horde of pestiferous officeseekers and the terrible anxiety of the existing financial crisis. . . .

Unfortunately Mr. Cleveland never learned to dictate easily to a stenographer. Practically all his letters, papers and addresses were written by his own hand. In the New York Academy of Medicine there is framed a formal address before the academy, every page of it laboriously hand written. I never received from him a note or a letter that was typewritten.

An Extensory Arrangement; No Baby Ruth

Cleveland is cited once in the *Oxford English Dictionary*, for the first and last example of *extensory* referring to an extension of time. The *OED* calls this a rare word. It comes in a ponderous paragraph of his December 1885 Annual Message to Congress: "In the interest of good neighborhood and of the commercial intercourse of adjacent communities, the question of the North American fisheries is one of much importance.

Following out the intimation given by me when the **extensory** arrangement above described was negotiated, I recommend that. . . ." The sentence goes on for another 64 words.

There's a well-known story that Cleveland was responsible for a famous brand name. The Baby Ruth candy bar was supposedly named after his first daughter, Ruth. That's a blatant lie. It was made up by the Curtiss Candy Company when it introduced its Baby Ruth bar in 1921, evidently so that the company could claim that the name had nothing to do with famous baseball star Babe Ruth. Ruth Cleveland was born in 1891 in the interval between her father's presidencies. She died of diphtheria in 1904, more than a decade before the Curtiss Company came into existence.

Benjamin Harrison

[1833–1901]
President 1889–93

Who is this John Sergeant Wise whose *Recollections of Thirteen Presidents*, published in 1906, has been mentioned so often? How was he able to meet 13 presidents in person? Well, he just happened to come from a nice Virginia and Pennsylvania family. His father, Henry A. Wise, was among other things a congressman, governor of Virginia, and a general in the Confederate Army. One grandfather, John Sergeant, was a congressman from Pennsylvania for seven terms; another grandfather, Major John Wise, was speaker of the Virginia House of Delegates in 1797 and 1798.

John S. Wise himself was a lawyer. He fought in the Confederate Army but maintained good ties with his northern relatives. Two decades after the Civil War he served a term as a congressman from Virginia. Soon afterwards he ran unsuccessfully for governor of Virginia—as a Republican—and then moved to New York City to practice law.

I introduce him here to vouch for his reliability as a character witness. He not only knew the presidents firsthand, but reported on their manner of speaking as well as their manners. And he knew Benjamin

Harrison particularly well, because Harrison came from a good Virginia family, though he grew up in Ohio. Here is Wise on Benjamin:

> *My father, who knew them all and loved them, . . . generalized Harrison traits by saying that he never knew a Harrison who was not a gentleman, but that they were inclined to run to extremes—some in the love of God, and others in the love of whisky.*
>
> *[Benjamin's] mother was from a typical New England family, and if there is a place in the world where the New Englander is more of a New Englander than he is in New England, it is the Western Reserve of Ohio, where Benjamin Harrison was born and reared by a mother of New England descent.*
>
> *In appearance, in manners in everything but name, he was as un-like a Virginian as a man could well be. . . .*
>
> *In private conversation his voice was inclined to a nasal drawl, but this disappeared when he spoke in public. There was a coldness and indifference in his manner in private which was very repellent, and absolutely different from the effect he produced when speaking. He was not only one of the wisest men of his time in all his public utterances, but, in public speaking, he warmed up and grew up to his thoughts in such manner that none of his contemporaries surpassed him in the power of arousing the enthusiasm of an audience.*

At the same time, Harrison was capable of saying, "I fear I am making an impression that I am garrulous! But the truth is that there is no man in the country that dislikes to make a speech so much as I do."

As mentioned in chapter 8, Benjamin Harrison of Ohio acted as if he didn't have Virginia connections. His voice, all 28 seconds of it recorded for posterity in the late nineteenth century, is *r*-ful, as befits an Ohioan rather than a Virginian.

The Latin American President

Harrison, who served as president after Cleveland's first term and before his second, provides the first *OED* evidence for *Latin American* (1890): "Our tariff laws offered an insurmountable barrier to a large exchange of products with the **Latin American** nations." The *OED* notes that until the twentieth century *Spanish American* was the customary term. This first for Harrison is particularly appropriate, since Benjamin was born in Rio de Janeiro while his versatile father was U.S. minister to Brazil.

Harrison is also quoted once in an example, by no means the first, of the use of the term *world power* (1901): "If the **World Powers** have any recognized creed, it is that it is their duty as 'trustees for humanity' to take over the territories of all the weak and decaying nations."

William McKinley

[1843–1901]
President 1897–1901

As explained in chapter 8, McKinley was an Ohioan but with a pronounced *r*-less and trilled-*r* accent. Perhaps his formal style was
the result of good training in elocution. At school in a private academy
in Poland, Ohio, near Youngstown in the northeast part of the state,
McKinley not only excelled in public speaking but was president of the
debate club.

He served in the Civil War, rising to the rank of brevet major, and
then became a lawyer, a congressman, governor of Ohio, and a prominent speaker on behalf of Republicans nationwide. Historian H. Wayne
Morgan of the University of Oklahoma explained in a 2001 talk:

> *The remarkable congressional campaign of 1894 illustrated his
> stature. In that year Republicans sensed the coming collapse of the
> second Cleveland administration under the weight of hard times and
> the Democratic party's internal stresses. McKinley responded then to
> almost every request from friends and other good Republicans to
> speak on their behalf. . . .*
>
> *The statistics of the contest were striking, almost incredible. He
> traveled 12,000 miles by rail, and spoke to an estimated two million*

*people in over four hundred speeches. He spoke twenty-three times in
one day, beginning in Des Moines at breakfast-time, and ending in
St. Paul at bedtime. He was not a spread-eagle orator, but spoke in a
clear precise voice, and had a special talent for making economic sta-
tistics and ideas human.*

Two years later, the election of 1896 was the first in which a candidate toured the country making campaign speeches. That candidate was
William Jennings Bryan, the Democrat. McKinley decided not to com-
pete by traveling but instead to bring supporters from all over the country to his front porch in Canton, Ohio. Eight years earlier, Benjamin
Harrison had received a few delegations at his Ohio front porch in his
successful bid for the presidency, but McKinley operated on a much
grander scale.

A delegation would arrive in Canton and march up the street to
McKinley's house. The leader of the delegation would make a short
speech—reviewed and edited in advance by McKinley—and McKinley
would respond with remarks directed at the issues raised by the visitors.
The delegates would then walk through the house and shake his hand.
By the time they were out the back door on their way to the railroad
station, another delegation was marching up the street to greet the candidate. "McKinley often appeared from dawn to evening, and had no
privacy, but never complained," according to Morgan. "He took the
gifts of food, flowers, live animals, crochet work, and all the rest in
stride, and never misspoke or appeared ruffled." Thanks to the efficient
organization of the visits, an estimated 750,000 people heard McKinley
in person between August 1896 and the election in November.

One of the two McKinley speeches preserved, at least in excerpts, in
the Vincent Voice Library at Michigan State University and discussed
in chapter 8 is from this front porch campaign. Here is a transcription
of that recording, the end of the speech. A vertical line marks a place
where McKinley paused.

I, fellow citizens, | think this event [the candidacy of Bryan?] *has
imposed upon the patriotic people of this country | a responsibility and
a duty greater than that | of any since the Civil War. | Then we fought
a struggle to preserve the government | of the United States. | Now it is
a struggle to preserve the financial honor | of the government.*

Our creed | embraces an honest dollar, | an untarnished | national credit, | adequate revenues for the uses of the government, | protection to labor and industry, | preservation of the home market, | and reciprocity | which will extend our foreign markets. | [Cheers] *Upon this platform we stand | and submit its declarations | to the sober and considerate judgment | of the American people.*

McKinley barely makes it into the *OED*, being quoted only once with an example, not the first, of *reunited*, from his 1896 presidential campaign: "We have demonstrated to the world that we are a **reunited** people."

Theodore Roosevelt

[1858–1919]
President 1901–09

Teddy Roosevelt is one of the language greats among American presidents. He has been celebrated in chapter 3 as the first of the Great Communicators and in chapter 7 as one of the great neologists. His patrician New York City accent has been covered in chapter 8. What's left for this final consideration?

It should certainly be mentioned that the familiar and beloved *teddy bear* owes not only its existence, but its name to him. The legend is that, on a hunting trip in Mississippi, President Roosevelt spared a bear cub rather than shooting it. That well-publicized act of kindness inspired a shopkeeper, Morris Michtom, to ask the president's permission to make toy stuffed bears and call them "Teddy's bears." The rest is history.

Before the rest, however, not all is history. The truth is that President Roosevelt went to Mississippi in November 1902 to try to end a border dispute between that state and Louisiana. After he finished that business, he did indeed go on a bear hunt. After several days of hunting in vain, his party's dogs found a bear near a water hole. Roosevelt's guide clubbed the bear and tied it to a tree for the president's convenience.

Declining this unsportsmanlike challenge, the president ordered the bear "put down" humanely. Cartoonist Clifford Berryman of the *Washington Post* took the opportunity to draw a sketch of Roosevelt turning his back on a bear held on a leash, with the caption, "Drawing the Line in Mississippi," referring to the border dispute as well as Roosevelt's refusal to shoot the bear. Soon the incident became transformed into the legend. Teddy bears were still going strong when they celebrated their recent centennial.

It should also be noted that, though Roosevelt doesn't quite match Jefferson as the leading neologist among presidents, he is the undisputed first among presidential neo-orthographists. That is, he alone among all presidents tried to change the way we spell words.

A poor speller himself, he was impressed with the work of the Simplified Spelling Board, an independent organization founded in March 1906 by philanthropist Andrew Carnegie. The first act of that board was to issue a pamphlet proposing simplified spellings for 300 words. A few months later, in August 1906 while Congress was on vacation, Roosevelt ordered the Government Printing Office to adopt those simplifications.

The changes were modest, including some already widely used in American English like *honor* for *honour* and *catalog* for *catalogue*. But the board also proposed, and Roosevelt ordered, more drastic changes, including *tho* for *though* and *thru* for *through*. In his letter to the public printer on August 27, 1906, Roosevelt explained that "the slight changes in the spelling of the three hundred words . . . represent nothing in the world but a very slight extension of the unconscious movement which has made agricultural implement makers and farmers write *plow* instead of *plough*. . . . It is merely an attempt to cast what slight weight can properly be cast on the side of the popular forces which are endeavoring to make our spelling a little less foolish and fantastic."

To Roosevelt's surprise, this proposal met with immediate outrage. Both Congress and the Supreme Court refused to allow the GPO to use the simplifications with their publications.

Roosevelt's Annual Message to Congress of December 3, 1906, delivered as usual in writing, was a last-ditch effort to keep the simplified spellings. Its final paragraph has two of them:

> *The Congress has most wisely provided for a National Board for the promotion of rifle* practise. . . . *We should establish shooting*

galleries in all the large public and military schools, should maintain national target ranges in different parts of the country, and should in every way encourage the formation of rifle clubs thruout *all parts of the land.*

But on December 13, 1906, Roosevelt gave up and rescinded the order to the public printer. Aware that this reform was futile and would cost him politically, Teddy never brought it up again.

Good to the Last Drop

One final Roosevelt legend. Supposedly, in 1907 while visiting the Hermitage in Nashville, Andrew Jackson's home, TR was served coffee from the Maxwell House Hotel, also in Nashville. Supposedly Teddy said it was "good to the last drop." This of course became the slogan of the Maxwell House brand that went nationwide in the 1920s. The authenticity of the story was said to have been vouched for by a witness who later became president of the Tennessee Historical Society.

It might be wise to take that legend with a drop of coffee. The *Nashville Banner* for October 23, 1907, reported that Roosevelt did indeed ask for coffee while at the Hermitage, but it didn't mention which brand, and it recorded him as saying, "This is the kind of stuff I like, by George, when I hunt bears."

William H. Taft

[1857–1930]
President 1909–13

As chapter 3 explains, Taft was better adapted to the modern era of communicators than his opponent in the 1908 election, William Jennings Bryan, who still kept to the old-fashioned oratorical style. As chapter 8 mentions, Taft spoke with an *r*-ful Ohio accent.

Maybe Taft's modernity was a necessity. Although he did give numerous speeches, his voice was a constant concern. As far back as 1907, while he was still vice president, he described in a letter the medical attention he sought for his voice: "Before delivering my address I went to consult Dr. Dean, a throat specialist, who blew me out as Dr. Richardson does. I fancy these fellows put some cocaine in their treatment." During the 1908 campaign he required repeated treatments by his Dr. Richardson.

In the fall of 1909, his first year as president, he traveled around the country making more speeches and losing his voice. He wrote about an October appearance in Houston: "The speaking platform was too high above the people, and the number of them was so great and my effort to make them hear so strenuous, that I strained my vocal cords, and haven't yet recovered their use." In St. Louis two days later, after making several speeches earlier in the day, he noted that, "My voice was in such condition as to make what I said very short and very formal and perfunctory."

As chapter 3 also notes, Taft was no match for the speaking abilities of his two opponents in 1912, Theodore Roosevelt and the victor, Woodrow Wilson. Taft was capable and fluent, but far from brilliant. Much later, in 1953, acerbic political columnist Westbrook Pegler remarked that William Howard Taft was "a dismal flop . . . when he tried to contend with Theodore Roosevelt as a phrasemaker." According to Pegler, Taft came up with "something like 'moneyfuggler,' seeming to mean an obfuscationist."

For whatever reason, nothing by Taft appears in the *Oxford English Dictionary.*

Woodrow Wilson

[1856–1924]
President 1913–21

Wilson was a man of letters: Ph.D. in particular—the only president
so far to have earned a doctorate. His was from the Johns
Hopkins University in Baltimore. His undergraduate degree was from
the College of New Jersey (known today as Princeton), to which he
returned in later years as professor of political science and then president. He was a Southerner, from Virginia, but far from the Tidewater
area of the first presidents; his birthplace and early home was Staunton,
in the Shenandoah Valley in the shadow of the Appalachians. As chapter 8 explains, that kept his speech *r*-ful though aristocratic.

His letters and speeches were typed—in itself not an innovation for a
president long after the invention of the typewriter, but he insisted on
typing them himself, at least at first.

Wilson was a capable speaker, less burdened by academic jargon
than one might think. Among his most persuasive and eloquent
speeches was his war message to Congress of April 2, 1917, in which he
asked for a declaration of war against Germany in response to that
country's unrestrained submarine warfare on neutral nations. There he
stated the famous goal of making the world safe for democracy:

We are glad, now that we see the facts with no veil of false pretense about them, to fight thus for the ultimate peace of the world and for the liberation of its peoples, the German peoples included: for the rights of nations great and small and the privilege of men everywhere to choose their way of life and of obedience. The world must be made safe for democracy. Its peace must be planted upon the tested foundations of political liberty. We have no selfish ends to serve. We desire no conquest, no dominion. We seek no indemnities for ourselves, no material compensation for the sacrifices we shall freely make. We are but one of the champions of the rights of mankind. We shall be satisfied when those rights have been made as secure as the faith and the freedom of nations can make them. . . .

America First

Wilson provides first evidence for two entries in the *Oxford English Dictionary*. He is the first cited for the slogan *America First*, in a 1915 speech while he still was keeping America out of the world war: "I am not speaking in a selfish spirit when I say that our whole duty for the present, at any rate, is summed up in this motto, 'America First.' Let us think of America before we think of Europe, in order that America may be fit to be Europe's friend when the day of tested friendship comes." The motto had legs; in the 1930s it became the slogan and name of a movement opposed to American involvement in World War II.

A much less momentous innovation is Wilson's earlier use of *capitalistically* (1889), the *OED*'s first instance for that word: "Churches are spiritually convenient; joint-stock companies are **capitalistically** convenient."

The Story of Okeh

Wilson was an *okeh* president. By using that spelling for *OK*, and by being a learned college president with a Ph.D., he imparted respectability to what had been a slang term. As the entry for Martin Van Buren explains, *OK* was invented back in 1839 by a Boston newspaper editor during a season of supposedly comic abbreviations; *OK* was a funny, totally misspelled way of abbreviating *all correct*. The term escaped oblivion the next year when Old Kinderhook's campaign sponsored "OK Clubs" in his vain attempt for reelection.

But *OK* limped along for the rest of the nineteenth century, shunned for whatever reason not only by many respectable writers, but even by famous users of slang like Mark Twain. Perhaps its origin was too humble and absurd. But by the time Wilson became president, the true origin of *OK* had been lost, not to be rediscovered until researcher Allen Walker Read published a famous series of articles in the 1960s. By Wilson's time many theories of the origin of *OK* had appeared, including a claim by a professor of English at the University of Alabama in the *Magazine of American History* for 1885 that it came from the Choctaw Indian language. He gave it the spelling *okeh*, and this was the one Wilson adopted. According to the published memoir of Wilson's widow, Edith, in 1939,

[The president] *would sit down beside his green-shaded lamp and take up one paper after another—and so work until the small hours. Approval was designated by "Okeh, W.W." on the margin of a paper. Someone asked why he did not use the "O.K." "Because it is wrong," Mr. Wilson said. He suggested that the inquirer look up "okeh" in a dictionary. This he did, discovering that it is a Choctaw word meaning "It is so."*

Warren G. Harding

[1865–1923]
President 1921–23

He had served less than one full term as president before he died, but he made such a mark that any way you look at presidential language, it's hard not to think of Warren G. Harding. As chapter 2 explains, Harding deserves notice for coming in as an orator when the age of oratory was over, so that his bloviations were the subject of mirth (or exasperation) rather than admiration. As chapter 6 explains, he was indeed a bloviator, but an intentional one, not a blunderer. As chapter 7 explains, he could count that word, *bloviate*, to his credit, as well as *normalcy* and *hospitalization*—for popularizing them, at any rate, though not for their first use. As chapter 8 explains, Harding was an *r*-ful Ohioan, and one who would emphasize every syllable of some words.

He has been such an amiable companion throughout the first part of this book that little is left to remark on here. We'll just give him one last opportunity to bloviate on "Liberty Under the Law," from a phonograph record of a short speech he made under that title. The speech is so grandly generic that a politician seeking platitudes to unite all Americans could easily employ it today with at most a minor change or two, if the politician wished to go against the current fashion of favoring diversity.

> *My countrymen, the menacing tendency of the present day is not chargeable wholly to the unsettled and feverish conditions caused by the war. The manifest weakness in popular government lies in the temptation to appeal to group citizenship for political advantage. There is no greater peril. The Constitution contemplates no class and recognizes no group. It broadly includes all the people with specific recognition for none, and the highest consecration we can make today is a committal of the Republican party to that saving constitutionalism which contemplates all America as one people and holds just government free from influence on the one hand, and unmoved by intimidation on the other.*

Calvin Coolidge

[1872–1933]
President 1923–29

From the outset, the young man from the hamlet of Plymouth Notch, Vermont, was recognized as a good speaker. Chosen as the student speaker at his Black River Academy commencement in 1890, he praised "Oratory in History." When he graduated from Amherst College in 1895, he was chosen to give the Grove Oration on behalf of his classmates.

His reputation as "Silent Cal" may have derived from his declaration while serving as vice president that "it is my duty to uphold the policies and actions of the administration one hundred percent," so that "when I cannot conscientiously agree with them, it is then my duty to keep silent." He enjoyed that epithet, but in fact he is said to have made more speeches than any previous president and was the first to make regular radio addresses.

Coolidge also continued Harding's practice of twice-weekly press conferences, though he insisted that they be off the record and was careful not to say anything worth recording.

But he didn't waste words. Silent Cal was known for his short pithy remarks rather than long drawn-out sentences. And it is said that he was the last president to write his own speeches. Here is a sample, the ending of a speech at Arlington National Cemetery in May 1924:

> *A mightier force than ever followed Grant or Lee has leveled both their hosts, raised up an united Nation, and made us all partakers of a new glory. It is not for us to forget the past but to remember it, that we may profit by it. But it is gone; we cannot change it. We must put our emphasis on the present and put into effect the lessons the past has taught us. All about us sleep, those of many different beliefs and many divergent actions. But America claims them all. Her flag floats over them all. Her Government protects them all. They all rest in the same divine peace.*

His reputation for New England thriftiness and laconicness was reinforced by his strong New England accent described in chapter 8.

The *Oxford English Dictionary* is silent about Coolidge's contributions to the English language. If it were a compendium of his short sharp wit instead of a dictionary, Coolidge couldn't be overlooked, although he was so deadpan that he was often misunderstood. Will Rogers, rather noted for humor himself, said that Coolidge "wasted more humor on folks than almost anybody." Two examples: When more money was urged for military aviation, Coolidge told his cabinet, "Why can't we just buy one airplane and have all the pilots take turns?" It was a joke—but some took him seriously. And his comment about a criticism of him that appeared in H. L. Mencken's waspish magazine *The American Mercury*: "You mean that one in the magazine with the green cover? I started to read it, but it was against me, so I didn't finish it."

Herbert C. Hoover

[1874–1964]
President 1929–33

L ong before he became president, Herbert Hoover's name was a
household word. A verb, in fact: to *hooverize*. It was coined at the
height of World War I in 1917 when Hoover, already known as the
Great Engineer and the Great Humanitarian, was appointed by President Wilson to the wartime position of United States food administra-
tor. He had organized relief for starving Belgium during the earlier
days of the war; now he took measures to make sure that Americans
would eat frugally to conserve the food supply for the war effort. Slo-
gans like "Do Not Help the Hun at Meal Time" got the point across. In
June 1917, one H. B. Gross, writing in the *New York Tribune*, suggested
that, since Hoover had "exhorted the public to exercise the utmost
economy in the use of foodstuffs . . . 'to Hooverize' be universally
adopted as expressing the assistance every one of us . . . can render in
that direction."

And Americans indeed hooverized their way through the war years,
planting War Gardens in their back yards, observing "Meatless Mon-
days" and "Wheatless Wednesdays"—and eating "liberty cabbage"
rather than sauerkraut.

While Hoover was president, another word using his name entered the vocabulary: *Hooverball*. This was a game invented by his White House physician to give the president an opportunity to exercise. It used a soft six-pound medicine ball, to be caught and immediately returned over a net as in volleyball, with scoring as in tennis. Every morning except Sundays during Hoover's presidency, from 7 a.m. till a nearby factory whistle blew at 7:30, Hoover and a half dozen or so of his "Medicine Ball Cabinet" would play Hooverball outdoors, regardless of the weather. When Hoover left the White House in 1933, the sport seemingly came to an end. But in 1988 it was revived for a National Hooverball Championship, now played every year as part of Hooverfest in Hoover's hometown of West Branch, Iowa.

The early 1930s brought the third and least flattering of the Hoover words: *Hooverville*. The Depression was at its height. People evicted from their homes lived in collections of makeshift shacks on the edges of towns called *Hoovervilles* in sarcastic reference to the president, who had declared in 1930 that "the Depression is over" and "nobody is actually starving," and who opposed involving the federal government in providing relief. There were other, shorter-lived Hoover namesakes: "Hoover blankets" were newspapers; "Hoover wagons" were old automobiles pulled by mules; "Hoover Pullmans" were empty railroad boxcars. And "Hoover flags" were empty pants pockets pulled out.

The Rugged Individual

Before he entered politics, Hoover had a long, distinguished career as an engineer. One of the two words in the *Oxford English Dictionary* for which he provides the earliest citation is *resuing*, which means removing the rock next to a vein of ore before mining the ore, used in his 1909 book *Principles of Mining*. He was neither the inventor of the technique nor the namer of it, however.

More relevant to Hoover the politician and statesman is his other first quotation in the *OED*. In a famous campaign speech on October 22, 1928, Hoover coined the phrase *rugged individualism*, which has resonated ever since for better or worse:

> *When the war closed, the most vital of all issues both in our own*
> *country and throughout the world was whether governments should*

continue their wartime ownership and operation of many instrumentalities of production and distribution. We were challenged with a peace-time choice between the American system of rugged individualism and a European philosophy of diametrically opposed doctrines of paternalism and state socialism. The acceptance of these ideas would have meant the destruction of self-government through centralization of government. It would have meant the undermining of the individual initiative and enterprise through which our people have grown to unparalleled greatness.

There isn't much to say about Herbert Hoover's pronunciation. He was an *r*-ful Iowan who grew up in *r*-ful Oregon with little that was remarkable about his accent. Nor was he remarkable as a speaker.

It has been said that Hoover "mumbled his dry words in a monotone." Judging from the recordings of his voice, "mumbled" is unfair. He articulates clearly. Nor does he stumble over his words. But "monotone" hardly does justice to the tone of his voice. The pitch is so level that he almost seems to be chanting, with a brief upturn or downturn at the end of a statement. In the midst of his statements there are occasional strange pauses, as if he were more concerned with catching his breath than with what he had to say. For example, in a radio speech from Elko, Nevada, at the close of the election campaign on November 7, 1932, he said in his monotone: "The action of our nation has been—(pause)—modified and benefited by the enfranchisement of women."

Still, his speeches were well engineered. He had nice things to say in his monotonous way. That election eve speech concludes:

Four years ago I stated that I conceived the presidency as more than an administrative office. It is a power for leadership bringing coordination of the forces of business and cultural life in every city and town and countryside. The presidency is more than an executive responsibility; it is a symbol of America's highest purpose. The president must represent the nation's ideals. He must also represent them to the nations of the world. After four years of experience, I still regard this as a supreme obligation.

Franklin D. Roosevelt

[1882–1945]
President 1933–45

Franklin Roosevelt has already made an appearance in chapter 3 as one of the twentieth century's great presidential communicators. He was also the last of the presidents with a patrician New York accent, as chapter 8 explains. There aren't likely to be more, because that accent is practically extinct.

FDR qualifies as a great presidential communicator not only for his innovative use of radio, but also for his virtuosity in older forms of public speaking. With help from excellent speechwriters, his inaugural addresses (and he had four of them, twice as many as any other president) introduced memorable phrases and phrasing. The first inaugural (1933) included the famous declaration, ". . . the only thing we have to fear is fear itself—nameless, unreasoning, unjustified terror which paralyzes needed efforts to convert retreat into advance." The second, third, and fourth all included hypnotic repetition of introductory phrases:

> *In this nation I see tens of millions of its citizens, a substantial part of its whole population, who at this very moment are denied the greater part of what the very lowest standards of today call the necessities of life.*

I see millions of families trying to live on incomes so meager that the pall of family disaster hangs over them day by day.

I see millions. . . . [three more times]

I see one-third of a nation ill-housed, ill-clad, ill-nourished. [second inaugural, 1937]

Democracy is not dying.

We know it because we have seen it revive and grow.

We know it cannot die because it is built on the unhampered initiative of individual men and women joined together in a common enterprise—an enterprise undertaken and carried through by the free expression of a free majority.

We know it because. . . . [three more times] [third inaugural, 1941]

And so today, in this year of war, 1945, we have learned lessons at a fearful cost and we shall profit by them.

We have learned. . . . [three more times] [fourth inaugural, 1945]

Cheerleader for the New Deal

Franklin Roosevelt provides more twentieth-century first quotations for the *Oxford English Dictionary* than any other president except his fifth cousin and role model, Theodore. Surprisingly, his earliest is the first *OED* example of *cheerleader*, from a 1903 letter: "I was one of the three **cheer leaders** in the Brown game."

And the good sport also has the first *OED* example of a figurative use of *scoreboard*, in a 1936 interview in the *New York Herald Tribune*: "From where I stand it looks as if the game was pretty well in the bag. . . . It's just plain **scoreboard** arithmetic. . . . Now, when the present management of your team took charge in 1933 the national **scoreboard** looked pretty bad." It wasn't the first use of *scoreboard*—the *OED* has examples going back to 1826—but the earlier examples are literal. Roosevelt put a spin on it, as well as a winning score.

Another word whose meaning FDR stretched is *Teapot Dome*. It is the name of a scandal during the Harding administration, mostly revealed after Harding's death. The *OED* quotes Roosevelt using it in 1936 as a generic name for a scandal, much as the suffix *-gate* from

Watergate would serve later in the century: "In spite of all the demand for speed, the complexity of the problem and all the vast sums of money involved, we have had no **Teapot Dome.**"

In a 1937 statement, Roosevelt provides the first *OED* example of *pump-priming* in the sense that government should spend money to get the economy going: "The things we had done, which at that time were largely a monetary and **pump-priming** policy for two years and a half, had brought the expected result, perfectly definitely."

Strangely enough, his is also the earliest example (1942) of *lift* referring to the capacity of an airlift. Winston Churchill quotes Roosevelt in his history of the Second World War: "The following shipping can be made available by the United States: . . . Transports, other than combat leaders, with a **lift** of 52,000 men."

More memorable were Roosevelt's ringing phrases. In his first inaugural address of 1933, Roosevelt announced a *good neighbor policy* towards Latin America. He wasn't the first to use the common phrase *good neighbor* in relation to Latin America; Herbert Hoover had used it himself back in 1928. After winning the election that year, Hoover made a point of visiting Latin America. While he was in Honduras he declared, "We have a desire to maintain not only the cordial relations of governments with each other but also the relations of **good neighbors.**"

Roosevelt took that notion and made it a policy. He explained it in a speech to the Pan American Union on April 12, 1933:

> *In my inaugural address I stated that I would "dedicate this Nation to the* **policy** *of the* **good** **neighbor**—*the neighbor who resolutely respects himself and, because he does so, respects the rights of others—the neighbor who respects his obligations and respects the sanctity of his agreements in and with a world of neighbors." Never before has the significance of the words* "**good** **neighbor**" *been so manifest in international relations. Never have the need and benefit of neighborly cooperation in every form of human activity been so evident as they are today.*

Even more famous as a Roosevelt slogan was *new deal*. Such a common phrase was hardly new; it has been easy to find earlier examples that go back as far as 1837. But Roosevelt made it memorable in his acceptance speech at the Democratic National Convention in 1932: "I pledge you—I pledge myself—to a **new deal** for the American people." It caught on so well that after he was elected his policies became known as the *New Deal.*

One more Rooseveltian phrase was the *four freedoms* announced in his January 1941 State of the Union address:

> *In the future days, which we seek to make secure, we look forward to a world founded upon* **four** *essential human* **freedoms.**
>
> *The first is freedom of speech and expression—everywhere in the world.*
>
> *The second is freedom of every person to worship God in his own way—everywhere in the world.*
>
> *The third is freedom from want—which, translated into world terms, means economic understandings which will secure to every nation a healthy peacetime life for its inhabitants—everywhere in the world.*
>
> *The fourth is freedom from fear—which, translated into world terms, means a world-wide reduction of armaments to such a point and in such a thorough fashion that no nation will be in a position to commit an act of physical aggression against any neighbor—anywhere in the world.*

And when America went to war, President Roosevelt even renamed the time. As *Time* magazine reported in its issue of February 9, 1942: "Franklin Roosevelt decided what he will call wartime daylight saving when it starts next week. Official name: War Time."

Harry S. Truman

[1884–1972]
President 1945–53

Harry Truman, our only president from Missouri, deservedly stars in chapter 5 as the one truly down-to-earth president. But he was truly unimpressive in formal speeches, especially in the early years of his presidency. He had an awkward reading style, sometimes going to the extreme of sounding out each syllable separately. Robert G. Nixon, White House correspondent for the International News Service, recalled in an interview at the Truman Library:

> *When they got to the White House, they got a voice tutor for him. Everything got fouled up. They were trying to make a President Roosevelt speaker out of what the president called "a Missouri clodhopper," which was impossible. It just didn't go over. When he would read his speeches to Congress, it became obvious that this wouldn't work. If he was going to be an effective speaker, he would have to be let alone to be himself.*

Finally, in June 1948 during his whistle-stop campaign, Truman was indeed let alone to be himself. The interview continues:

> *Truman began to just talk. He spoke, in contrast to the conscious reading of words that were not his words at all. As I say, he began to talk, instead of orating. He used his Missouri dialect. He became natural in every way. . . .*
>
> *It took a little time for it to happen, but it gradually came into being. It happened even in his prepared speeches like the ones at Berkeley and Los Angeles. He began to deliver them in a natural manner, rather than like a schoolboy making a classroom oration of the Gettysburg speech. . . . At times he simply tore up the set speech that he had prepared for him by his staff, and made his own speech right off the top of his head. When he did that he was most effective of all, because he was just saying what he wanted to say. He was dealing with subject matter that was in his own mind. He was particularly good later when he began to tear into the 80th Republican Congress.*

Truman wasn't so bad at news conferences, where he could be plain and direct. But he had a problem there too, according to Robert Nixon:

> *We get back again to these Missouri mannerisms and dialect, his proneness to use direct sentences with a maximum of ten words. Sometimes he just said "yes" or "no." Rarely did he ever develop a subject. . . . It was just: "No, they're not going to get it." We had to go with the rest.*

Truman relished denouncing his enemies, often employing his pet abbreviation *s.o.b.*, if not the fully spelled out phrase. A man he found truly worthy of his denunciation was Richard Nixon. One of Truman's typical comments about Nixon was, "I don't think the son of a bitch knows the difference between telling the truth and lying."

The Buck Stops with Harry

For all his plain speaking, Truman made his mark in the *Oxford English Dictionary*. He is credited there for the phrase *fair deal*, which he included in his State of the Union address in 1949: "I hope for cooperation from farmers, from labor, and from business. Every segment of our population and every individual has a right to expect from our Government a fair deal." This first use of the phrase had only its ordinary meaning, but *Fair Deal* soon became the name for Truman's programs, just as *New Deal* had been for his predecessor, Franklin Roosevelt.

Shortly before that State of the Union address, in his one inaugural address in January 1949, Truman made a number of specific proposals. The fourth soon became a full-fledged program that was called *Point Four*. In that speech also, Truman provides the first *OED* example of *underdeveloped* referring to the less prosperous regions of the world:

> *Fourth, we must embark on a bold new program for making the benefits of our scientific advances and industrial progress available for the improvement and growth of* **underdeveloped** *areas.*
>
> *More than half the people of the world are living in conditions approaching misery. Their food is inadequate. They are victims of disease. Their economic life is primitive and stagnant. Their poverty is a handicap and a threat both to them and to more prosperous areas.*

But formal speaking is not what people remember about "Give 'em hell Harry." He was noted for his earthy plain speaking in conversation and on the campaign trail. The other *OED* citations of Truman are words of this kind. Truman gets *OED* credit for earliest use of *The buck stops here* from a 1952 speech at the National War College: "You know, it's easy for the Monday morning quarterback to say what the coach should have done, after the game is over. But when the decision is up before you—and on my desk I have a motto which says '**The Buck Stops Here**'—the decision has to be made." The Truman Library in Independence, Missouri, has that sign on display. It was made in a prison in Oklahoma and sent by a friend to Truman in October 1945.

The *OED* also uses Truman as first evidence for two humorous deliberate misspellings. Both are from private letters to his wife, Bess, written long before he became president but published long after he had been president, in 1983. One misspelling is the nickname for the mail-order retailer *Montgomery Ward* (1912): "Nor **Monkey Ward**'s nor the ten-cent store." A 1918 letter provides the first *OED* example of a humorous spelling of *melodrama*: "It was good old **mellerdramer**." It's very unlikely that Truman was the wit who invented either of these twists on familiar items, but even the new *Random House Historical Dictionary of American Slang* finds no earlier examples.

Down-to-earth Truman also provides the *OED* with a fistful of non-first examples: for *fifth wheel, pinhead, screwball, trickle-down, visiting fireman,* and *country jake,* the latter in a 1941 letter: "You'd think I was Cicero or Cato. But I'm not. Just a **country jake** who works at the job."

Dwight D. Eisenhower

[1890–1969]
President 1953–61

Like Truman, Dwight Eisenhower, of Kansas and of a military career, was plainspoken, but he wasn't as earthy. His vice president, Richard Nixon, could say of him with a straight face in his third 1960 television debate with John Kennedy:

> *And I can only say that I'm very proud that President Eisenhower restored dignity and decency and, frankly, good language to the conduct of the presidency of the United States.*

Chapter 6 exculpates Eisenhower from well-known charges of blundering. In fact, he was capable of a well-turned phrase more often than not. He spoke clearly and emphatically. But he was definitely in favor of plain speaking. Meena Bose and Fred I. Greenstein wrote in 2002:

> *In working with his speechwriters on public addresses, he chose language that was at once elevated and simple. As he put it in a prepresidential cabinet review of his 1953 inaugural address, "I deliberately tried to stay at the level of talk that would make as good reading as possible at the Quai d'Orsay or at No. 10 Downing," but that also "would sound good to the fellow digging the ditch in Kansas."*

Ex-general Eisenhower has four firsts in the *Oxford English Dictionary*. The earliest, in a 1946 report, is the first example of *killing ground:* "Allied guns ringed the ever-shrinking '**killing-ground**' and . . . the ordinary German infantry gave themselves up in ever-increasing numbers." Another non-*OED* source predates that with a 1944 quotation, but still Eisenhower's: "The battle of Falaise will be the greatest **killing-ground** of the war."

As president, Eisenhower provided the first *OED* evidence for the *domino theory*, the theory that if one country should fall to Communist rule, others would follow. It was in a *New York Times* article in 1954: "You had broader considerations that might follow what you might call the '**falling domino**' principle. You had a row of dominoes set up, and you knocked over the first one, and what would happen to the last one was the certainty that it would go over very quickly."

Someone in the State Department apparently invented *counterpro-ductive*, but it was Ike who introduced it to the world at large in a press conference on August 3, 1959: "The holding of a summit meeting . . . would be . . . absolutely impractical and as the State Department says, **counterproductive**." Two years later an article in the *Minneapolis Tribune* encapsulated its subsequent success, at a time when it was still new enough to require explanation: " '**Counter-productive**' was first used, so far as memory goes, by President Eisenhower in a press conference. Then GOP chairman Thruston Morton picked it up and used it a few times. Now Bundy. '**Counter-productive**' means unwise, worse than useless, contra-indicated, and lousy."

Eisenhower's most famous coinage was *military-industrial complex*, first spoken in his farewell address of January 17, 1961. (In this case, as in so many others, the coinage actually came from a speechwriter. The author of this one was Malcolm Moos.) Eisenhower's use of *industrial-military* slightly later in the speech indicates that the phrase wasn't thought of as a special coinage in this initial use. The context of the phrase is a warning that has not been heeded since:

> *Until the latest of our world conflicts, the United States had no ar-maments industry. American makers of plowshares could, with time and as required, make swords as well. But now we can no longer risk emergency improvisation of national defense; we have been compelled to create a permanent armaments industry of vast proportions. Added*

to this, three and a half million men and women are directly engaged in the defense establishment. We annually spend on military security more than the net income of all United States corporations.

This conjunction of an immense military establishment and a large arms industry is new in the American experience. The total influence—economic, political, even spiritual—is felt in every city, every statehouse, every office of the federal government. We recognize the imperative need for this development. Yet we must not fail to comprehend its grave implications. Our toil, resources and livelihood are all involved; so is the very structure of our society.

In the councils of government, we must guard against the acquisition of unwarranted influence, whether sought or unsought, by the **military-industrial** complex. The potential for the disastrous rise of misplaced power exists and will persist.

We must never let the weight of this combination endanger our liberties or democratic processes. We should take nothing for granted. Only an alert and knowledgeable citizenry can compel the proper meshing of the huge industrial and military machinery of defense with our peaceful methods and goals, so that security and liberty may prosper together.

Akin to, and largely responsible for the sweeping changes in our **industrial-military** posture, has been the technological revolution during recent decades. . . .

John F. Kennedy

[1917–63]
President 1961–63

John F. Kennedy had that Boston accent. But, as former U.S. Representative Ken Hechler recalled of the 1960 Democratic primary in
West Virginia,

> *Many of the national media felt that since West Virginia was 95 per-*
> *cent Protestant, we would follow the practice that we had recorded in*
> *1928 when we refused to back Alfred E. Smith, who was running for*
> *president, because of his Catholicism. Of course, there was a tremen-*
> *dous lot of personal difference between Al Smith and John F.*
> *Kennedy. John F. Kennedy looked like an average person, whereas Al*
> *Smith looked like an eastside New Yorker and spoke like an East Side*
> *New Yorker. Kennedy's Boston accent never seemed to hurt him here*
> *in West Virginia.*

A gifted communicator, skilled debater, charismatic—what can't be said
about John Kennedy as a speaker? Well, he wasn't an orator. Not because
he couldn't be, but because oratory wasn't the style of the later twentieth
century—or of the earlier, for that matter, as Warren G. Harding had

demonstrated by his bloviating. An oration builds an argument; a modern communication makes points. Kennedy made brilliant points.

His greatest speeches were ones he wrote in collaboration with Theodore Sorensen. Looking back, Sorensen summarized:

> *Our chief criterion was always audience comprehension and comfort, and this meant: (1) short speeches, short clauses and short words, wherever possible; (2) a series of points or propositions in numbered or logical sequence, wherever appropriate; and (3) the construction of sentences, phrases and paragraphs in such a manner as to simplify, clarify and emphasize.*
>
> *The test of a text was not how it appeared to the eye, but how it sounded to the ear. His best paragraphs, when read aloud, often had a cadence not unlike blank verse—indeed at times key words would rhyme. He was fond of alliterative sentences, not solely for reasons of rhetoric but to reinforce the audience's recollection of his reasoning.*

Here too Sorensen focuses on "points or propositions," not overall argument.

The Missile Gap

Kennedy is represented with three firsts in the *Oxford English Dictionary*. Two of them have to do with the nuclear threat in the Cold War.

He made the *missile gap* a political issue, starting with a dramatic speech in the U.S. Senate in 1958. The gap was the supposed deficit of U.S. nuclear warheads compared with those of the Soviet Union. His 1958 speech is the first example for the term in the *OED* and probably also the actual first use of it: "Our Nation could have afforded, and can afford now, the steps necessary to close the **missile gap**." Two years later he made the missile gap a major theme of his successful campaign for the presidency, though after he had been in office for a year or two he decided that the gap had never existed.

Another nuclear term for which Kennedy provides the first *OED* example is *megatonnage*. In 1962 he stated, "When we start to talk about the **megatonnage** we could bring into a nuclear war, we are talking about annihilation."

The other Kennedy first in the *OED* is just the abbreviation of a name in 1961—*A.I.D.*, standing for the new *Agency for International Development* that was created at the start of his administration.

The *OED* pays Kennedy some attention for other words too. His words are used as examples, though not the first, for *head count, menace, minister* (in government), (diplomatic) *mission, moon*—all of them recent additions in the third edition of the *OED*. Other Kennedy quotations, also not first, appear in *OED* entries for *dedication, as far as, Territorial Army*, and even the basic word *safe*.

Lyndon B. Johnson

[1908–73]
President 1963–69

L yndon Johnson of west Texas was a master politician and a fairly
good speaker. Actually, he could be great at campaign speeches
before live audiences, where he either knew his text by heart or spoke
completely extemporaneously, as he did in a fiery speech for civil rights
to a New Orleans audience during the 1964 presidential campaign.
With formal speeches he sometimes struggled. But he could also rise to
the occasion, as with his March 1965 speech to a joint session of Congress demanding voting rights legislation:

> *At times history and fate meet at a single time in a single place to
> shape a turning point in man's unending search for freedom. So it
> was at Lexington and Concord. So it was a century ago at Appomat-
> tox. So it was last week in Selma, Alabama. There, long-suffering
> men and women peacefully protested the denial of their rights as
> Americans. Many were brutally assaulted. One good man, a man of
> God, was killed.*
>
> *There is no cause for pride in what has happened in Selma. There
> is no cause for self-satisfaction in the long denial of equal rights of*

millions of Americans. But there is cause for hope and for faith in our democracy in what is happening here tonight. . . .

There is no Negro problem. There is no Southern problem. There is no Northern problem. There is only an American problem. . . .

Many of the issues of civil rights are very complex and most diffi-cult. But about this there can and should be no argument. Every American citizen must have an equal right to vote. . . .

As might be expected, this major address was written in the first instance by a speechwriter—in this case, Richard Goodwin. But it included very personal remarks by LBJ:

My first job after college was as a teacher in Cotulla, Texas, in a small Mexican-American school. Few of them could speak English, and I couldn't speak much Spanish. My students were poor and they often came to class without breakfast, hungry. They knew even in their youth the pain of prejudice. They never seemed to know why people disliked them. But they knew it was so, because I saw it in their eyes. I often walked home late in the afternoon, after the classes were finished, wishing there was more that I could do. But all I knew was to teach them the little that I knew, hoping that it might help them against the hardships that lay ahead. Somehow you never for-get what poverty and hatred can do when you see its scars on the hopeful face of a young child.

He concluded by asking his former colleagues to do him and the coun-try a favor:

And so at the request of your beloved speaker and the senator from Montana; the majority leader, the senator from Illinois; the minority leader, Mr. McCulloch, and other members of both parties, I came here tonight—not as President Roosevelt came down one time in person to veto a bonus bill, not as President Truman came down one time to urge the passage of a railroad bill—but I came down here to ask you to share this task with me and to share it with the people that we both work for. I want this to be the Congress, Republicans and Democrats alike, which did all these things for all these people. . .

The *Oxford English Dictionary* is much more fond of Johnson's wife, Lady Bird, identified in the dictionary as "Mrs. L. B. Johnson," than it is of the president himself. A reader for that dictionary must have decided that her *White House Diary*, published in 1970, would be a good source of contemporary usage, because the *OED* includes more than 200 quotations from that book. In most cases they are not the first evidence but rather modern examples of the words in context.

Lady Bird does provide, however, the earliest *OED* example for *advance* meaning an advance briefing (1968): "I knew that I was about to go home by car for a fifteen-minute **advance** before the press arrived at the Ranch on the bus." Hers is also the first *OED* evidence for the verb *to motorcade* (1965; the noun goes back to 1913): "We **motorcaded** into Madison Square Garden—the streets lined with cheering people." And her diary gives the *OED* its first example of *porta-crib* (1969): "On the last trip [on Air Force One] I must be sure to take off . . . Patrick Lyn's **porta-crib**."

Finally, of all things, she provides the first *OED* example for *Strategic Arms Limitation Talks* (SALT, 1968): "When and where the talks would start, we do not know. They are being referred to as **Strategic Arms Limitation Talks.**"

LBJ himself has a grand total of two appearances in the *OED*. He provides the first example for *training program* (1971): "Our manpower **training programs** focused on preparing unskilled men and women for jobs." And Lyndon Johnson also provides an example of *aboard*, but by no means the first.

Richard M. Nixon

[1913–94]
President 1969–74

R ichard Nixon, with his unremarkable *r*-ful California accent, was a skilled debater even in high school. He had his lapses, as in the first presidential debate with John Kennedy in 1960, discussed in chapter 3, but more often than not he won the argument.

Until he became president, he wrote his own speeches—or rather, for the most part, he wrote notes for them, then set the notes aside, because he got better audience response when he spoke without notes. When he became president he acquired some excellent speechwriters, including conservative Patrick Buchanan and witty William Safire, but he still would rework a speech into his own style. And for important presidential speeches he would read from a manuscript.

He preferred a plain style. This is evident in perhaps his most effective speech, the one he gave to a television audience on September 23, 1952, while he was the Republican candidate for vice president on the ticket with Eisenhower. In this speech he replied to charges that he had used a secret trust fund for personal expenses. His method was to offer full details of the fund, to show that it was neither secret nor personal. Not only that, he recounted his personal finances from his childhood to the present day, presenting himself as an honorable man of small means, using simple short statements:

> Well, that's about it. That's what we have. And that's what we owe. It isn't very much. But Pat and I have the satisfaction that every dime that we've got is honestly ours. I should say this, that Pat doesn't have a mink coat. But she does have a respectable Republican cloth coat, and I always tell her she'd look good in anything.

It's remembered as the "Checkers" speech because of the statement that immediately followed:

> One other thing I probably should tell you, because if I don't they'll probably be saying this about me, too. We did get something, a gift, after the election. A man down in Texas heard Pat on the radio mention the fact that our two youngsters would like to have a dog. And believe it or not, the day before we left on this campaign trip we got a message from Union Station in Baltimore, saying they had a package for us. We went down to get it. You know what it was? It was a little cocker spaniel dog, in a crate that he had sent all the way from Texas, black and white, spotted, and our little girl Tricia, the six-year-old, named it Checkers. And you know, the kids, like all kids, love the dog, and I just want to say this, right now, that regardless of what they say about it, we're gonna keep it. . . .

His speech brought tears to people's eyes, but that wasn't all of it. He also went on the offensive, pointing out the financial misdeeds of his Democratic opponents, and declaring that only his running mate could save the country from communism.

> And now, finally, I know that you wonder whether or not I am going to stay on the Republican ticket or resign. Let me say this: I don't believe that I ought to quit, because I'm not a quitter. And, incidentally, Pat's not a quitter. After all, her name was Patricia Ryan and she was born on St. Patrick's day, and you know the Irish never quit. But the decision, my friends, is not mine. I would do nothing that would harm the possibilities of Dwight Eisenhower to become President of the United States. . . .

The mixture of the intensely personal with the intensely political was characteristic of Nixon's whole career. He made famous remarks on other occasions, too. Perhaps his most famous came at the end of a 16-minute press conference on November 7, 1962, after he had lost the election for governor of California. He uttered a prophecy that subsequent events proved untrue:

> *Last point: I leave you gentlemen now; and you will now write it, you will interpret it, that's your right. But as I leave you, I want you to know* [chuckle]*—just think how much you're going to be missing. You won't have Nixon to kick around anymore, because, gentlemen, this is my last press conference. And it will be one in which I have welcomed the opportunity to test wits with you. I have always respected you, I have sometimes disagreed with you, but unlike some people, I have never canceled a subscription to a paper; and also, I never will. I believe in reading what my opponents say.*
>
> *And I hope that what I have said today will at least make television, radio, the press, first recognize the great responsibility they have to report all the news; and second, recognize that they have a right and a responsibility, if they're against a candidate, to give him the shaft; but also recognize that if they give him the shaft, put one lonely reporter on the campaign who will report what the candidate says now and then. Thank you, gentlemen, and good day.*

He had begun that press conference declaring, "I have no complaints about the press coverage; I will never complain about it."

That language and even the contradictory statements are typical for Nixon in conversation. Amidst dignified formal vocabulary and phrasing he inserts vigorous slang. In private, of course, as we know from the secret recordings made public during the Watergate investigation, Nixon had a facility for what would appear in printed transcripts as "(expletives deleted)."

On the Fast Track

Nixon provides the earliest evidence in the *Oxford English Dictionary* for *fast track* extended beyond its long-established reference to horse racing. Nixon's *fast track* innovation appeared in the *New York Times*

Magazine in 1965: "New York . . . is a place where you can't slow down—a fast track. Any person tends to vegetate unless he is moving on a fast track."

He also has the first example of *to scatter-gun* (1968), although *scattergun* the noun goes back to 1836: "If we scatter-gun too much we are not going to have an impact."

Quite a few other quotations from Nixon are in the *OED*, though not as first examples. He provides later examples for *audit, loose cannon, in spades, decommissioning, open (administration), tie-breaking, unsubtle, showerhead, toll-house cookies, wiretapper, workfare, welcome mat, worship service,* and *tape* (1978): "I was not comfortable with the idea of taping people without their knowledge." (But he did it anyhow.)

Gerald R. Ford

[1913–]
President 1974–77

Gerald Ford, the only president from Michigan, was appointed vice
president when Spiro Agnew resigned in disgrace, then became
president when Nixon resigned in disgrace. Ford made a point of avoid-
ing disgrace in his speeches and statements. In that he succeeded, but
in other respects he earned very honorable mention among the blunderers in chapter 6, where his speeches are discussed at length.

Because of his difficulties in pronouncing big words, Ford's speechwriters were given lists of words to avoid in his speeches. One such
word, according to former speechwriter Craig Smith, now a professor at
California State University, Long Beach, was *judgment*, which Ford pronounced "judge-uh-ment." But, Smith added, "The lists were confidential and not published," so we know only a few examples. Another,
according to James C. Humes, who also wrote speeches for Ford, was
nuclear, "in which he added an extra syllable. One wrote *atomic*
instead."

The *Oxford English Dictionary* picks up only one quotation from Ford,
the rather unremarkable abbreviation *NRC* for the U.S. Nuclear Regulatory Commission. When he signed the agency into law on October 11,

1974, Ford used the abbreviation several times: "NRC will be responsible for the licensing and regulation of the nuclear industry under the provisions of the Atomic Energy Act. This means that NRC will be fully empowered to see to it that reactors using nuclear materials will be properly and safely designed, constructed and operated to guarantee against hazards to the public from leakage or accident. NRC will also. . . ."

Jimmy Carter

[1924–]
President 1977–81

A true *r*-less Southerner from Georgia, Jimmy Carter wasn't the worst of speakers, but he was certainly not the best. In presidential campaign debates in 1976 he was able to outclass Gerald Ford, especially when Ford slipped up and declared, "There is no Soviet domination of Eastern Europe," but four years later he was no match for the Great Communicator, who knocked him out with a simple "There you go again." Carter had seemed in the catbird seat as he warned against the dangerous views of his challenger:

> *Governor Reagan, as a matter of fact, began his political career campaigning around this nation against Medicare. Now we have an opportunity to move toward national health insurance, with an emphasis on the prevention of disease, an emphasis on out-patient care, not in-patient care; an emphasis on hospital cost containment to hold down the cost of hospital care for those who are ill; an emphasis on catastrophic health insurance, so that if a family is threatened with being wiped out economically because of a very high medical bill, then the insurance would help pay for it. These are the kinds of elements of*

a national health insurance, important to the American people. Governor Reagan, again, typically is against such a proposal.

But Reagan nimbly replied, turning defense into attack:

There you go again. When I opposed Medicare, there was another piece of legislation meeting the same problem before the Congress. . . .

Carter attained a grim low point in presidential addresses with what became known as his "malaise speech" on July 15, 1979. Concerned about the energy crisis, he had met with a wide variety of national leaders at Camp David for ten days to determine what should be done. He wanted to rally the American people to heroic efforts to solve the crisis. Yet the speech soon ran off the tracks as he quoted statements from the people he had talked with:

This from a Southern governor: "Mr. President, you are not leading this nation—you're just managing the government."
"You don't see the people enough any more."
"Some of your Cabinet members don't seem loyal. There is not enough discipline among your disciples. . . ."
This rather summarized a lot of other statements: "Mr. President, we are confronted with a moral and a spiritual crisis."

What happened to the energy crisis? Well, he returned to it now and then, but he often veered away to declare, for example,

Our people are losing that faith, not only in government itself but in the ability as citizens to serve as the ultimate rulers and shapers of our democracy. . . .
One of the visitors to Camp David last week put it this way: "We've got to stop crying and start sweating, stop talking and start walking, stop cursing and start praying. The strength we need will not come from the White House, but from every house in America."

Carter finally did get around to declaring his new energy policies, to be established by that same government people were losing faith in. He ticked off point after point, six points in all. Here are a few:

Point one: . . . Beginning this moment, this nation will never use more foreign oil than we did in 1977—never. . . . I am tonight setting the further goal of cutting our dependence on foreign oil by one-half by the end of the next decade, a saving of over four and a half million barrels of imported oil per day.

Point two: To ensure that we meet these targets, I will use my presidential authority to set import quotas. I'm announcing tonight that for 1979 and 1980, I will forbid the entry into this country of one drop of foreign oil more than these goals allow. . . .

Point three: To give us energy security, I am asking for the most massive peacetime commitment of funds and resources in our nation's history to develop America's own alternative sources of fuel. . . . Moreover, I will soon submit legislation to Congress calling for the creation of this nation's first solar bank, which will help us achieve the crucial goal of 20 percent of our energy coming from solar power by the year 2000.

Carter wanted just a little sacrifice from the American people:

I ask Congress to give me authority for mandatory conservation and for standby gasoline rationing. To further conserve energy, I'm proposing tonight an extra $10 billion over the next decade to strengthen our public transportation systems. And I'm asking you for your good and for your nation's security to take no unnecessary trips, to use carpools or public transportation whenever you can, to park your car one extra day per week, to obey the speed limit, and to set your thermostats to save fuel. Every act of energy conservation like this is more than just common sense. I tell you, it is an act of patriotism.

All this for a government we didn't trust. His speech and his policies were a massive failure, though oil imports did in fact decline somewhat during the next decade before they rose again.

Carter's frustrated speechwriters said he didn't care much for speechwriters or public speaking, and it shows. "He just hates to use texts and he hates to practice to improve his delivery," according to speechwriter James Fallows. In fact, Carter distrusted anything but the plainest matter-of-fact language. His poem "On Using Words," published in 1994, concludes:

Now when I seek efficient words
to say what I believe is true
or have a dream I want to share
the vagueness is still there.

No words of Jimmy Carter's are in the *Oxford English Dictionary*.

Ronald Reagan

[1911–]
President 1981–89

In chapter 3, Ronald Reagan had his due as the Great Communicator; in chapter 9, as the Hollywood fantasy president made reality. How would an actor perform as president? people wondered during the 1980 campaign. Very well, as it turned out. His award-winning role was not in any of the 60 movies he made, but as president of the United States. And in an introduction to a recent book on presidential speechwriting, Martin J. Medhurst notes, "Reagan's own speechwriters have consistently credited him with being the foremost speechwriter in the White House."

What else? Well, he deserves recognition for an innovation in the venerable State of the Union address. By its very nature, the State of the Union inclines to the soporific, since the president needs to cover a laundry list of specific topics and issues. President Reagan found a way to wake up his audience. At the end of the speech, to a standing ovation, he introduced "heroes in the balcony": ordinary citizens who had performed heroic deeds, living embodiments of the American virtues of courage and initiative. Conveniently, they would be sitting with his family in the visitors' gallery. The first such introduction came at the end of his 1982 State of the Union:

Just two weeks ago, in the midst of a terrible tragedy [an airplane crash] *on the Potomac, we saw again the spirit of American heroism at its finest—the heroism of dedicated rescue workers saving crash victims from icy waters. And we saw the heroism of one of our young government employees, Lenny Skutnik, who, when he saw a woman lose her grip on the helicopter line, dived into the water and dragged her to safety.*

In his 1984 address, he not only named a hero, but addressed him directly:

Sergeant Stephen Trujillo, a medic in the Second Ranger Battalion, 75th Infantry, was in the first helicopter to land at the compound held by Cuban forces in Grenada. He saw three other helicopters crash. Despite the imminent explosion of the burning aircraft, he never hesitated. He ran across 25 yards of open terrain through enemy fire to rescue wounded soldiers. He directed two other medics, administered first aid, and returned again and again to the crash site to carry his wounded friends to safety.

Sergeant Trujillo, you and your fellow service men and women not only saved innocent lives; you set a nation free. You inspire us as a force for freedom, not for despotism; and, yes, for peace, not conquest. God bless you.

He doubled the number in his 1985 State of the Union, introducing both a young refugee from Vietnam, Jean Nguyen, who was in the 1985 graduating class at West Point, and an elderly woman, Mother Hale of Harlem, who took care of babies born to heroin addicts. In 1986, he doubled the number again, this time showing off four young people: a college student who designed an experiment for the space shuttle, a 12-year-old gospel singer, a 13-year-old rescuer of another child in a traffic accident, and a 13-year-old suburban youth who brought blankets and food to the inner-city homeless.

Maybe that was enough; he didn't have any heroes in the balcony for his last two State of the Union addresses. But he had established a model that later presidents would often follow. When President George W. Bush addressed a guest during his 2004 State of the Union, he was continuing what had become a conventional feature of that speech:

And tonight we are honored to welcome one of Iraq's most re-
spected leaders: the current president of the Iraqi Governing Council,
Adnan Pachachi. Sir, America stands with you and the Iraqi people
as you build a free and peaceful nation.

Reagan provided one quotation for the *Oxford English Dictionary*, an illustration of *warmongering*. It's their most recent example for that word rather than the first. A 1981 article in the *New York Review of Books* quoted him as saying, "It is not **war-mongering** to say that some things are worth dying for."

George H. W. Bush

[1924–]
President 1989–1993

George Bush the Elder, from Connecticut, but not east enough in Connecticut to have developed a New England accent, suffered from speechwriters too clever by half. That's an occupational hazard for a presidential speechwriter: the temptation to let rhetorical fireworks fly from the lips of the most listened-to political figure in the nation. Credit then goes to the clever president and to the clever writer who spelled out the words. But sometimes the words will bite the one who said them.

In the Nixon years, speechwriter William Safire was wise enough to vent his "nattering nabobs of negativism" through the voice of an insignificant vice president rather than to hang those words around a president's neck. But George H. W. Bush, in his sparkling speech accepting the Republican nomination for president in 1988, not only was given "I want a kinder, gentler nation" and "a thousand points of light" by his speechwriters, but also "Read my lips—no new taxes." That was brilliant and unforgettable, especially when, less than two years later, Bush called for new taxes. Someone promptly coined *bushlips* and said it meant "insincere political rhetoric."

310

Sometimes Bush was fine as a speaker, sometimes not. One of his speechwriters, Craig R. Smith, later commented:

> When he took advantage of logographers [speechwriters!] and rehearsals, he could be formidable. When he spoke extemporaneously, he often mangled syntax and used incredibly cryptic phrases obviously assuming the audience could read his mind or that they possessed the same special knowledge he did. . . .
>
> The main problem with Bush's presidential rhetoric was Bush himself. He disdained rehearsal. His love of substance often caused him to neglect style, particularly in speeches he delivered from the Oval Office to television audiences. . . . His press conferences were tremendous demonstrations of sagacity, wit, and humanity. But he did not want to appear to be imitating Reagan, so he refused to hold his press conferences at night when all of the nation could have seen them.

The elder Bush is the last president so far to have a quotation in the *Oxford English Dictionary*. He is quoted twice, in fact, but not with the first instance in either case. He provides an example of *new world order*, a term he didn't invent, but that nevertheless was a key phrase in his policies. He used it in his State of the Union address in 1991, and later that March when the first war with Iraq had come to a successful conclusion: "And now, we can see a new world coming into view. A world in which there is the very real prospect of a **new world order**."

He is also quoted for *go ballistic*, on an earlier occasion (1988): "I get furious. I **go ballistic**. I really do and I bawl people out."

Bill Clinton

[1946–]
President 1993–2001

Brilliant, compassionate, charming, and educated at those top-of-the-line establishments Georgetown, Oxford, and Yale, Arkansawyer Bill Clinton was one of our most verbally gifted presidents. He loved the bully pulpit of the presidency and never was at a loss for words. In his speeches, town meetings, and interviews with the press and on television, Clinton was fluent, and his speeches were copious, sometimes expanding to twice their intended lengths.

Until he became president, Bill Clinton wrote his own speeches. "Wrote" is probably the wrong word, because for almost all speeches even after he became president, except for something as formal as the State of the Union, he extemporized. He would have notes and drafts beforehand, his own and those of his speechwriters, but he continually revised them and would often deviate from the text he had prepared. His ad-libbing made his speeches long, and longer than planned.

Yet his fluency was also his undoing. Other presidents earned nicknames like Old Hickory, Honest Abe, the Great Humanitarian, and the Great Communicator, but the soubriquet that stuck with Clinton was "Slick Willie." He was too glib for his own good.

Collections of Clinton quotations include this one from his 1993 inaugural address: "There is nothing wrong with America that cannot be cured with what is right in America." But he is remembered more for his ringing declaration during the 1992 campaign: "When I was in England, I experimented with marijuana a time or two, and I didn't like it. I didn't inhale, and never tried it again." Earlier he had ingeniously, though not ingenuously, declared, "I have never violated the laws of my country."

Even more memorable are his excruciating equivocations during the Lewinsky year, 1998, starting with a televised address on January 26, heavy with sincerity: "But I wanna say one thing (pause for emphasis) to the American people. I want you to listen to me. I'm gonna say this again. I did not (pause) have (pause) sexual (pause) relations with that woman (pause), Ms. Lewinsky." And later that year, before a grand jury, President Clinton was asked in regard to his intern: "Is there a relationship?" He gave what seemed a hyper-legalistic reply:

> It depends on what the meaning of the word is is. If the—if he—if is means is and never has been, that is not—that is one thing. If it means there is none, that was a completely true statement. . . . Now if someone had asked me on that day, are you having any kind of sexual relations with Ms. Lewinsky, that is, asked me a question in the present tense, I would have said no. And it would have been completely true.

And finally his later statement, again dripping with sincerity: "It is important to me that everybody who has been hurt (pause) know that the sorrow I feel is (pause) genuine."

Bill Clinton's presidency brought to prominence a person who subsequently became a U.S. Senator from New York: Hillary Rodham Clinton, a much-mentioned possibility for president herself later in the twenty-first century. Just in case, it should be noted here that she grew up in the Chicago suburb of Park Ridge, Illinois, and speaks with a cultivated, unobtrusive r-ful accent not so different from that of other presidents from the north central states.

George W. Bush

[1946–]
President 2001–

Just when you think you've heard everything from a president, along comes George W. Bush. He combines a down-home Midland, Texas, accent with a unique gift for misunderapprehending words as they float to his consciousness and out through his lips.

Purely on merit, his manner of speaking has earned him eminence in this book. As a presidential blunderer, he's in a class of his own, as chapter 6 explains. And as a presidential neologist (chapter 7), he's in a class with Thomas Jefferson—Jefferson at the head of the class and Bush at the back, to be sure, but the same class nevertheless. What he shares with Jefferson is the unusual ability to be comfortable with new words, indeed to relish them. The difference is that Jefferson coined them consciously and conscientiously.

And then there is his accent (chapter 8), much more West Texas than East Coast Establishment. Here are a couple of samples of his informal speech:

> *It's gettin' worse. That's what people have gotta understand up there in Washington, or over there in Washington, down there in Washington,*

314

wherever—thought I was in Crawford for a minute. (Speech in Scranton, Pennsylvania, January 16, 2003)

First of all, I appreciate the wisdom of Chairman Greenspan [chairman of the Federal Reserve Board, about the economy]. *He uses the word, "soft spot." I use the word, "bumpin' along."* (After a cabinet meeting in the White House, November 13, 2003)

Even in formal statements, Dubya will use a *sh* sound for *s* in words like *lasht* for *last, fashter* for *faster, yeshterday* for *yesterday, intereshted* for *interested, frushtration* for *frustration.* He'll reduce two consonants to one at the end of a word or syllable: *Polan* for *Poland, shiel* for *shield, invesigators* for *investigators, fasses* for *fastest, dismanling* for *dismantling. However* comes out as *hahever.* He'll sometimes use the *ah* pronunciation for the long *I* vowel in words like *I* itself and *united.* And the final consonants of words that might have a *z* sound—*members* and *citizens,* for example (though spelled with *s,* they are most often sounded *z*)—come out with a strong *s.* Similarly, words that generally end with a *d* sound, such as *trained,* come out with *t.* He says *remenants* for *remnants* and *ambasser* for *ambassador* and pronounces *insurance* with emphasis on the first syllable.

Nuke 'em

Though he doesn't read newspapers, which now and then comment on his pronunciation, Bush surely has advisers and speechwriters who have called his attention to his pronunciation of *nuclear* as *nucular.* In vain. He may make an occasional effort to tidy up his speech in other ways, but he evidently likes the sound of *nucular,* the preferred military pronunciation. In his 2004 State of the Union address, he used *nucular* exclusively—four times.

What does Dubya think about his language? He knows he trips over his words, but he trips on them too, to use a sixties' expression. Early in his presidency, at the seventh annual Texas Celebration of Reading, he kept an audience in continual laughter by reading from the recently published *George W. Bushisms: The Slate Book of the Accidental Wit and Wisdom of Our 43rd President.* It's only fair to let Dubya have the last word about his language:

It's not exactly a world transformed, but I'm kind of proud that my words are already in book form. And I thought tonight I would share a few quotable passages with you. It's kind of like thoughts of Chairman Mao. Only with laughs and not in Chinese.

Here's one. And I actually said this. "I know the human being and fish can coexist peacefully." Now, that makes you stop and think. Anyone can give you a coherent sentence, but something like this takes you to an entirely new dimension. . . .

Now, most people would say this when they're talking about the economy: "We ought to make the pie bigger." However, I said this: "We ought to make the pie higher." It is a very complicated economic point I was making then. But believe me—believe me, what this country needs is taller pie. . . .

John Ashcroft, by the way, attributes the way I talk to my religious fervor. In fact, the first time we met, he thought I was talking in tongues.

Then there is my famous statement, "Rarely is the question asked, is our children learning?" Let's analyze that sentence for a moment. If you're a stickler, you probably think the singular verb is *should have been the plural* are. *But if you read it closely, you'll see that I'm using the intransitive plural subjective tense. And so the word* is *are correct.*

Now, ladies and gentlemen, you have to admit, in my sentences, I go where no man has gone before. But the way I see it is, I am a boon to the English language. I've coined new words like misunderestimate *and* Hispanically. *I've expanded the definition of words themselves, using* vulcanize *when I meant* polarize, Grecians *when I meant* Greeks, inebriating *when I meant* exhilarating. *And instead of* barriers and tariffs, *I said* terriers and barrifs.

It's no coincidence that these light-hearted remarks, along with Bush's light-hearted advocacy of neology on Jefferson Day as noted in chapter 7, came before September 11, 2001. Until that day it didn't seem to matter much to the life of our country who was president in the early twenty-first century; the economy was doing pretty well, and the rest of the world seemed at a distance, so much that Bush's foreign-policy advisors could light-heartedly nickname themselves the "Strategery Group," adopting the pseudo-Bushism invented by *Saturday Night Live.*

After the terrorist attacks of September 11, however, the Bush presidency of necessity became much more serious. Until that date, it seemed as if George W. might be a president remembered most for his language; after that date, for better or worse he would be remembered for his deeds. His inadvertent inventiveness with the English language continued unabated, proving that his manner of speaking was the real thing and not an act. The change of focus in his presidency was a reminder that substance is as important as style.

But in all seriousness, his language still is important. So it wasn't trivial when, shortly after September 11, Bush remarked, "This crusade, this war on terrorism, is going to take a while," while Pentagon planners thoughtlessly referred to the invasion of Afghanistan as Operation Infinite Justice. Both terms offended Muslims: *crusade* because it evoked the original Crusades, religious wars carried out by European Christians who invaded the Muslim-ruled holy lands; and "infinite justice" because that is the realm of the Almighty, not mere mortals. Bush has since avoided speaking of crusades, and the Pentagon quickly changed the name to Operation Enduring Freedom, but the damage had been done. Words matter.

Index

A

fellow citizens, my fellow citizens, 3
Fields, W.C., 49
fifth wheel, 287
Fillmore, Millard, **223–224**
fireside chats, 51, 52, 58
Fleming, Andrew, 163
follow, 246
Fonda, Henry, 161, 162, 169
foppling, 119–120
Ford, Gerald R. *See also* debates,
    presidential
    blunders, in speaking, **101–103**
    profile, **301–302**
    speaking style/accent, 108, 156,
      160, 301
    speechwriters, 79, 301
Ford, Harrison, 167, 170
Ford, John, 161
fortify, 246
"...Four Freedoms..." (Roosevelt, F.),
    78, 283
Freberg, Stan, 6
French, neologisms and, 121–122,
    129
frock-dress, 230
Fronde, 208

G

"Gamalielism," 38
Garfield, Bob, 177
Garfield, James A.
    death, *xi,* 10
    inaugural speech, 85
    as neologist, 112
    as orator, 29, 33–34
    profile, **250–252**
    speaking style/accent, 94
gascoigny, 118
-gate (suffix), 281
German, neologisms and, 129
get through, 246
Gettysburg Address, 25, 161, 233,
    236

ghostwriting. *See* speechwriters
Gilliam, Mays, 164
"Give 'em hell Harry." *See* Truman,
    Harry S.
go ballistic, 311
gold standard, 16
Goldwater, Barry, 64, 155
Gompers, Samuel, 136
good neighbor policy, 113, 282
"...good to the last drop..." (Roosevelt,
    T.), 267
Goodwin, Richard, 79, 295
Gorbachev, Mikhail, 68, 69
graffage, 132
Grammer, Kelsey, 162
Grant, Hugh, 141
Grant, Ulysses S., 112, **244–247**
Great Bloviator, the. *See* Harding,
    Warren G.
Great Commoner, the. *See* Bryan,
    William Jennings
Great Emancipator, the. *See* Lincoln,
    Abraham
Great Pacificator, the. *See* Clay,
    Henry
Greenstein, Fred I., 288
Greenwood, Bruce, 162
Griffith, D.W., 161
Gross, H.B., 277
Ground Zero (New York, NY), 181
grown up (crowded), 246
growth, 246
Guiteau, Charles J., 251
gullied land, 116
gunning, 246

H

Hale, Mother, 308
half...half, 236
Hamilton, Alexander, 72, 117, 187,
    200
Harding, Warren G.
    death, *xi*

fear..." (Kennedy), 79
Levy, Lillian, 98
Lewinsky, Monica, 313
Lewis and Clark, 126, 196
Libya, 79
lift, 282
Lincoln, Abraham
  death, *xi*
  inaugural address, **25–29**, 74, 178
  letters, 75–76
  movies, depiction in, 161
  as neologist, 112, **236–239**
  as orator, 17, 25–29
  as presidential model, 82
  profile, **231–239**
  speaking style/accent, 140, 179,
    232–236
  speechwriters, 74–76, 77
  voice, 39, 233–234
liquor law, 236
Livingston, Edward, 73
lobbyist, 247
logged, 116
long-felt, 239
looped, 222
loose cannon, 300
Louisiana Purchase, 203
lunarium, 125
lunatic fringe, 109, 112, 134
lying (idle), 246

M

Madison, James
  as neologist, 112, **200–202**
  profile, **197–202**
  speaking style/accent, 94, 141
  Washington and, 72, 73, 185–186,
    187
  writing ability, 73, **198–200**
magical, 202
magnum bonum plum, 116
magotty bay bean, 116
major-generalcy, 246

malapropisms, 105, 137
mal de mer, 121
maneuver, 119
manifestation, 205, 207
mannequins' debate, 40–41
man (the guns), 246
Marconi, Guglielmo, 50
margravate, 129
Markebronn, 129
Marsalla, 129
Marx, Rabbi Robert J., 135
Mason, Charles, 125
Mason and Dixon's line, 125
Massey, Raymond, 161
Mathews, Chris, 166
Max, Daniel, 176
maxim (premise), 202
Maxwell House Hotel, 267
McAdoo, William G., 94
McClendon, Sarah, 97, 100
McCullough, David, 189
McKean, Erin, 139
McKinley, William
  Bryan and, 16
  death, *xi*
  Hay and, 76
  profile, **262–264**
  speaking style/accent, 146–147
  voice, recorded, 40
Meader, Vaughn, 153
mean (average), 202
Medhurst, Martin J., 307
media-savvy, 40
megalonyx, 126
megatherium, 126
megatonnage, 113, 292
mellerdramer, 286
menace, 293
Mencken, H.L., 37, 38, 94, 276
Menlo Park (Edison, NJ), *xiii*, 41
mential, 137
merit, 202
metairie, 129
meter, 126
Michigander, 112, 236–237

Michtom, Morris, 265
"...military-industrial complex..."
(Eisenhower), 78, 113, 289
Mill, John Stuart, 77
milliard, 129
millionaire, 112, 129
Milton, John, 119
mineral coal, 126
mineralized, 126
mingled, 202
minister (government), 293
Mirabilis, 126
misadjustment, 112, 251–252
misanthropism, 132
misjudged, 202
missile gap, 113, 292
mission (diplomatic), 293
Missourian, 212
Missouri Compromise, 220
misthinking, 201
misunderestimate, *ix*, 80, 109, 113,
137, 139, 316
Mme. (Madame), 129
modus agendi, 129
Moffat, Donald, 170
Mohr, Charles H., 100
Mondale, Fritz, 180
Mondale, Walter, 179
moneyfuggler, 269
Monkey Ward's, 286
monocrats, 127
monotonously, 130
Monroe, James, 73, 77, 141,
203–205
Monroe Doctrine, 30, 73, 205
moon mission, 293
Moos, Malcolm, 78, 289
more so, 202
Morgan, H. Wayne, 262
Morse, John T., 192
Morton, Thruston, 289
mosseux, 129
movies, presidents in, *xii*, 160–161
as action hero, 167–169
historical, 161–163

hypothetical, 163–170
muckraker/muck rake, 45, 46, 86,
109, 112, 133, 139
municipally, 128
muniments, 135
mussel-mud, 120
mussurana snake, 132
"...mystic chords..." (Lincoln), 74

N

"...nail jelly to the wall..." (Roosevelt,
T.), 113, 133
nameable, 122
Native Americans, 31, 84–85, 196
"...nattering nabobs of negativism..."
(Agnew), 101, 310
neologists, presidents as, 109–111.
See also Adams, J.; Bush, G.W.;
Jefferson; Lincoln; Roosevelt,
T.; Washington
"New Deal" (Roosevelt, F.), 282, 286
New Town Pippin (apple), 116
new world order, 311
New Yorker, 118
Nguyen, Jean, 308
Nicolay, John G., 238
Nixon, Patricia Ryan, 298
Nixon, Richard M. *See also* debates,
presidential
Eisenhower and, 97–98, 100, 288,
298
finances, 297–298
impeachment, 10
movies, depiction in, 161,
162–163
as neologist, 113
profanilty, use of, 83, 90, 179,
299
profile, **297–300**
resignation, *xi*
speaking style/accent, 156
speeches/speechwriters, 77, 298
temperament, *x*

Nixon, Robert G., 284, 285
non-effective, 118
non-exportation, 128
non-intercourse, 128
normalcy, 109, 113, 136–137, 139
North Korea, 79
Novak, Robert, 166
noyade, 121
NRC (National Regulatory
    Commission), 301–302
nuclear, pronunciation of, 107–108,
    152, 156, 301, 315
Nullification Proclamation (1832),
    73–74

O

objectioner, 118
odometer, 115, 125
OED. *See* Oxford English Dictionary
    (OED)
OK, okeh, 113, 213–214, 271–272
"Old Hickory." *See* Jackson, Andrew
"Old Kinderhook." *See* Van Buren,
    Martin
"Old Man Eloquent." *See* Adams,
    John Quincy
on the creen, 132
ooching, 138
open (administration), 300
operations (military), 246
orators, great
    Adams, J., 17–24, 189
    Adams, J.Q., 29–33
    age of, *xii*, 12–13
    Garfield, 33–34
    Harding, 34–38
    Lincoln, 25–29
    nonpresidents as, 13–16
oratory, defined, 12
Orben, Bob, 79
outpost, 118
Oxford English Dictionary (OED), *xiii*,
    114–133, 135, 137, 139

P

Pachachi, Adnan, 309
palinoidal, 132
patricidal, 130
patton-cotch, 239
Pearl Harbor, 52–55, 78
Pearson, Drew, 89
pecuniary, 5
pegging away, 236
Pegler, Westbrook, 88, 269
peter out, 236
"phonautograph," *x*
phonograph, invention of, *xiii*, 39,
    40. *See also* recordings, presi-
    dential voices
pick up, 246
Pierce, Franklin, 112, **225–228**
Pierce, William, 198
pileus, 119
pinhead, 287
pistareen, 122
plagiat, 122
plateau, 116
plexi-chronometer, 125
Poats, Rutherford M., 96
points, 112, 246
point well taken, 238
Polk, James K., 14, **219–220,** 229
polygraph, 125
porta-crib, 296
post-note, 127
"preacher president." *See* Garfield,
    James A.
predilection, 4
preordinate, 132
presidency, the
    constitutional limits on, 9–10
    requirements of, *x*, 176
    terms of, *xi*, 2, 21
    transition, *xi*, 20
President's Mansion/President's
    House, 220
press conferences
    Bush, G.W., 104

strategery, 107, 316
Strategic Arms Limitation Talks
   (SALT), 296
struggle, 236
Stuart, Gilbert, 7
subliminable, 137
sulla, 126
Sully, Thomas, 110
Sutherland, Kiefer, 171
swear, 225, 226
"swimmer's breath," 101

T

Taft, William H.
   profile, **268–269**
   speaking style/accent, 148,
      268–269
   speeches, 42–43
   voice, recorded, 40–41
tamanoir, 126
tape/taping, 300
Taylor, Zachary, *xi*, **221–222**
Teapot Dome, 281, 282
technology, impact of, 16, 39–40, 50,
   70
teddy bear, 112, 265, 266
telegraph/telephone, invention of, 39
television. *See also West Wing, The*
   Kennedy and, 55
   presidential debates and, 57–62
   presidents depicted on, *xii*, 162,
      170–174, 175
   press conferences, 99
Territorial Army, 293
terrorism/terrorists, 171, 317
that few, 236
the most, 202
"...the only thing we have to fear..."
   (Roosevelt, F.), 52, 78, 280
"...there is nothing wrong with
      America..." (Clinton), 313
Thornton, Billy Bob, 170
"...thousand points of light..." (Bush,

G.H.W.), 310
tie-breaking, 300
Tiers Etat, 121
Tilden, Samuel J., 248
tin can, 112, 116
tinings, 116
"Tippecanoe and Tyler, too," 215, 217
to average, 112
Tocqueville, Alexis de, 179
toll-house cookies, 300
to motorcade, 296
to net, 119
to quirt, 132
Totenberg, Nina, 165
towpath, 116
training program, 296
Trewhitt, Henry, 180
trickle-down, 287
Trout, Robert, 51
Trujillo, Sergeant Stephen, 308
Truman, Harry S.
   assuming the presidency, 11
   movies, depiction in, 162
   as neologist, 113
   Nixon and, 60–61, 89, 285
   profanity, use of, 89–90, 285
   profile, **284–287**
   speaking style/accent, **87–90,**
      152, 179
Twain, Mark, 11, 272
Tyler, John, **217–218**

U

uncommerciable, 131
unconciliatory, 131
unconstitutionality, 117
underdeveloped, 286
United States Supreme Court, 32–33
unlocated, 131
unsubtle, 300

Picture Credits

Title page

Herbert Hoover addressing a joint session of Congress Library of Congress, LC-USZ62-22162

Half-title page

detail of George Washington's first inaugural address Library of Congress, Manuscript Division, A115

The Language of the Presidency

George Washington's first inauguration Corbis/Bettmann **George Washington's dentures** Courtesy of the National Museum of Dentistry, Baltimore, Maryland **Henry Clay** Library of Congress, LC-USZ62-689 **William Jennings Bryan** Corbis/Bettmann **Abraham Lincoln's second inauguration** Library of Congress, LC-USA7-16837 **Theodore Roosevelt's speech with bullet hole** Smithsonian Institution, Archives Center, National Museum of American History, negative number 2000-6101 **Franklin D. Roosevelt radio address** Corbis/Bettmann **Richard Nixon and John F. Kennedy televised debate** AP/Wide World Photos **Ronald Reagan** Corbis/

Bettmann **John Hay** Library of Congress, LC-DIG-cwpbh-00650 **Theodore Sorenson** Corbis/Bettmann **Andrew Jackson** Picture History (7.011) **Harry S. Truman whistlestop** Corbis **Dwight D. Eisenhower press conference** Courtesy of the National Park Service and the Dwight D. Eisenhower Presidential Library and Museum **George W. Bush and José Maria Aznar** AP/Wide World Photos- J. Scott Applewhite **Thomas Jefferson** Library of Congress, LC-USZ62- 13003 and the U.S. Senate Collection, #31.00006, *Thomas Jefferson*, attributed to Thomas Sully **Harry S. Truman sign** Courtesy of the Harry S. Truman Presidential Library and Museum **George Washington's farm** Library of Congress, LC-USZ62-3912 **Boston Tea Party** National Archives and Records Administration **Warren G. Harding recording** Library of Congress, LC-USZ62-64386 **Thomas Edison** Library of Congress, LC-DIG-cwpbh 04044 **William McKinley** Corbis/Bettmann **New York Times article** *New York Times*, Wednesday, April 13, 1921 **Herbert Hoover radio address** Corbis/Bettmann **Dwight D. Eisenhower at Silver Spring,**

Maryland Corbis/Bettmann **John F. Kennedy press conference** Corbis/Bettmann **Dennis Haysbert** Courtesy of the Fox Broadcasting Company **Martin Sheen** Photo © 2004 Warner Bros. Entertainment Inc., All rights reserved. **George W. Bush at Ground Zero** AP/Wide World Photos-Doug Mills

Profiles of the Presidents

Library of Congress: **George Washington** (LC-USZ62-117116), **John Adams** (LC-USZ62-13002), **Thomas Jefferson** (LC-USZ62-117117), **James Madison** (LC-USZ62-13004), **James Monroe** (LC-USZ62-117118), **John Quincy Adams** (LC-USZC4-5801), **Andrew Jackson** (LC-USZ62-117120), **Martin Van Buren** (LC-USZ62-13008), **William Henry Harrison** (LC-USZ62-87283), **John Tyler** (LC-USZ62-13010), **James K. Polk** (LC-USZ62-13011), **Zachary Taylor** (LC-USZ62-13012), **Millard Fillmore**, **Franklin Pierce** (LC-USZ62-13014), **James Buchanan** (LC-USZ62-13015), **Abraham Lincoln** (LC-USZ62-13016), **Andrew Johnson** (LC-USZ62-13017), **Ulysses S. Grant** (LC-USZ62-13018), **Rutherford B. Hayes** (LC-USZ62-13019), **James A. Garfield** (LC-USZ62-13020), **Chester A. Arthur** (LC-USZ62-13021), **Grover Cleveland** (LC-USZ62-13022), **Benjamin Harrison** (LC-USZ62-13023), **William McKinley** (LC-USZ62-97097), **Theodore Roosevelt** (LC-USZ62-13026), **William H. Taft** (LC-USZ62-13027), **Woodrow Wilson** (LC-USZ62-065033), **Warren G. Harding** (LC-USZ62-13029), **Calvin Coolidge** (LC-USZ62-39282), **Herbert C. Hoover**

(LC-USZ62-4747)

Courtesy of the Franklin D. Roosevelt Presidential Library and Museum: **Franklin D. Roosevelt** (48-22:3830, 19)

Courtesy of the Harry S. Truman Presidential Library and Museum, U.S. Army Photo: **Harry S. Truman** (58-486)

Courtesy of the Dwight D. Eisenhower Presidential Library and Museum: **Dwight D. Eisenhower**

Courtesy of the John Fitzgerald Kennedy Presidential Library and Museum & Cecil Stoughton, The White House: **John F. Kennedy** (STC237163)

Courtesy of the Lyndon B. Johnson Presidential Library and Museum: **Lyndon B. Johnson** (D-3007-16)

Courtesy of the Nixon Presidential Materials Staff: **Richard M. Nixon** (C8341)

Courtesy of the Gerald Ford Presidential Library and Museum: **Gerald R. Ford** (A0381)

Courtesy of the Jimmy Carter Presidential Library and Museum: **Jimmy Carter**

Courtesy of the White House, Michael Evans: **Ronald Reagan**

Courtesy of the White House, David Valdez: **George H. W. Bush**

Courtesy of the White House: **Bill Clinton**

Courtesy of the White House, Eric Draper: **George W. Bush**